Advance praise for **Black**

"*Black Women in Leadership* is a book that re[...] ven more importantly it is a book that speaks about Bla[...] on Black men in higher education is very important and [...] [...]ust of all this attention to men, research on Black women often falls through the cracks. As educators and scholars, we need to know and internalize the stories of both Black men and women. In this book, Dannielle Joy Davis and Cassandra Chaney, along with their various authors, bring the lives of Black women to life and demonstrate these women's perseverance, intellect, and strength."—MARYBETH GASMAN, UNIVERSITY OF PENNSYLVANIA

"As I began reviewing this book I was intrigued by its scope. It includes topics focusing on Black women in history to how Black women currently view the leadership of Michelle Obama. In terms of research formats, one chapter provides a case study and other chapters include the findings of research with much larger data bases. The book has a broad range of topics, with one chapter providing an overview of how Black women got where they are today to another chapter which highlights issues of Black women in the workplace. As I began skimming the first chapters, I couldn't wait to read each chapter in its entirety. The topics and content of the chapters are compelling and are of interest to scholars in a wide range of disciplines. It is likely that I will use the book in future courses when I teach about diversity and family life. I also see this book being of interest to those without an academic background but who want to know more about the role of Black women in society."—LINDA SKOGRAND, PROFESSOR, FAMILY, CONSUMER, AND HUMAN DEVELOPMENT, UTAH STATE UNIVERSITY

"*Black Women in Leadership* covers the diverse leadership roles of Black women by highlighting noteworthy contributions we make in the field of education, in our communities, and within our families. This text is unique because the authors address the relationship between leadership and self-care for Black women, a topic that is all too often neglected in published literature. As an educator, I am excited to see a text that incorporates multiple perspectives by highlighting the accomplishments of our historic and modern Black women leaders. The diversity of our personal and professional identities is rarely depicted accurately in books or other media. I appreciate Dannielle Joy Davis and Cassandra Chaney for capturing the true essence of our most precious gems and sharing it with the world!"—RENÉE A. MIDDLETON, DEAN, THE GLADYS W. & DAVID H. PATTON COLLEGE OF EDUCATION, OHIO UNIVERSITY

"*Black Women in Leadership* is an unsentimental, meticulous presentation of African American women's leadership. It examines leadership with a broad brush. Dr. Davis and Dr. Chaney wisely incorporate a strong historical flavor in their book, which challenges what we think we know about African American women and simultaneously accords these women the political, social, and intellectual autonomy that they deserve. This clearly written, thoroughly documented book rejects the perception that African American women's leadership is a recent phenomenon, showing instead the divergent forms that this leadership has taken in a range of venues from family to education to church to the political arena. This scholarly and engaging womanist critique provides a compelling picture of African American women's legacy of leadership."—IRIS CARLTON-LANEY, PROFESSOR, SCHOOL OF SOCIAL WORK, UNIVERSITY OF NORTH CAROLINA AT CHAPEL HILL

"By examining distinct views on the meaning of leadership in multiple settings, *Black Women in Leadership* appeals to a wide academic audience. Editors Dannielle Joy Davis and Cassandra Chaney have created an engaging work that highlights the little-told and often-discounted stories of the conviction and character of selected Black women leaders. Their interdisciplinary perspective is a distinguishing factor of this examination of the many forms of leadership provided by Black women historically and currently. It is a welcome addition to the literature exploring the leadership of women of color."—BEVERLY L. BOWER, DON A. BUCHHOLZ ENDOWED CHAIR, UNIVERSITY OF NORTH TEXAS, AND AUTHOR OF *ANSWERING THE CALL: AFRICAN AMERICAN WOMEN IN HIGHER EDUCATION LEADERSHIP* AND *WOMEN AT THE TOP: WHAT WOMEN UNIVERSITY & COLLEGE PRESIDENTS SAY ABOUT EFFECTIVE LEADERSHIP*

Black Women in Leadership

Rochelle Brock and Richard Greggory Johnson III
Executive Editors

Black Studies on Leadership
Judy A. Alston, Series Editor

Vol. 36

The Black Studies and Critical Thinking series
is part of the Peter Lang Education list.
Every volume is peer reviewed and meets
the highest quality standards for content and production.

PETER LANG
New York • Washington, D.C./Baltimore • Bern
Frankfurt • Berlin • Brussels • Vienna • Oxford

Black Women in Leadership

Their Historical and Contemporary Contributions

EDITED BY Dannielle Joy Davis & Cassandra Chaney

PETER LANG
New York • Washington, D.C./Baltimore • Bern
Frankfurt • Berlin • Brussels • Vienna • Oxford

Library of Congress Cataloging-in-Publication Data

Black women in leadership: their historical and contemporary contributions /
edited by Dannielle Joy Davis, Cassandra Chaney.
p. cm. — (Black studies and critical thinking; v. 36)
Includes bibliographical references.
1. African American women in the professions—United States.
2. African American women executives—United States.
3. African American women educators—United States.
4. Leadership in women—United States. 5. Occupations and race.
I. Davis, Dannielle Joy. II. Chaney, Cassandra.
HD6054.2.U6B53   303.3'4082—dc23   2012010516
ISBN 978-1-4331-1652-0 (hardcover)
ISBN 978-1-4331-1682-7 (paperback)
ISBN 978-1-4539-0829-7 (e-book)
ISSN 1947-5985

Bibliographic information published by **Die Deutsche Nationalbibliothek**.
Die Deutsche Nationalbibliothek lists this publication in the "Deutsche
Nationalbibliografie"; detailed bibliographic data is available
on the Internet at http://dnb.d-nb.de/.

The paper in this book meets the guidelines for permanence and durability
of the Committee on Production Guidelines for Book Longevity
of the Council of Library Resources.

© 2013 Peter Lang Publishing, Inc., New York
29 Broadway, 18th floor, New York, NY 10006
www.peterlang.com

Printed in the United States of America

Contents

PART III: LEADERSHIP AND SELF-CARE AMONG BLACK WOMEN

Foreword

Linda C. Tillman

The consistent leadership of Black women has received minimal attention in both historical and contemporary literature. While the subject of women in leadership is much discussed and often written about, the discourse continues to focus primarily on White women. It should not surprise us that many of the historical and contemporary images, perceptions, expectations, and negative portrayals of Black women are, to a great degree, defined by what we see in the media. Thus, the life experiences and leadership of Black women reflect age-old stereotypes: Black women as maids, mammies, and welfare mothers or Black women as aggressive, loud, uneducated, and angry. Despite the many accomplishments of Black women in leadership roles, media portrayals continue to cast us as dressed-up versions of Prissy in *Gone with the Wind*.

The publication of this book represents a significant step in telling our stories—stories of Black women as successful and influential leaders in every level of life: from politics to business, from motherhood to ministry, and from education to the pinnacle of Black female leadership—the First Lady of the United States of America. The publication of this book also provides counter-narratives to Eurocentric stories, media portrayals, and commonly accepted definitions of who Black women leaders are. Chapters in this book offer theoretical and empirical evidence of the powerful roles Black female leaders play in today's society and provide us with a broader understanding of the challenges they face when working within the matrix of race, class, and gender. The authors contributing to this book remind us of a powerful truth: Black women have always and continue to provide strong leadership to their families, communities, and society.

The women whose work you will read in this book represent the promises of Black female leadership—strength, resilience, intelligence, beauty, and a boundless determination to make a difference. Let us applaud them and all Black women who are leaders in all walks of life. . . who, despite circumstances, always rise, rise, rise!

— Linda C. Tillman, Ph.D.
University of North Carolina

Acknowledgments

Dannielle Joy Davis

To my mother, Linda Marilyn Davis, whose love, encouragement, and use of supplemental homeschooling has made me into the woman I am today. Thank you for cuddling with me on the coach daily and teaching me to read by the age of two. Thank you for the weekly mandatory book reports, frequent trips to the library, and encouraging me to write poetry throughout my early years. Because of you, writing for me is a joy, rather than a chore, and thinking about ways to promote equality and positive change in people's lives is as natural as play. Your leadership skills as an award-winning elementary school teacher transferred to the home, modeling for me both intellectual leadership and motherhood. Thank you.

Thank you to my father, Rochester Davis, Jr., who has been a wonderful father and life coach. You were my main cheerleader during my doctoral studies and now in your own way continue to encourage. I also am grateful to my grandmother, Sophia Buckner, and my grandfather, Joseph Buckner, for being models of creativity and strength.

Thank you to my son Bryce for giving me the motivation to continuously reach higher goals and constantly reminding me to see the joy in life. Thank you Dr. Cassandra Chaney for being a longtime friend and colleague. You are a remarkable woman. Finally, I wish to thank Drs. Jim Huffman, Phil Waldrop, and Michael Allen, who provided various forms of support during the final phase of this work's production. Thank you.

Cassandra Chaney

To my beautiful mother Helen, for always providing unconditional love and support, for being the strong woman that you are, and for providing for me a model of strong Black female leadership that is the foundation of who I am today, I thank you. Because of you, I have learned to commit to life, leadership, and love. You are my mother, but most of all, I am so very proud to call you my friend. From the bottom of my heart, I love you. To my beautiful sisters Alana and Tameka that have known me the longest and know me the best. I am so very proud of the women that you are today. With each passing day, I have a stronger appreciation and respect for the courage, determination, and honor that are inherent to you both. I am so fortunate to have you both in my life and to be a part of yours. The best is unfolding with each passing day. I love you both. To my nieces (Parris, Patia, Darling, Arionne, Elliyah, and Anna), and my nephew (Ariel), my wish is that you emulate the strength and courage of your beautiful mother and that you grow up to be beacons of strong leadership for future generations, within and outside of your family. My wish for Reece, Corran Jr., and Jairett is that you all grow up to be men who make it your aim to always appreciate, nurture, and encourage Black women to greatness. To my aunts Brenda and Anita, my cousin Nathan, my Uncle Lawrence, Aunt Margie, cousin Katrina, her son (Derek Jr.) and daughter (LaBella), my cousin Marcus, Marcus, Jr., my cousin Erica and her family (Andante, Deondre, Brendon, and Rae-Lynn), my cousin Brianne and her family (husband Darryl, daughters Brittany, Brianya, and Taelah; and sons Darryl Jr. and Victor), my cousin Tressa and her family (husband Alvin and daughter Shayna), my Aunt Gail and her family (husband Marion, son Rodney), my cousin Jacquelyn and her sons, as well as my cousin Jonathan and his family, thank you for making the word "family" synonymous with the words "love," "laughter," and "fun."

In addition to my family, I would like to thank my trusted mentors, Dr. Robin L. Jarrett and Dr. Jennifer Hamer for the invaluable advice, support, and encouragement that they have provided me over the years. In addition to these powerhouse women, I would also like to thank others that have made me smile, laugh, and encouraged me when I most needed it, namely: Dr. Eric Clausel, Mrs. Linda Smith-Griffin, Dr. Lashunda Anderson, Dr. Stephanie Jefferson, Dr. Michelle Easy, Dr. Isiah M. Warner, Dr. Thomas Durant, Dr. Saundra Y. McGuire, Dr. Colita Fairfax-Nichols, Dr. Kamesha Spates, Dr. Janice Johnson-Diaz, Dr. Teri Brown, Valerie Thomas, Mrs. Chante Warren-Pryor, Michelle Savage, Dr. Shawn Bediako, Dr. Theda Daniels-Race, Dr. Paul Race, Dr. Juan Barthelemy, and Dr. Stephen Finley. Given our collective passion for helping create stronger families and communities, I would also like to thank the following very special people that worked tirelessly under the direction of the Administration for Children and Families (ACF) and have continuously supported my scholarly commitment to understanding and strengthening Black families over the years, namely: Ms. Joyce Thomas, Ms. Elma Goodwin, Mr. Leroy McCowan, Ms. Diane Dawson, and Mr. Vander Green.

Last but not least, I owe a special thank you to my beautiful and special "sister colleague," Dr. Dannielle Joy Davis. Joy, your name certainly fits you. I can say, without reservation that this collaboration has been a real pleasure because of who you are. In addition to your sharp mind, determination, and high work ethic, over the years, you have consistently been a "joy" to be around. Joy, thank you for setting high standards for yourself because by doing so, you consistently raise the bar and encourage me to always present my best self. You are a remarkably strong woman!

Part One

Leadership within Communities and Families

Chapter One

Introducing Black Women in Leadership

Their Historical and Contemporary Contributions

Dannielle Joy Davis and Cassandra Chaney

(1) Identities

This edited volume explores the leadership of Black women within both macro and micro systems of society. Macro systems featured include public education, industry, social services, and civic organizations. Micro systems discussed include Black women's influence within families, as well as in the church. This collection provides historical and contemporary examples of leadership within these contexts. The work holds significance as scholarship regarding the leadership of Black women currently often focuses merely upon professional administrative (i.e., business) contexts and experiences. In fact, with few exceptions (e.g., Rosa Parks, Fannie Lou Hamer, Shirley Chisholm, Dorothy Height, Daisy Bates, Angela Davis), the accomplishments of Black female leaders have historically been ignored, minimized, or primarily linked to those of prominent Black men (e.g., Dr. Martin Luther King Jr., Malcolm X, Colin Powell, and President Barack Obama). The purpose of this work is not to minimize the historical contributions of Black men, but rather to elucidate factors that motivate the leadership of Black women, to create their own strong identities, and become leaders in their own right. This interdisciplinary work views leadership from a variety of contexts, as this volume highlights the historical barriers and multiple obligations held by Black women in leadership roles. In particular, the work examines strategies underlying Black women's leadership, which in turn, encourages members of the Black community to actualize their individual and collective potential. The book reveals the diversity of forces that shape and enhance Black women's leadership.

There are several distinctive features of this work. First, it moves beyond examining the administrative experiences of Black women. In particular, the volume examines the various contexts (i.e., historical, societal, and familial) that foster Black women's leadership in their families and communities. Second, this work highlights the unique ways Black women model, demonstrate, and practice leadership. Third, the work explores the individuals and institutions that support Black women's leadership. Fourth, it examines the ways that Black women support and are supported by Black men and racial others. The work examines the cultural zeitgeist that allowed Black women to move from tertiary positions of support to those of national and international prominence. The volume also explores various theoretical frameworks that are applicable to the race, gender, and class experiences of Black female leaders. Finally, the book places Black women at the center of the leadership experiences they create and maintain.

Black Women in Leadership works to answer the following questions: (1) How do Black women define leadership? (2) How do Black women demonstrate leadership? (3) What societal conditions foster the leadership of Black women? (4) How do religion and the Black church support or hinder Black female leaders? (5) How do race, class, and gender influence Black female leaders? (6) What are the greatest challenges of leadership among Black women? (7) What are the greatest joys of leadership among Black women? (8) What type of identities must Black women embrace in order to become leaders? (9) How salient is the role of Black women in their communities? (10) How does the media portray Black female leaders? (11) How do young, educated Black women perceive Black female leaders? (12) How do Black female leaders strengthen the Black community? (13) What theoretical frameworks are compatible in examining the experiences of Black female leaders? (14) What similarities and differences exist between how Black women demonstrate leadership historically and in contemporary society?

Black women have exhibited strong leadership throughout human history, from ancient periods as demonstrated via Egypt's Queen Hatshepsut to the contemporary leadership of Canada's former Governor General Michaelle Jean. The study of Black women in leadership is unique given their double minority status. As a Black woman, the first author has exhibited leadership via the Sisters of the Academy Institute's Leadership Team (Davis & Sutherland, 2008) and as a leader of various faculty writing groups (Davis, Provost, & Major, 2012). Yet this work moves beyond leadership within the professoriate and toward leadership exploration within a variety of venues at the micro and macro levels. The double minority status of Black women and the multifaceted leadership roles they take on in varied contexts (i.e., home, civic life, church, the workplace) positions the group to yield unique approaches to problem solving and decision making. These intersectional roles and leadership traits have been passed down in a number of Black families from mothers to their daughters for centuries. Learning from this population may offer strategies for leadership development programs geared toward Black women. In doing so, this work holds the potential to influence practice through program development. The following briefly summarizes the chapters of this work.

Part I of the work centers upon leadership within communities and families. It begins with Brown's study of Black women's legislative influence and the intersectionality of being Black and female while serving in political roles. Thompson-Rogers then moves into the realm of spirituality in her demonstration of how Black women have historically held leadership roles in the church. In Chapter 4, Tickles offers a case study illustrating the leadership of an African American mother.

Part II explores the leadership of Black women in education, both historically and in contemporary society. It opens with two historical pieces, "Each One, Teach One: Black Women's Historical Contributions to Education," by McPherson and "Black Women's Historical Leadership in African American Home Education," by Hudson and Davis. The work of Esnard and colleagues then features the experiences of Black female educational leaders in K–12 settings. Illustrations of Black female leadership at the postsecondary level follow, including chapters on the organization Sisters of the Academy, Chaney's study of Black female college students' perception of the leadership of First Lady Michelle Obama, and an autobiographical, reflective piece on leadership by Clark.

Leadership and Self-care among Black Women serves as the topic for Part III of the book. It begins with "The Double Outsider's Challenges to Professional Success: Implications for Black Women's Leadership," by Tassie and Givens, which is complemented by Marn's work on overcoming gender and race issues in the workplace. Scott's work on "The Role of Vicarious Traumatization in Black Female Mental Health Professionals" follows, emphasizing the importance of self-care among the population. The leadership of senior African American women is also highlighted in Ferguson and King's "Honoring the Lateness of the Day: Opportunistic Shifts in the Personal Leadership Sojourns of African American Professional Women at Second Adulthood."

Recent books have chronicled the history of leadership for Black women, particularly their work in the Black Power and Civil Rights movements (Collier-Thomas & Franklin, 2001; Dossett, 2008). While other work examines the contemporary experiences of Black female administrators in higher education (Bower & Wolverton, 2009) or business, this book offers a unique interdisciplinary exploration of Black women's leadership in multiple contexts while highlighting past and current examples. This reflection upon the past illustrates that leadership among Black women is not a recent phenomenon, but a legacy in which current women of African descent continue.

Bibliography

Davis, D. J., & Sutherland, J. (2008). Expanding access through doctoral education: Perspectives from two participants of the Sisters of the Academy Research Boot Camp. *Journal of College Student Development, 49*(6), 606–608.

Davis, D. J., Provost, K., & Major, A. (2012). Working for work-life balance: HBCU and PWI faculty share their stories as writing group leaders. In J. E. Groccia (Ed.), *To improve the academy: Resources for faculty, instructional, and organizational development*, vol. 31 (pp. 31–42). San Francisco: Jossey-Bass.

Chapter Two

Black Women's Legislative Influence

Nadia Brown

As American political institutions become increasingly diverse, African American female political elites experience unprecedented challenges and opportunities based on their identity as minority women. In particular, Black female state legislators have developed political tactics to demonstrate their legislative effectiveness within institutions that purport being free of gender and racial bias, yet fail to live up to that ideal.[1] Studies have indicated that their race and gender further serve to marginalize African American women's legislative effectiveness even when they achieve seniority and occupy leadership positions (Hawkesworth, 2003; Smooth, 2001). Black female state legislators have been able to meet these challenges based on their race and gendered identities to assume leadership positions, as well as to exert legislative influence.

Because most institutions, including state legislatures, mediate power through unique, historically established norms and preferences, it is important to understand how these factors influence the decision-making process. Gender and race simultaneously affect the legislative experiences of women of color, specifically their ability to garner legislative influence. My interest in studying the legislative influence of African American female state legislators is prompted by studies showing that the intersection of race and gender identities impedes legislative suc-

---

1 Throughout the paper, I use the terms *Black* and *African American, Hispanic* and *Latino*, and *White* and *"Anglo"* interchangeably. I capitalize *Black* because "Blacks, like Asians, Latinos, and other 'minorities,' constitute a specific cultural group and, as such, require denotation as a proper noun" (Crenshaw, 1988, 1332 n.2, citing MacKinnon, 1982, 516).

cess for them. This study explores the self-perceived legislative influence of Black female legislators. The study also examines the Maryland legislature to consider whether women of color experience additional hardships because of their race and gender.[2]

In this study, I focus on the impact of race and gender identity on Black women's legislative influence. I begin this analysis by assessing Black women's legislative leadership and assessing their legislative influence. I then analyze Black women legislators' self-perceptions of their own legislative influence and agency. By centering on Black women's voices, my approach empirically tests the theorized concept of intersectionality. Intersectionality theory avoids privileging one aspect of identity (i.e., either race *or* gender) and instead recognizes that Black women occupy specific race and gender categories simultaneously (Crenshaw, 1991). The effects of such intersectional experiences cannot be understood as simply the effect of adding race to gender or vice-versa. Rather, the combination of these competing identities exerts a unique impact on Black women's representational style. As such, "race constructs the way Black women experience gender; gender constructs the way Black women experience race" (Mansbridge & Tate, 1992, 488). Thus, while it might be instructive, it is not sufficient to examine the effects of either gender or race alone. Working within this framework, I explore the effects of race and gender on Black women's legislative influence.

Legislative Influence

Studies on the influence exercised by African American state legislators find that the traditional sources of legislative influence, such as tenure, leadership positions, and prestigious committee memberships, are often closed to Black legislators. Simply put, Black legislators experience marginalization based on their race. Scholarship has shown that, with few exceptions, African American legislators are unable to integrate themselves effectively into legislative bodies. For example, King-Meadows and Schaller (2000) build upon Rosenthal's (1995) claim that Blacks are excluded from the most influential leadership positions—speaker and majority leader. Similarly, Nelson (1991) finds a negative relationship between the proportion of leadership positions held by minority lawmakers and the enactment of their policy preferences. Browning, Marshall, and Tabb (1984) contend that minority representatives must be incorporated into the dominant political

---

2   While the term "women of color" is problematic because it marks minority women as the other and Whites as identity-free, this catchall term for minority women is the best descriptor for this population that is currently in widespread use. While the term denotes all non-White persons, it is often taken to be synonymous with Black women, who were the first scholars to theorize feminist ideologies that were different from those of White women (hooks, 1991; Collins, 2000). Additionally, while there is not an immense body of research on women of color, research on African American women as political actors outweighs scholarship on other women of color.

regime in order to exert influence over policy decisions. African Americans lack institutional incorporation—the ability of minority lawmakers to hold formal positions within a representative body—which diminishes their influence over policy decisions (Deering & Smith, 1990; Francis, 1989; Jewell & Whicker, 1994; Preuh, 2006). When African Americans gain a significant level of institutional incorporation, however, there is a positive correlation with their policy preferences (Haynie, 2001).

Scholars have examined the extent to which the racialization of a legislature impedes the influence of Black legislators. Racialization within a legislature is most readily seen where racial cleavages persist despite the adoption of pluralistic institutional mechanisms designed to ensure color-blind legislative influence. Racialization dramatically reduces African American legislators' ability to exert legislative influence. Wright, Osborn, and Winburn (2005) illustrate, for example, that in Southern state legislatures, where liberal coalitions are nonexistent except where a handful of Black and liberal White legislators work together, racism is the underlying factor that guides partisan affiliation (Valentino & Sears, 2005).

Racialization can also be seen in the types of formal positions afforded to minority legislators. In this context, formal leadership positions such as Committee Chair and Party Leader are assigned to White legislators to ensure that the interests of the dominant racial group are not threatened (Orey, 2000). In turn, racialization produces negative outcomes insofar as the proportion of Black representation in non-leadership positions is not reflected in policy outcomes benefiting Blacks (Critzer, 1998; Nelson, 1991). Racialization also generates subjective evaluations of Black legislative influence (Smooth, 2001; Hedge, Button, & Spear, 1996) and of the ability of Black legislators to successfully navigate the legislative process (Bratton & Haynie, 1999; Hamm, Harmel, & Thompson, 1983). Last, racialization also reduces the volume of successful legislation introduced by Blacks. Hedge, Button, and Spear (1996) find that Black-sponsored legislation is subject to lower rates of passage than White-sponsored bills in state legislatures.

Women find it especially difficult to access powerful leadership positions. Blair and Stanley (1991) find that women legislators believe that in most cases an "old boys' club" remains the center of legislative power and influence. Female legislators are excluded from such networks, which in turn greatly reduces their legislative abilities and hinders the advancement of their policy priorities. Additionally, such exclusionary, male-dominated centers of legislative power discourage other legislators from viewing women legislators as equals. As a result, female legislators are not as influential in the legislative process as their male counterparts. Regarding such male legislative elites, Rosenthal finds that there is resistance and little adaptation "on the part of male [legislative committee] chairs when women hold greater institutional power" (2000, 41).

Scholars who study the role and experiences of women in politics track committee membership on the part of women to indicate their progress in legislative influence (Norton, 1995; Winsky Mattei, 1998). Focusing on women's legislative and leadership styles, scholars suggest that women pursue cooperative legislative strategies, while men prefer competitive, zero-sum tactics. Also, women are more likely to pursue consensus, preferring less hierarchical, more participatory, and more collaborative approaches than their male counterparts (Thomas, 1994; Jewell & Whicker, 1994; Rosenthal, 2000). These tactics have helped women legislators be more successful in passing preferred legislation, which consequently increases their legislative influence (Dodson & Carroll, 1991; Saint-Germain, 1989; Kathlene, 1994; Thomas, 1991, 1994). As such, Cramer Walsh contends that women are afforded three distinct mechanisms through which to exert legislative influence: "contributing to distinct perspectives in issue framing, enlarging the consideration of which constituents are likely to be affected by a specific policy, and providing personal testimony that includes perspectives distinct from those provided by male legislators" (2002, 373). As congressional scholars contend, those who wield institutional power are those most likely to influence policy, regardless of gender (Hall, 1996). Institutional status helps to determine the success or effectiveness of women's policy efforts.

The Intersections of Race and Gender on Legislative Influence

Studies of elected women of color consistently document forms of marginalization, including stereotyping, invisibility, their exclusion from leadership positions within legislatures, and a lack of institutional responsiveness to the policies that they champion (Bryce & Warwick, 1977; Bratton & Haynie, 1999; Smooth, 2001; Barrett, 1995; Hawkesworth, 2003). Early research on African American women in politics depicted Black female political elites as suffering from a double disadvantage (King, 1988) as both women and African Americans. By situating Black female legislators at the center of my analysis, I argue that while institutional barriers may serve to marginalize African American female legislators, they are able to find innovative ways to exert legislative influence.

Hedge, Button, and Spear (1996) and Barrett (1995) find that Black female legislators report that they must work harder than their racial and gender counterparts do to overcome the effects of their race and gender. Smooth (2001) investigates Black female state legislators' influence to better understand the impact of increased diversity on the allocation of institutional power. She documents alternative approaches that African American women employed in the effort to acquire institutional power, which include forming coalitions with the executive branch, building alliances with the African American and women's caucuses, and engaging in individual acts of resistance on the House floor. Smooth finds in particular that African American female legislators' influence comprises policy areas in which Black women are policy experts. As such, Black women do not enjoy all-encompassing legislative influence (2001, 284). Moreover, White legislators were less likely to view African American women as exercising influence within a legislature. Smooth concludes that, while democratic institutions may hold the promise of equality, the lived reality of Black female legislators continues to illustrate that existing power structures exclude them.

Smooth (2005) demonstrates that experiences of marginalization are not mitigated by seniority or leadership positions for African American female state legislators. She finds that the longer Black women have served in office and the more powerful the positions they hold within legislative institutions, the stronger are their feelings of exclusion. As a result, Smooth contends that marginalization of Black women state legislators does not disappear at the onset of legislative success. While it is reasonable to suppose that seniority and leadership positions lead to increased legislative influence, this is not true for African American women. Women of color who are legislators are often silenced or made to be invisible in key legislative functions such as committee negotiations or floor discussions.

To explain why Black women are not afforded greater or significant legislative influence, Hawkesworth (2003) argues that legislative institutions are both raced and gendered, a condition that produces a range of effects for legislators at the intersections of these identities. The somatic norms of Whiteness and maleness found in such institutions lead to advanced marginalization of legislators who are not White males. Racialization and gendering can play a distinct role in organizational practice by recreating and reproducing symbols as well as identities. The interactive processes of racing and gendering generates and maintains systems of power and disadvantage consisting of institutional processes, practices, images, ideologies, and distributional mechanisms (Acker, 1989, 1992; Kenney, 1996). The obstruction and demoralization that racing and gendering causes can make it difficult for minority female legislators to achieve the objectives that motivated them to enter politics (Kathlene, 1994; Thomas, 1994). Furthermore, a theory of racing and gendering explicates the ways in which masculinity and femininity are raced and that race is intimately connected to constructions of gender.

In contrast to the double disadvantage that scholars cite in explaining the marginalization of Black female legislators, other scholars have posited that minority women are afforded opportunities that others are not. Fraga and colleagues (2006) find that Latina legislators employ *strategic intersectionality*—the combination of substantive policy focus on education, healthcare, and jobs—and enjoy multiple-identity, gender-inclusive advantages providing them with strategic leverage in the legislative process. Fraga and associates argue that the intersection of gender and ethnicity positions Latina legislators to choose from "a richer set of strategic options, relative to Latino male legislators" (2006, 7). For example, strategic intersectionality affords Latina state legislators the ability to enter into coalitions, position themselves distinctly from their male counterparts on salient issues that are supported by a women's caucus, as well as serve on education and health and human services committees. A strategic intersectionality model provides for a more nuanced understanding of the complexity of representation and legislative influence of minority female legislators. While minority female legislators may not exercise sweeping legislative influence, they are able to use their identity to their advantage. As such, minority female state legislators' race, ethnicity, and gender may in some cases serve to increase their legislative influence. The remainder of this study takes up this position to illustrate the ways in which Black female state legislators articulate how their identity affects their perceived legislative influence.

Data and Methods

Due to the small number of African American women serving in state legislatures across the country, I chose to study the Maryland legislature because it held the largest number of Black women state legislators during the 2009 legislative session (20, distributed among 15 delegates and 5 senators). Furthermore, Maryland was the only legislature addressing social issues during the 2009 legislative session, as many legislatures were overwhelmingly concerned with economic issues.

The Maryland legislature is highly professionalized and comprises part-time representatives who dedicate a 90–day period annually to law making. Maryland's political culture is regarded as individualistic, akin to that of a business, where individual legislators broker deals and orchestrate political favors. While the party structure is highly organized, legislators have the ability to act as individuals, especially regarding policy areas in which some have specialized knowledge (Smooth, 2001). The General Assembly includes 47 senators and 141 delegates elected from 47 districts. The multimember districts are comprised of four representatives— one senator and three delegates. Maryland was selected as the case study for this research because of its large number of Black female legislators and a legislative structure favorable for research, as it allowed for greater control in analyzing how race and gender influenced decision making in the 2009 legislative session dealing with social issues.

The data for this study comes from 51 in-depth, semi-structured, and open-ended interviews that I conducted with Democratic Maryland state legislators during the 2009 legislative session. All 20 of Maryland's African American legislators were asked to place themselves on a scale from 1 to 7, where 1 represents the margin of power and 7 represents the center of power, in response to the question, "Where in relation to the center of power in the Maryland legislature would you place yourself?" When asked to assess their influence, Black female legislators ranged from those who do not believe that gender and race affected their legislative influence to those who believed their race and gender afforded them particular advantages in finding successful legislative tactics.

Because this study relies solely on self-reports of legislative influence, it is difficult to measure the veracity of claims. These women are, after all, politicians and are therefore given to carefully measured responses that shift subtly from one audience to another. There can be a gap between what legislators say on the record and what they believe. Indeed, as Smooth (2001) asserts, self-reports may never tell the entire story of legislative influence. There is also often a rift between how legislators see themselves and how their colleagues view them, regardless of the measured outcomes of their legislative success. Nor do the tactics that these Black female legislators employ represent prevalent norms for all the Black female legislators who fall within the purview of this study. Self-reports also do not illustrate very clearly how these tactics affect various Black women's legislative initiatives. Despite these limitations, exploring Black female legislators' self-perceived influence should benefit scholars who work to understand agency in a structure that practices racing and gendering.

The remaining sections of the chapter present Black female legislators' perceptions of institutional influence. These women do not indicate that they feel marginalized or powerless. Instead, the legislators in this study perceive themselves as succeeding despite the obstacles they encounter due to racism and sexism.

Findings

This section thematically presents Black female legislators' perceptions of institutional influence. Many of the study participants viewed their power strictly in terms of leadership and tenure. As such, the first theme centers upon Black female legislators' leadership roles in the Maryland state legislature. Second, I illustrate how African American female legislators without leadership roles are able to acquire legislative influence in a myriad of nontraditional mechanisms and channels. Last, the subjects of the study use their race and gender to their advantage by drawing on their experiences, expertise, and institutional knowledge to influence colleagues in leadership positions.

Leadership & Tenure

Many of the Black female legislators under study viewed their power strictly in terms of leadership and tenure. Specifically, a few of the study participants' comments reflect the traditional definitions of influence as mediated by seniority and tenure within the legislature. Some African American women involved in the study largely did not attribute their legislative influence to their intersectional identity. Instead, they gauged their legislative effectiveness by leadership status.

As evidenced by their comments, Black women in the legislature hold various positions of leadership. These positions directly relate to their perceived level of influence. In rating her influence one participant shared:

> I would [rate my influence as] a six because I am second in command of the House. (African American Female Delegate)

Another held:

> I'm a freshman; I've only been here for three sessions. I don't suffer any delusions of grandeur. I'm not at the center of power. Probably somewhere in the middle, I'd say a four. (African American Female Delegate)

> I'm in the middle. I'm new enough to know I don't have that much power. Especially the newer members, you have to pay your dues here to move yourself to the top. But I have formed enough allegiances with people that I do have some power. (African American Female Delegate)

> I am in the hierarchy of leadership. I came in as part of the leadership hierarchy. I came in as assistant deputy majority rep[resentative] my first year. I am now deputy majority rep. I hold the record of the passage of most bills by a new senator. (African American Female Senator)

Maryland state legislators appear to equate legislative influence and effectiveness with holding leadership positions. This professionalized legislature places significant emphasis on the prestige of committee chairs due to the small number of committees within the legislative structure. The legislators quoted above regard holding formal leadership positions as synonymous with being influential. Influence is also measured by policy expertise, tenure, or committee membership. While African American women in the Maryland legislature are afforded leadership opportunities, low-level party leadership positions do not offer institutional prestige and influence. However, due to the legislature's large leadership structure and focus on consensus building, few decisions are made in secret.

Playing the Game

Some of the African American female state legislators interviewed said that, although they do not occupy formal leadership positions or have served in the institution for a relatively short amount of time, they are still able to exert legislative influence in certain respects. Viewing her institutional power in terms of her ability to negotiate desired policy outcomes, one delegate with 37 years of tenure in the Maryland legislature finds that her institutional power is derived from legislative bargaining:

I look at it from a point of how much power do I have, what can I get out of it, [and] do they need me? From a seat of power, the power that I bring by being able to help them [White men] means a lot. It means a lot to me because I can change things for them. And it means a lot to them because they never thought I could do that. They didn't think I had that much power.

This response was predicated on power differences afforded to White men and Black women in the Maryland House of Delegates, of which the delegate is clearly well aware. She contends that White male delegates speak to her only when they need her legislative support. In turn, she finds that because the White male power brokers need her assistance to accomplish their legislative goals, she is vested with informal power in a system built on established hierarchies.

When asked to expand on why she believes that her colleagues do not think that she has much power, she pointed to her skin color. On the other hand, she acknowledges fellow legislators who realize that she can help them achieve their legislative priorities, have been willing to work with her, and regard her as an influential member of the institution. In this sense, she can turn her racial identity into an advantage. Indeed, this strategy has paid off. According to the delegate, "When I was named as Chairman of the Rules and Executive Nominations Committee everybody began to look at me totally different."

Another study participant referenced her legislative tenure as the major component in achieving legislative success. However, when she learned to play the game—bartering, making compromises, offering political favors, and expending political capital—she gained legislative influence. This delegate learned that seniority is not the only important factor in achieving one's legislative priorities. She found that cooperation or being a team player is an asset in gaining legislative success that can provide as much or more influence as holding a leadership position within the legislature would.

One freshman delegate participant was asked to sponsor a bill by the chair of the judiciary committee. The chair informed this delegate that he approached her to serve as sponsor on an important piece of legislation because "everyone liked her." She acknowledges that, because she is likable and amenable, the committee chair asked her to work with the judiciary committee to serve as a sponsor of their bill. The committee chair felt that colleagues would be more likely to support a bill that was sponsored by someone whom they liked. Because of this opportunity, this delegate was able to make valuable connections with the leadership of the judiciary committee. She finds that the opportunity to establish such political relationships is the most important factor in enabling freshman legislators to build a strong legislative record. This delegate's intersectional identity as a Black woman seemingly did not play a large role in helping her to establish these relationships. She attributed this instead to her likeable personality. Her character and individual traits opened the door to establishing connections with powerful and more senior members of the legislature.

Extra-institutional Measures

Recognizing the advantages of more formalized power, another delegate participant acknowledged that she needed institutional backing in some cases to gain influence in the Maryland legislature. However, she found that there were alternative channels through which she could have a voice on issues of particular importance to her and her constituents. When asked about her status regarding the institutional power scale, the delegate answered:

> I'd say I am slightly before the middle, closer to marginalized. I think that I'm not marginalized. When I speak on an issue, it is recognized and not put to the side. But I don't have the power without "the machine" with me or the leadership behind me to get legislation passed. [Nevertheless] I have been very effective in opposing legislation or bringing it to the forefront and the consciousness of the public.

This delegate said that she uses the media and community outreach efforts to engage with and mobilize the public, communicating through traditional media outlets and new social media such as Facebook and Twitter to express her opposition to legislation. She observed that her ability to mobilize the community and garner news coverage helped her maintain an active legislative profile. There is little mention in the literature of such a strategy for integrating the use of outside institutional channels into legislative activity. During my fieldwork, this delegate held two press conferences addressing police brutality toward African Americans in Baltimore. I attended one such press conference, which was held in the State House. The delegate spoke in depth with a television reporter about the mistreatment of African American inner-city youth at the hands of law enforcement. She stayed later and talked at greater length than other Baltimore City delegates who attended the event. Perhaps the delegate's methods are a necessary response to racing and gendering or a natural option for a freshman legislator who has yet to establish an institutional voice. Her use of extra-institutional communication channels represents another avenue through which to acquire legislative influence.

Institutional Prestige Is Unnecessary

Another delegate understood that her influence within the Maryland legislature diverged from traditional conceptualizations of institutional power. The following quote shows that her influence was felt on bills that directly affected her constituents:

> I do not have a reputation down here in putting in a lot of bills. African American women are not selfish. I came down [to Annapolis] and began to look at the

bills that are being put forth. When I get up to speak on the floor, people listen because of my years of experience and because of the knowledge I bring to the table. I can come with the history and the facts. It helps tremendously in the kind of influence that I can levy here relative to the package of [certain] bills. I don't consider myself ineffective, no. I am very effective when it comes to ensuring that legislation either passes or fails. . . and that has a positive or negative impact on the people I serve.

The delegate's understanding of legislative power and influence does not fit standard models posited by legislative studies scholars. Instead, she defines her influence in terms of what she can do for the people she serves. Her office is adorned with pictures of influential Black women, such as Winnie Mandela, Harriet Tubman, Oprah Winfrey, Shirley Chisholm, and Sojourner Truth. Alongside these pictures are handmade drawings from elementary schoolchildren thanking her for her many years of service to the Baltimore School System. Next to these drawings are inspirational quotes on leadership, success, and motivation by notable African Americans, as well as biblical scriptures. She pointed to her office decorations several times during our conversation to imply that these people, the quotes, and scriptures inspire her legislative agenda in Annapolis. She clearly judges the importance of her legislative influence solely by her ability to affect the daily lives of her constituents.

This study participant stated that she is not concerned with formal institutional power or influence. Does this mean that she is ineffective? Because she sees her role as a legislator as one of working to advance the priorities of her constituents, she is not pursuing legislative prestige, in the traditional sense, for its own sake. This is not to say that this Black female delegate could not be more effective as a legislator were she to occupy a formal leadership role, serve on a prestigious committee, or specialize in a relevant policy area. But this is not her explicit goal. She seeks to advance the priorities of her constituents in the legislature, not personal accolades.

Intersectional Identities: A Different Perspective

One of the participants in the study was among the few healthcare professionals in the Maryland legislature and an immigrant from Jamaica who saw her experiences, gender, race, and immigrant status as helping to make her an effective legislator. Because this delegate was not in a leadership position, she rated herself as a 5 on the 7–point scale indicating institutional influence. However, she found that her legislative influence was based on her opportunity to persuade colleagues to adopt her views on issues about which she had superior expertise. As a member of the Health and Government Operations Committee, this delegate's professional nursing background lent her credence with many of her colleagues. "I think that gives a certain amount of respect that I gain from my colleagues. . . who I am and the type of legislation I put forth." The expertise that this delegate brought to her committee was also affected by her race and gender, as she supported legislation that reflected lessons she learned from her experiences as a Black woman. She found that such positionality helped her to understand certain sensitivities that others might not understand. "Being a Black woman, I understand the social determinants of health. I understand racism,. . . culture. . . disparities, [and] the healthcare disparities that exist within the African American and other minority communities." Because her colleagues respected her, they were willing to listen to her racial and gendered perspective on health care.

This delegate was also aware of the legislative consequences of speaking on behalf of one's constituency based on a racial and gendered perspective. She found that while the majority of her colleagues respected her opinion, others despised her "cause they can't stand my legislation and can't take it because of who I am." When asked to explain this comment, she mentioned a bill addressing cultural competence and the phrasing of one particular healthcare-related bill:

> When. . . talking about cultural competence in healthcare, you are talking about all races and all ethnic groups. We all have our own cultures and beliefs and norms that we come with, but [one colleague] still wanted to make it look like I was just looking at stuff from the African American perspective. So I had to kind of make it quite clear that, as a nurse, I understand the pain from a clinical cultural competency component. You have to know your colleagues. And so with that it gives me a different little edge [on] some of the questions that they ask.

These remarks indicate that this participant was feeling that her colleagues pigeonholed her expertise as applying only to African Americans, as though she would have little interest in addressing the healthcare concerns of Whites, Asian Americans, or Hispanics. Her response signifies that her professional expertise as a nurse, the only nurse in the Maryland state legislature, is not based solely on race even if she does call attention in her legislative work to healthcare disparities affecting people of color and women. This African American female delegate noted that although her expertise is broad based, she focuses on minority health concerns as the only healthcare professional serving on the Health and Government Operations Committee. Both her nursing background and her identity as a Black woman enhanced her authority among her colleagues during committee hearings.

Additionally, this study participant wanted to make it clear that most of her colleagues did not view her in the same way as the one highlighted in the previous quote does. She added that for the most part, other legislators viewed her professional experiences as an asset and respected the bills she supported. Using both her identity and her professional background to her advantage, this African

American female delegate navigated around difficult colleagues who do not value her policy preferences.

A state senator who had not allowed potential gendered or racialized legislative handicaps to undermine her effectiveness, acknowledges:

> I always believe that the power was at the urinal. I always believe that they stood there and just. . . did stuff. My mentor around here was Delegate Pete Rawlins, who is now deceased. He was the most powerful person in the House,. . . it was just nice having him around. I used to say to him, "I think they [male legislators] are making plans at the bathroom and I think you're tricking me." He said, "What do you mean?" And I'd say, "I know they are doing stuff and I don't know what it is." I do believe that there are probably some things going on that I'm missing. I know stuff is happening, but I don't know what it is. But it's not hurting me that I'm missing stuff. I'm not going to worry about what I'm missing because obviously it's not important.

This senator's quotes indicate that she paid little attention to racing and gendering disadvantages, although she also acknowledged that her race and gender kept her from accessing powerful networks. She observed that as the Deputy Majority Whip she was influential as the bills that mattered most to her successfully passed. Instead of worrying about how she was silenced or marginalized, she concentrated on factors that she could control. She was in charge of her legislative agenda and did not allow her intersectional identity to pigeonhole her into a disadvantaged legislative position.

Still another example of a participant who believed that her race and gender as a Black woman gave her an advantage in the Maryland legislature was a delegate who when asked about her institutional influence asserted, "I have a lot of clout." Although this delegate had been a member of the legislature since 1983, she did not attribute her institutional status to seniority: "First off, as a Black woman, I have to feel that way [that I have legislative power]. Nobody else is going to feel that way unless I do it myself." This delegate further surmised that Black women have an intuitive skill that helps them in the legislature, namely the ability to discern the difference between what people say and their real intentions. Her advice would be to "listen to the people and watch their eyes. People will tell you [who they are]." She attributes this skill to her mother, who taught her at an early age that she must be self-sufficient and protect her own interests. The ability to discern between what people say and how they behave is a powerful asset in politics. When coalition building is predicated upon personal trust, legislators must be able to have confidence in a colleague's word.

The African American female delegate attributed her long and successful career in the Maryland legislature to this skill. She added that many politicians sought her advice in navigating the legislature. She noted that successful legislative interaction depended on how a member talked to her colleagues. "I always tell new legislators, 'You can't talk to people like they are in a classroom; they aren't students.'" This participant credited her successful communication style to her ability to do what Black women have always done in order to distinguish friend from foe.

Finally, consider the experience of a study participant who was among the most powerful senators in the Maryland legislature. She was Chair of the Education, Health, and Environmental Affairs Committee, one of the four standing committees in the Maryland Senate. Partly because of her leadership position, she rates herself as a "5 or 6" on the study's 7–point institutional influence scale. This Black woman senator believed that her personality traits helped her achieve her leadership position. She stated that "because of my aggression, commitment, and insistence, I'm the only African American woman Committee Chair in the Senate. I'm the only chairwoman of the four committees. They are all White males and I'm a double minority." This senator pointed out that she made history as the first Black female committee chair in Maryland's legislative history. She attributed her achievement to her persistence and unwillingness to "take no for an answer." Her comments reflected the ethos of the American creed that privileges individual talent and effort. Articulating that creed may indeed be a prerequisite for success in mainstream politics in a "post-racial" era. However, I found this senator's assertion that personality and hard work enabled her to become the first Black female committee chair to imply that she had to work harder and be smarter than White colleagues to overcome the institutional racing and gendering that often stymies Black female legislators. Her case seems to illustrate Williams' finding that the "old adage that Black parents often tell their children, 'You've got to work twice as hard to get half as far,' seems to partially explain the puzzle of Black women's success" (2001, 314).

This participant had not only worked hard and persistently enough to achieve a leadership role, she also believed that intersectional identity distinguished her from other committee chairs in the legislature. She believed she was elected to help her constituents, to fight for causes that she felt were important to the Black community and women, and to improve the quality of life for all Maryland residents. She acknowledged that her colleagues did not, share this perspective. She observed that they:

> . . . really don't want to help people. For me, it's about all people—it's not just about constituency. It's not about industry. [For them] it's about what do I get out of it and that's not why we are here. That's what I tell them on the floor. See. . . they don't want to hear that because that is what embarrasses them.

This Black female senator was also known for her directness. She unabashedly promoted the interests of all Maryland's citizens, not just those of her own constituents, and certainly not those of major business lobbies. She credited this quality with catapulting her into the position of the first Black female Vice Chair, which made it possible for her to become Chair when that post was vacated. In this leadership position, she used her intersectional experiences in the legislative process to advocate for people whose interests were too often excluded by her colleagues.

It is perhaps worth noting that all of the minority female legislators interviewed for this study insisted that I interview this particular senator. They all stated that they were immensely proud of her. As a trailblazer, she set a positive example for all female legislators of color in Maryland. Another Black female praised this senator as her role model, adding that she felt extremely fortunate to have such a legislative mentor whose work as the chair of a powerful committee resonated among all minority female legislators.

Conclusion

The Black female legislators who participated in this study were able to use their social positioning and strategic intersectionality to their advantage (Fraga et al., 2006). This study suggests that while Black female legislators experience some negative effects of racing-gendering (Hawkesworth, 2003), they are skilled at negotiating around them, using their identity in various ways to achieve their desired outcomes. As expected, based upon double disadvantage literature, some of the Black female legislators studied acknowledged differences in legislative influence due to their race and gender, while others cited neither their identities nor marginalization based on race and gender as factors in building legislative influence.

Black female legislators have discovered effective strategies for overcoming adversity to achieve their legislative priorities. The self-perceived influence of African American women in the Maryland legislature indicate that while political, institutional, and societal discrimination based on patriarchy, hegemony, racism, and classism have disadvantaged Black women, these legislators did not allow themselves to be marginalized. While institutional norms and preferences, as well as discrimination based on both race and gender, may inhibit their legislative success the findings in this work indicate that these Black women have found ways to exert their influence by means other than traditional legislative channels or institutions. Even those who did not feel they worked near the center of power readily admitted that the legislative culture has changed enough to provide them with a measure of influence. These women may measure influence differently or emphasize atypical mechanisms of legislative activity. They used the tools available to them to achieve their legislative priorities in a raced and gendered institution.

This study mirrors the work of Smooth (2001, 2006), who found that African American female state legislators, in particular Maryland state legislators, were able to exert legislative influence. While Black female legislators did not represent themselves as wielding broad-based legislative influence, they echoed Smooth's findings that they were influential with public policy issues that directly affected their constituents. Building upon extant research on female legislators of color and legislative influence (Smooth, 2001, 2006; Hawkesworth, 2003; Fraga, 2006), this study demonstrates that identities are privileged and marginalized within American legislatures. As such, the somatic norm of Whiteness and maleness (Puwar, 2004) remains a barrier that Black female legislators must overcome. Nevertheless, I find that these legislators can and do use their identities to their advantage in gaining legislative leadership and influence. Black female legislators expressed a range of concerns about, challenges within, and disadvantages in pursuing the legislative process based on their social positioning. Yet, they were largely successful in developing tactics based on their identities that enhanced their institutional power. This study concludes, based on its survey and analysis of Black female legislators' self-perceptions of their own legislative influence and agency, that Black women in the Maryland state legislature perceive themselves as successful in circumventing marginalization.

Moreover, the Black women interviewed in this study found that their race and gender could be attributes in navigating the legislative process. Their policy priorities were sometimes facilitated by their intersectional identities. These Black women understood that their identities need not matter in the legislative process, even though they were certainly not blind to racism and sexism within society as well as in the legislature. Instead, armed with this understanding, they confronted patriarchy and racism by using their race and gender to their advantage.

Bibliography

Acker, J. (1989). Hierarchies, job bodies: A theory of gendered organizations. *Gender and Society, 4,* 139–158.

Acker, J. (1992). Gendered institutions: From sex roles to gendered institutions. *Contemporary Sociology, 21,* 565–569.

Barrett, E. J. (1995). The policy priorities of African American women in state legislatures. *Lesgislative Studies Quarterly, 20*(2), 223–247.

Blair, D. D., & Stanley, J. R. (1991). Personal relationships and legislative power: Male and female perceptions. *Legislative Studies Quarterly, 16,* 485–507.

Bratton, K.A., & Haynie, K. (1999). Agenda setting and legislative success in state legislatures: The effects of gender and race. *Journal of Politics, 61,* 658–679.

Browning, R. P., Marshall, D. R., & Tabb, D. H. (1984). *Protest is not enough: The struggle of Blacks and Hispanics for equality in urban politics.* Berkeley: University of California Press.

Bryce, H. J., & Warrick, A. E. (1977). Black women in electoral politics. In M. Githens and L. J. Prestage (Eds.), *A portrait of marginality: The political behavior of the African American woman* (pp. 395–400). New York: David McKay.

Cramer Walsh, K. (Ed.). (2002). *Female legislators and the women's rights agenda.* Norman: University of Oklahoma Press.

Crenshaw, K. (1991). Mapping the margins: Intersectionality, identity politics, and violence against women of color. *Stanford Law Review, 43*(6), 1241–1299.

Critzer, J. W. (1998). Racial and gender income inequality in the American states. *Race and Society, 1*(2), 159–176.

Deering, C. J., & Smith, S. S. 1997. *Committees in Congress* (3rd Edition). Washington, D.C.: CQ Press.

Dodson, D. L., & Carroll, S. J. (1991). *Reshaping the agenda: Women in state legislatures.* New Brunswick, N.J.: Center for the American Woman and Politics.

Fraga, L.R., Lopez, L., Martinez-Ebers, V., & Ramirez, R. (2006). Gender and ethnicity: Patterns of electoral success and legislative advocacy among Latina and Latino state officials in four states. *Journal of Women, Politics & Policy, 28*(3–4), 121–145.

Francis, W. L. (1989). *The legislative committee game: A comparative analysis of the fifty states.* Columbus: The Ohio State University Press.

Hall, Richard L. (1996). *Partcipation in congress.* New Haven, CT: Yale University Press.

Hamm, K. E., Harmel, R. & Thompson, R. (1983). Ethnic and partisan minorities in two southern legislatures. *Legislative Studies Quarterly, 8*, 177–189.

Hawkesworth, M. (2003). Congressional enactments of race-gender: Toward a theory of race-gendered institutions. *American Political Science Review, 97*(4), 529–550.

Haynie, K. L. (2001). *African American legislators in the American states.* New York: Columbia University Press.

Hedge, D., Button, J., & Spear, M. (1996). Accounting for the quality of Black legislative life: The view from the states. *American Journal of Political Science, 40*, 82–98.

Jewell, M. E., & Whiker, M. L. (1994). *Legislative leadership in the American states.* Ann Arbor: University of Michigan Press.

Kathlene, L. (1994). Power and influence in state legislative policymaking: The interaction of gender and position in committee hearing debates. *American Political Science Review, 88*, 560–576.

Kenney, S. (1996). New research on gendered political institutions. *Political Research Quarterly, 49*, 445–466.

King, D. (1988). Multiple jeopardy, multiple consciousness: The context of Black feminist ideology. *Signs: Journal of Women in Culture and Society, 14(1)*, 42–72.

King-Meadows, T., & Schaller, T. F. (2000). *The institutionalization of Black state legislative power.* Paper presented at the Annual Meeting of the American Political Science Association, Washington, DC.

Mansbridge, J., & Tate, K. (1992). Race trumps gender: The Thomas nomination in the Black community. *PS: Political Science and Politics, 25*(3), 488–493.

Nelson, A. (1991). *Emerging influentials in state legislatures.* New York: Praeger.

Norton, N. (1995). Women, it's not enough to be elected: Committee position makes a difference. In G. Duerst-Lahti Kelly & M. R (Eds.), *Gender power, leadership and governance* (pp. 115–140). Ann Arbor: University of Michigan Press.

Orey, B. D. (2000). Black legislative politics in Mississippi. *Journal of Black Studies, 30*(6), 791–814.

Orey, B. D., Smooth, W., Adams, K. S., & Harris-Clark, K. (2006). Race and gender matter: Refining models of legislative policy making in state legislatures. *Journal of Women, Politics, & Policy, 28*(3–4), 97–119.

Preuhs, R. R. (2006). The conditional effects of minority descriptive representation: Black legislators and policy influence in the American states. *Journal of Politics, 68*(3), 585–599.

Puwar, N. (2004). *Space invaders: Race, gender and bodies out of place.* Oxford: Berg Publishers.

Rosenthal, C. S. (1995). The role of gender in descriptive representation. *Political Research Quarterly, 48*(3), 599–611.

Saint-Germain, M. (1989). Does their difference make a difference? The impact of women on public policy in the Arizona legislature. *Social Science Quarterly, 70*(4), 956–968.

Smooth, W. G. (2006). Intersectionality in electoral politics: A mess worth making. *Politics and Gender, 2*(31), 400–414.

Smooth, W. G. (2001). *Perceptions of influence in state legislatures: A focus on the experiences of African American women in state legislatures.* Dissertation, University of Maryland.

Smooth, W. G. (2005). African American woman and electoral politics: Journeying from the shadows to the spotlight. In Susan J. Carroll & Richard Fox (Eds.), *Gender and Elections: Shaping the future of American politics.* New York: Cambridge University Press.

Thomas, S. (1991). The impact of women on state legislative policies. *Journal of Politics, 53*(4), 958–976.

Thomas, S. (1994). *How women legislate.* New York: Oxford University Press.

Valentino, N. A., and Sears, D. O. (2005). Old times there are not forgotten: Race and partisan realignment in the contemporary south. *American Journal of Political Science, 49*(3), 958–976.

Williams, L. F. (2001). The civil rights-Black power legacy: Black women elected officials at the local, state, and national levels. In Bettye Collier-Thomas & P. V. Franklin (Eds.), *Sisters in the struggle: African American women in the civil rights-Black power movement.* New York: New York University Press.

Winsky Mattei, L. R. (1998). Gender and power in American legislative discourse. *Journal of Politics, 60*(2), 440–461.

Wright, G., Osborn, T., and Winburn, J. (2005). *Parties and representation in the American legislatures.* Paper presented at the Midwest Political Science Association.

Chapter Three

Black Women and Leadership in the Church

Kaye Thompson-Rogers

As a middle-aged Black woman, I know from experience the struggles that Black women endure. Whether they are wives, mothers, homemakers, students, single parents, divorcees, parents that support their children's extracurricular activities or civic organizations within and outside of their church organizations, Black women are doers for the home and family (Onyuku-Opukiri, 2000). The Black church has served as one of the greatest sources of strength for many Black women. Since slavery, Black women participated in and assumed leadership roles in religion, particularly the Black church (Carpenter, 2001).

Western Black religion, which takes root in traditional African religious practices meshed with Christianity or Islam, assisted Blacks in coping with slavery (Carpenter, 2001) and is still employed by many African Americans to successfully deal with life's challenges. Black religion and religious institutions facilitate the liberation of people of African descent. The spiritual foundation of the Black church formed a relationship with the Black community. This connection has yielded freedom movements for Black people (Simmons & Thomas, 2010) throughout the world which continues to this day.

Black churches and religion have offered Black women spiritual tools to deal with racism, sexism, and day-to-day trials and tribulations. During Sunday morning service, Black women are given an opportunity to renew themselves emotionally and spiritually, which prepares them for another week to face the challenges of family, supervisors, colleagues, and others they encounter. For many

Black women it takes constant praying and the companionship of God to make it through each day (Jones & Shorter-Gooden, 2003). My work on Black females and religion features Black female abolitionists, ministers, lay women, and others providing various forms of leadership in the church.

Research indicates that countless women find their involvement with religious organizations and institutions to be encouraging, nurturing, and satisfying. A review of five national studies by Robert Joseph Taylor of the University of Michigan and several of his colleagues suggested that Black people hold stronger religious feelings than Whites and that Black women were more religious than Black men (1999). It has been indicated that African American women are perhaps the most spiritually committed persons in the United States. Another survey by the National Survey of Black Americans revealed that more than 71% of Black women attend religious service several times a month and that Black women's membership often make up more than 68% of a church or its congregation (Taylor, Mattis & Chatters, 1999).

National Survey of Black Americans data found that prayer was the second most common strategy to cope with stressful episodes in the lives of Black women and men. Black women were more likely to use prayer as a strategy to manage the stress of health issues, emotional situations, or interpersonal problems (Bowman, 1996). Black women know that religious participation is health enhancing, as research has confirmed. Studies also show that Black women who attend church services regularly and are more religious are less likely to be depressed and more likely to be happier and experience satification in their lives (Jones & Shorter-Gooden, 2003).

Another survey in 2009 by Barna Group shows the number of Black female senior pastors in Protestant churches has doubled to 10% since 1999 (Bradley, 2010). Fifty-eight percent of those women work in major area churches, which includes the United Methodist Church. Protestant Christian churches have ordained women for five decades (Bradley, 2010). Today the historical, sociological, biblical, theological, and preaching contributions of Black women, both past and present, are readily available (Carpenter, 2001). A study by Marian Whitson utilized focus-group data in 1991 and 1992 of 100 Black female church members that also included clergy. Whitson wanted to know the women's perceptions of sexism and gender issues in the Christian Methodist Episcopal Church. The results of the study found that the majority of participants witnessed limited female leadership, sexual harassment, and other forms of sexism. The women were disturbed about the church not speaking out against these types of issues and the pervasive silence within the house of worship surrounding them (Whitson, 1997).

This chapter intends to highlight the salience of religious participation as it relates to Black female leadership in the Black church. In particular, it highlights the religious experiences and trajectories of 17 Black laywomen, religious activists, and pastors. Black women historically have preached for numerous reasons. They wanted their lives to be rich legacies of spirituality and activism, to claim their full humanity, overcome subordination in the church, and to socially and spiritually uplift the enslaved.

Ella Mitchell is credited with helping African American women find their voices, frame their thoughts, focus their messages, and speak in a profession historically dominated by men. The featured women of this chapter consist of Jarena Lee, Zilpha Elaw, Rebecca Cox Jackson, Sojourner Truth, Maria W. Stewart, Julia A. Foote, Harriett Tubman, Harriet A. Cole Baker, Lizzie Woods Robinson, Mary Lena Lewis Tate, Nannie Helen Burroughs, Anna Pauli Murray, Ella Muriel Pearson Mitchell, Barbara C. Harris, Prathis L. Hall, Claudette A. Copeland, and Renita Weems. Given the salience of their contributions, it is important to give scholarly attention to the role of these Black women (Carpenter, 2001)[1] as their religion continues to guide and influence many communities (Lowen, 2011).

A large body of research has found religion and religious participation to be especially important for Black women (Ross, 2003). Given the importance of religion in their lives, one may find it ironic that few Black women hold positions of leadership in the Black church. Currently, twice as many female senior pastors exist compared to a decade ago in the United States. Although women have proved their effective leadership in many denominations, they have yet to head pulpits as large as their male counterparts (Holley, 2009). As women assume greater leadership roles in the church, some are faced with more obstacles and challenges than male counterparts. For example, in some African churches, female ministers are not allowed to enter the altar, pulpit, or participate in administering the Lord's Supper.[2] In some cases, even the founders of these churches are not allowed to participate in these practices (Onyuku-Opukiri, 2000). For Black women, spiritual beliefs incorporate the center of their being. Hence, participating in religious organizations often leads to lifelong commitments (Taylor, Mattis & Chatters, 1999). The following section traces the involvement and roles that Black female ministers, laywomen, and abolitionists played and how their contributions benefited society in terms of faith, spirituality, and the church.

Black Women as Leaders during Slavery and Beyond

Black female religious leaders have historically used spiritual exaltation as a means of serving God. Their ancestors laid the foundation for prayer, often asking God to bring them out of bondage, poverty, and towards racial uplift (Ross, 2003). During the period of institutionalized slavery (and beyond), families would gather together

1   The terms *Black* and *African American* will be used interchangeably in this chapter.
2   The same as communion, a Christian sacrament that commemorates Jesus Christ's Last Supper, with the priest or minister consecrating bread and wine consumed by the congregation.

to sing Negro spirituals. These songs inspired them to praise God, increased their faith, and served as signals that fellow slaves were attempting to escape. During such times, songs such as "Steal Away" or "Swing Low, Sweet Chariot" were sung (Moon, 2010). Spiritual exaltation and singing was customary during this period and still serve as vital components of Black spiritual communities today.

During slavery, Black women determined the social needs necessary to improve the lives of the Black masses in their communities (Ross, 2003). These needs involved the desire for political freedom, independence, self-sufficiency, and well-being for the African American community (Carpenter, 2001). Black women prayed and met the needs of their neighbors and families as they followed the "Word of God."

Religious Black women led and followed, volunteering in various movements to increase racial justice within society during the Civil Rights era. In this respect, many Black women began their ministries as evangelists. They also served as missionaries in Africa, Liberia, and Angola, taking positions as leaders in the early years of the church. For example, Lavina Johnson (1845), Sarah Simpson (1860), Susan Collins (1902), and Martha Drummer (1906) were Black female missionaries who worked in the field until their retirement (Carpenter, 2001).

According to Ross (2003), Joyce Ladner, a former Student Nonviolent Coordinating Committee (SNCC) worker and sociologist stated, "Black women's social responsibility derived from practices of our Black ancestors wanting to sustain and improve African American life" (p. 4). This practice followed African Americans through their religious experiences and continued for future generations. Dorothy Height often said, "Black women are the backbone of every institution" (Nichols & Bello, 2010). In a recent article, Marc Morial, President of the National Urban League, stated that women are the backbone of the Black family and when women hurt, the American family suffers. In this article, Morial held, "By uplifting Black women, especially those struggling hardest to keep their families together and their dreams on track, we lift up every American community" (Woods, 2008, p.1). The remainder of this chapter highlights Black female religious leaders from colonial times to the present.

Jarena Lee

Jarena Lee (1783–ca. 1850), one of the first African American women to preach the gospel in the 13 colonies (Simmons & Thomas, 2010), made it known to Reverend Richard Allen—founder of the African Methodist Episcopal (AME) Church—that she believed it was her duty to preach the gospel. Allen replied to Lee saying "as to preaching. . . that our discipline knew nothing at all about it, that it did not call for women preachers." Not deterred by Allen's response, she later joined Zilpha Elaw to travel throughout the country and preach the gospel (Williams, 1993) as a traveling evangelist (Moon, 2010). During the time of Jarena Lee, women in the community would open their homes to female preachers, while Black males in authority would not ordain them and denied them use of the church or other buildings (Williams, 1993). In spite of this, Lee earned the distinction of being the first female preacher in the AME Church (Carpenter, 2001).

At the time of the 1800 census, approximately 25% of African Americans in the United States considered themselves Methodist or Baptist. In the northern United States, free Negro Christians faced a great deal of prejudice and discrimination from Whites within several churches and denominations. Thus, enslaved and free Blacks began to establish their own places to worship independently from Whites. Over time, Black congregations and denominations continued to expand and develop in the northeastern and southern parts of the United States. During this time, large churches were built in Fayetteville, North Carolina; Boston, Massachusetts; Wilmington, Delaware; Mobile, Alabama; and New Orleans, Louisiana (Moon, 2010).

Zilpha Elaw

Zilpha Elaw (ca. 1790–ca. 1840), born near Philadelphia, Pennsylvania, during colonial times, visited slave states to preach: a dangerous venture which could have cost her her life. Elaw, a bold Black woman who preached the gospel and was considered a heroine, worked unsponsored by any organization, board, or denomination (Simmons & Thomas, 2010).

In her late 20s, she attended her first camp meeting and gave her first public prayer in 1817. For the next five years she spent time attending meetings, praying for people, and doing the Lord's work. During her travels in 1819, she became ill and had a vision of future health. The vision directed her to go to a camp meeting. A year after her illness, she attended the meeting and felt the divine word telling her to preach. Methodist Church elders gave their approval for her to preach, but other church members discouraged her to step into a role that generally was reserved for men. Even though her husband expressed disapproval of her preaching, she continued. Due to a decline in his health, her husband died on January 27, 1823.

After the death of her husband, Elaw became a domestic caring for her 11–year-old daughter. With the help of Quaker friends, she subsequently opened a school for Black children. She ultimately returned to Philadelphia in 1827 to preach. When she arrived in Burlington, New Jersey, in 1828, she had just enough money to pay her debt and to take care of her child. She eventually started another preaching tour, heading towards Maryland, Washington, D.C, and areas in the South (Simmons & Thomas, 2010). Her mastery of preaching and public speaking led her to become well known in her travels (Simmons & Thomas, 2010).

Elaw continued preaching in the northeastern states in 1830, and in spite of hostility she received from some congregations, she continued her mission. In many of her sermons, she criticized the racist practices and immorality demonstrated by many Whites at the time. She preached thousands of sermons drawing upon the scriptures using straightforward and precise words (Simmons & Thomas, 2010).

Rebecca Cox Jackson

Rebecca Cox Jackson (1795–1871) was born outside of Philadelphia at the turn of the 19th century. A married, free Black Methodist woman and seamstress, Jackson's religious beliefs and experiences propelled her to become a preacher and founder of the Black Shaker community. She believed she was chosen by God to reveal his will and discovered the presence of a divine inner voice instructing her how to use her spiritual gifts. In 1830, at age 35, she experienced a spiritual rebirth and set out on her religious journey. She became an itinerant preacher who believed in sanctification, experienced divine grace, and inspired both Whites and Blacks. Jackson along with other Black Methodist women preached throughout the 19th century (Jackson, 1981).

Jackson ended up in Albany, New York. While there, she became associated with a group named the Religious Perfectionist, most of whom were White. They were impressed with her gifts, so she stayed among them for four years in Watervliet, New York. She soon became dissatisfied with the group's outreach to Blacks, which caused conflict. Hence, she returned to Philadelphia with her companion and protégé, Rebecca Perot. Together, Jackson and Perot started the Black Shakers in Philadelphia. The group, who combined elements of Shaker theology and Black female praying band traditions, consisted of a dozen to 20 members. Other Black Shakers living throughout Philadelphia joined the group for services. After the death of Rebecca Jackson in 1871, Rebecca Perot took the name "Mother Rebecca Jackson" and took leadership of the Philadelphia family, which survived another 40 years (Jackson, 1981). Rebecca Cox Jackson was known as a gifted visionary and religious activist who mentored and paved the way for future Black female leaders.

Sojourner Truth

A Black religious female activist during the antebellum period, Sojourner Truth (1797–1883) (a.k.a. Isabella Baumfree and Isabella Van Wagener) was born in bondage in Ulster County, New York. During the mid-19th century, she believed God summoned her to flee from servitude to speak against slavery, fight for women's rights, and free the enslaved. During 1826, Truth escaped from slavery and in 1843 changed her name to Sojourner Truth. From this point on, she established herself as an extraordinary preacher (Ross, 2003).

Truth began lecturing against slavery. Her first speeches took place in Northampton, Massachusetts, and in New York in 1845. Later, William Lloyd Garrison invited her to speak. At his invitation, she joined the antislavery lecture circuit. Lecturing from a religious perspective, Truth's reputation as a powerful speaker grew. She spoke on women's rights and the abolition of slavery (Ross, 2003).

Throughout Sojourner's life, she prayed, practiced holy living, witnessing, and testifying. Unable to read, she depended on children to read the scriptures to her. She preferred children because they would not give her their interpretation of the scripture. She believed in divine interaction and expected divine intervention within her life. Truth modeled leadership guided by her religious perspective and activism. She inspired women and girls to be educated, to believe and trust in God, and to become lifelong learners (Ross, 2003). Just as Sojourner worked towards equal rights, Maria Stewart pursued a similar mission.

Maria W. Stewart

Born in Hartford, Connecticut, in 1803, Maria W. Stewart held a philosophical religious faith and served as an abolitionist and advocate for women's rights. Stewart's public speaking was inspired by the Bible. She was very intellectual and led a spiritual life informed by her for five years in Sabbath School (Carpenter, 2001). On August 10, 1826, Maria married James W. Stewart and began her career as a teacher in New York. By 1845, she had taught more than 60 Black scholars. She was appointed assistant principal under the direction of Hezekiah Green in 1847 (Stewart, 1987).

Stewart's husband became sick in December 1829. He died on December 17, leaving Maria a widow about three years after their marriage. After the death of her husband, she was stripped of a substantial inheritance that was willed to her by her husband by a group of White business men. Stewart continued to preach against slavery, taught pride to Blacks, and self-help among her people, as she constantly defended her right to preach in the church. Within a year of her leaving Boston, Black and White women began walking down her path to podiums, speaking at churches and meeting halls to proclaim the social gospel of liberation and justice (Stewart, 1987).

Julia A. Foote

Born in Schenectady, New York, Julia A. J. Foote (1823–1900) experienced a Christian conversion after her family moved to Albany. She believed God "plucked her out of the burning path" to preach and teach. As a result, she went against her husband and followed her spiritual pursuits. Later, Foote was asked to leave the Boston African Methodist Episcopal Zion Church (AMEZ) by Reverend Jehiel C. Beman. Some believe that Beman was bothered that Foote was a bold female and that he did not agree with her use of Methodist tenets in sermons and teaching (Simmons & Thomas, 2010). Foote's faith was so strong that nothing deterred her from her aspirations. Her impact on Black women and religion paved the way for other Black women with similar ambitions, including Harriet Tubman.

Harriet Tubman

Harriet Tubman (1820–1913) was referred to as "Moses," which was a reference to a prophet in the Bible's book of Exodus who led the Hebrews to freedom. As "the Moses of Her People," Tubman led more than 300 slaves to freedom using the Underground Railroad. The railroad consisted of tunnels, makeshift dirt roads, and safe houses along various routes (Clinton, 2005). She was born into slavery as Araminta "Minty" Ross in Dorchester County, Maryland (Moon, 2010). As a child, she was told that she was a native of the Ashanti Region of Ghana. It is believed that she adopted her name Harriett either from her mother as a part of her religious conversion or in honor of a sister that had disappeared (Clinton, 2005).

In her teens, Tubman suffered a head trauma as a result of an overseer throwing a two-pound weight at her as she protected a slave trying to run away. Tubman married a free Black man around 1844 and became ill again around 1849 which decreased her value as a slave. The illness prompted her master to try to sell her, as she was unable to successfully pull her workload. She prayed and asked God to make her owner change his mind about selling her, yet it looked as if the sale would be finalized. Suddenly, she changed her prayer and asked the Lord to kill him as he would not change his ways. Ironically, her owner, Mr. Brodess, died within a week and his wife began selling off the slaves. Tubman told her husband that she was not going to allow the Brodess family to decide her destiny, so she ran to her freedom, eventually ending up in Philadelphia, Pennsylvania (Moon, 2010).

During her life, she was a conductor of the Underground Railroad, a feminist, a Union spy, a political leader, a spiritual leader, a cook, an armed scout, a nurse, and an abolitionist. The railroad was in operation from the early colonial period until the end of the Civil War. Tubman was affiliated with the African Methodist Episcopal Zion Church (Moon, 2010).

Harriet A. Cole Baker

Harriet A. Cole Baker (1829–1913) was born a free woman in Havre de Grace, Maryland. She was one of seven children and the daughter of William and Harriet Cole. At the age of 11, her father passed. She married William Baker, a fugitive slave, at age 16. Seven months after their child was born, they left Maryland and moved to Pennsylvania. Her husband was later captured, yet with the help of some friends, Baker was able to pay for his freedom (Simmons & Thomas, 2010).

Baker was called to preach in 1872, yet her husband did not support this decision. Her husband, in particular, was not in favor of her leaving the children. He stated that if something happened to the children during her travels, he would never forgive her. Unfortunately, two children became ill and died less than 12 months later while she was on her journey. In later years, Baker had three more children. Around 1875, the African Methodist Episcopal Church (AME) authorized Baker to preach. During her travels, for more than 15 years, she preached at camp meetings and revivals.

In 1889, the Philadelphia Conference of the AME Church appointed Baker pastor of St. Paul's Church in Lebanon, Pennsylvania. The church congregation was small, but there were both Black and White members. *The Colored Lady Evangelist*, the autobiography of Reverend Harriet A. Cole Baker was published in 1892. Because of her skills and the fact that she was received by both Blacks and Whites, she was well known on the East Coast. Baker was the first Black female pastor appointed by an AME Conference (Simmons & Thomas, 2010). The loss of her children and her husband's disapproval did not weaken Baker's determination. Meanwhile, other strong Black women came forward to preach and teach.

Lizzie Woods Robinson

Lizzie Woods Robinson (1860–1946), also referred to as Lizzie Woods Roberson, was born on April 5, 1860. After the Civil War, she, her mother, and four siblings were left without a male to help provide financially. Lizzie's mother never learned to read, but she was determined to send her children to missionary school so they could be taught. Around the age of 8, Lizzie could read the Bible to her mother. When Lizzie was 15, her mother died (Simmons & Thomas, 2010). Later, Lizzie joined a Black church in Pine Bluff, Arkansas, embraced Christianity, and became involved with the Baptist Academy in 1901.

Lizzie became active in the Church of God in Christ (COGIC) and received the baptism of the Holy Ghost in 1911. She eventually left the Baptist Academy and later that year was appointed as supervisor of the COGIC's women's work. Mother Robinson was the first African American to serve in this position. Robinson and her family moved to Omaha, Nebraska, and established its first Church of God in Christ. Presently known as the Robinson Memorial—which was named for the family—the Church of God in Christ has been placed on Nebraska's National Register of Historic Places. Robinson is considered one of the greatest organizers among Christian women. In the women's ministry for the COGIC, the women were called evangelists, revivalists, Mothers, or missionaries. A strict woman, Robinson established a dress code and rules that governed women's behavior. While her methods seemed extreme to some, her primary motivation was to solidify and uplift the African American community (Simmons & Thomas, 2010).

Mary Lena Lewis Tate

Mary Lena Lewis Tate (1871–1930) was born in Steel Spring, Tennessee, on January 5, 1871. During the time of her birth, slavery was unconstitutional, yet racism and lynching were prevalent. She spent the majority of her early years in the south. Reading and writing were very important to her mother, so she made sure that her children were equipped with these skills. Mary married David Lewis in 1888 and from their union came two sons (Simmons & Thomas, 2010).

Lewis Tate became an organizer of a faith community and her sons joined her in the ministry. She was not concerned with approval from men as her vision demonstrated approval from Jesus Christ through her works. She was educated and dealt with challenges of transportation by using any means necessary to accomplish her goals. She prevailed by walking, using barges, steamships, old cars, wagons pulled by mules, and Jim Crow trains to reach her destinations (Simmons & Thomas, 2010).

Lewis Tate had a reputation for always trying to do the right thing and thus earned the nickname, "Ms. Do Right." Around 1895, she established a group of religious adherents called "The Do Rights" whose purpose was to expand her religious empire and purchase property. Lewis preached in Tennessee, Kentucky, Illinois, Missouri, Alabama, Georgia, and other states in the eastern portion of the United States. Finally, Lewis and the Do Rights formally established the Church of the Living God, The Pillar, and Ground of the Truth in the year 1908. By 1918, 20 more of these churches were established in surrounding states (Simmons & Thomas, 2010).

In addition to these accomplishments, Lewis Tate was responsible for establishing the New and Living Way Publishing House in Nashville, Tennessee. Much of the early church literature was written by Tate. These included the *First Decree Book*, written in 1914, as well as the *Constitution, Government, and General Decree Book* in 1923. She completed her last preaching tour in the winter, arriving in Philadelphia in 1930. Lewis Tate died from complications from frostbite, gangrene, and diabetes, yet her strong leadership and preaching lived in the hearts and minds of many for years to come[3] (Simmons & Thomas, 2010).

Nannie Helen Burroughs

Nannie Helen Burroughs was born in Orange, Virginia, to John and Jennie Poindexter Burroughs. Although the exact year of her birth is unknown, it has been recorded as May 2, 1879, or 1883. Burroughs was an educator, religious leader, and social activist who helped found the Women's Auxiliary of the National Baptist Convention (NBC) and the National Training School for Women and Girls. At age 5, her mother took her to Washington, D.C., as there were more educational opportunities for Blacks there (Easter, 1995).

Burroughs' involvement in the 19th Street Baptist Church started at an early age. After she moved to Washington, D.C., she became active with the Sunday school and the young people's organization. She studied business and domestic science and graduated with honors from the M Street School in 1896. Burroughs

---

3   In Christianity, Holy Spirit is understood as the spiritual force of God.

went on to organize the Harriet Beecher Stowe Literary Society. The society gave students an opportunity for literary and oratorical expression. Unable to find a job in Washington, D.C., or Tuskegee, she accepted a job in Philadelphia as an associate editor for a paper known as the *Christian Banner* (Easter, 1995).

Burroughs returned to Washington, D.C., hoping to obtain a position as a clerk, but temporarily worked as a janitress at an office building until finding desired employment. She later took a position as a bookkeeper and editorial secretary under the direction of Reverend L. G. Jordan, corresponding secretary to the National Baptist Convention's Foreign Board (NBC). The board moved its headquarters to Louisville, Kentucky, in 1900. Hence, Burroughs felt compelled to move as well. Burroughs attended the National Baptist Convention (NBC) in 1900, giving a talk entitled "Hindered from Helping." Her speech was intended to set the tone to establish a Women's Convention (WC). After Burroughs' speech, her friend and advisor Reverend Jordan recommended that the Women's Convention be approved (Easter, 1995).

Burroughs became president of the Woman's Convention in 1948. Under her leadership, she proposed the development of a national young people's camp. She eventually raised the money and reported to the Convention in 1959 when funds were available. The camp opened in 1960 and operated during the months of June, July, and August each year. It offered youth training and fellowship, as well as (1) mission studies; (2) worship training and church programs; (3) exercise and recreation; (4) communal-societal interaction; and (5) theater art, drama, and music (Easter, 1995).

Burroughs' lifetime dream was to open a school for girls in the District of Columbia's school system. Burroughs mentioned the establishment of the school at the 1901 Women's Convention and in 1904 President S. Willie Layten endorsed her recommendation. The location of the school was decided upon and announced at the January 1907 Convention in Washington, D.C. The dedication of the site took place on September 14, 1907. The school opened with Burroughs as president on October 19, 1909, and was debt free.[4] The aim of the school centered upon training the head, hands, heart, and overall development of individuals interested in contributing to human welfare. To accomplish this aim, the school sought to cultivate a Christian atmosphere. Under the motto "We Specialize in the Wholly Impossible," the Burroughs School combined industrial training and liberal arts with a Christianity. She maintained her own publishing house, trained women missionaries, and educated African American women to be self-sufficient wage earners. Her school was influential in the "uplifting of the race" for women and girls throughout the country. The school was eventually named the Nannie Helen Burroughs School with the street name being changed to Nannie Helen Burroughs Avenue. The District of Columbia declared it a historical landmark in

---

4   This is property that was paid in full with no balance.

1991 (Easter, 1995). Playing an instrumental role, Burroughs also advocated that churches establish Woman's Day Observances (Carpenter, 2001). Women's Day, now called Mother's Day, is celebrated in the United States on the second Sunday of each May thanks to Nannie and others that followed in her footsteps.

Anna Pauli Murray

Anna Pauli Murray (1910–1985) was born Anna Pauline Murray in Baltimore, Maryland. She lost both parents at an early age and was raised by her maternal grandparents and aunts (Simmons & Thomas, 2010) in Durham, North Carolina (Wise, 2010). Murray served as a lawyer, activist, poet, and priest (Vaughn, 2010). She addressed race, gender, and class throughout her work. Issues that were most important to her were the abuse of White men towards Black slave women, as well as the disparate treatment of African Americans (Vaughn, 2009). Her passion for multiracial issues was linked to her multiracial heritage, as Murray was African American, White, and Native American (Vaughn, 2010).

After many years as an active Episcopal laywoman, Murray earned ordination toward the end of her life (Carpenter, 2001), serving as the first female African American Episcopalian priest (Vaughn, 2010). She was also the only woman and first in her graduating class at Howard University Law School in 1944. In addition, she was the first African American to be awarded a Doctor of Juridical Science degree from Yale University Law School; the first African American to serve as Deputy Attorney General in the state of California; and the first African American woman to publish a lead article in a law review for the journal, *The University of California Law Review* (Simmons & Thomas, 2010).

Another significant achievement was Murray's authoring of a legal brief that ended state laws denying women the right to serve on juries in the *White v. Cook* case. Title VII of the Civil Rights Act of 1964, which prohibited discrimination in employment including women, was an amendment advocated by Murray (Simmons & Thomas, 2010).

Murray authored several publications, including *States' Laws on Color and Race* (Simmons & Thomas, 2010); *Proud Shoes; Dark Testament and Other Poems; The Autobiography of a Black Activist, Feminist, Lawyer, Priest and Poet;* and *Song in a Weary Throat: An American Pilgrimage*, which was published two years after her death (Murray, 1987). Murray's publication, *States' Laws on Color and Race*, encourages Christian women to work towards changing unjust laws (Carpenter, 2001).

The Duke Human Rights Center at the John Hope Franklin Humanities Institute in Durham, North Carolina, chose Murray's home to provide a history of human rights. The project intends to use Murray's legacy to explore Durham history and dialogue, which may lay the foundation for a proposed Museum of History in Durham (Vaughn, 2009).

Ella Muriel Pearson Mitchell

Ella Muriel Pearson Mitchell (1917–2008), the daughter of a Presbyterian minister from Charleston, South Carolina, graduated from Avery Institute, Talladega College (1939), Union Theological Seminary in New York, Columbia University (1943), and completed her doctorate at the School of Theology at Claremont in California in 1974. She also studied at Fresno State, the University of California–Los Angeles, and the University of Massachusetts (Simmons & Thomas, 2010).

She met her husband, Henry H. Mitchell, while attending college, and they married in 1944. Throughout her career, she served churches in New York and Los Angeles as a minister of church education. In addition, she served as a public school teacher in Fresno and Claremont, California, and taught for the Oakland-Berkeley Council of Churches. She also taught at the American Baptist Seminary of the West, the former Berkeley Baptist Divinity School, Compton College, Claremont School of Theology, and the Proctor School of Theology of Virginia Union University in Richmond from 1982 to 1986, where she was Associate Professor of Christian Education and Director of Continuing Education. Mitchell was ordained as a minister in 1978 (Simmons & Thomas, 2010).

In 1986, Mitchell was appointed as Dean of the Sisters Chapel at Spelman College in Atlanta, Georgia. Later, she and her husband began team-teaching as Visiting Professors at the Interdenominational Theological Center in Atlanta. Eventually, they taught at the United Theological Seminary in Dayton, Ohio, in its doctoral program. *Ebony* magazine listed her as one the top 15 Black female preachers in America in 1997.

Barbara C. Harris

Barbara C. Harris (1930–) worked within the Civil Rights Movement, participating in freedom rides, voter registration campaigns, and accompanying Martin Luther King Jr. during his march on Selma, Alabama. Harris' interest in the priesthood began while working at the Sun Company in public relations as a senior staff consultant from 1949 to 1978. She was called to the diaconate in September 1979 and ordained as an Episcopal priest in 1980. When called to the priesthood, she made her experience in journalism and public relations work for her while in charge of St. Augustine of Hippo Church in Norristown, Pennsylvania, serving as its priest from 1980 to 1984. Barbara provided leadership in county activities that included being chaplain for the Philadelphia County prisons and counselor for the industrial corporations for public policy issues and concerns. She was also appointed Executive Director for the Episcopal Publishing Company and publisher of *Witness* magazine (Simmons & Thomas, 2010).

Harris' continued preaching was spurred by her passion for advocacy, justice, diversity, and the belief that women should be included and receive all benefits that men hold in the church. She was elected Assistant Bishop of the Diocese of Massachusetts and later as a consecrated Bishop in 1989. Harris was the first woman to be ordained to the episcopate in the Anglican Communion–Worldwide. Protests occurred as some were not pleased with her being elected bishop. Further disturbance took place when several priests severed relationships with the Anglican Church and several top leaders in England refused to acknowledge female bishops. Harris stood strong and met challenges of opposition faced in her new position as bishop. Harris received numerous honorary degrees from colleges, universities, and theological schools. She is a celebrated preacher and was an outspoken advocate for "the least, the lost, and the left out" (Simmons & Thomas, 2010).

Prathia L. Hall

Prathia L. Hall (1940–2002) was born in 1940 to Berkeley and Ruby Hall in Philadelphia, Pennsylvania, and was one of four children. She was licensed and ordained by her father, a pastor. After college, she joined the Civil Rights Movement. Hall was married and later divorced. In that union, she had a son and daughter, yet her daughter died at an early age from a stroke. She was educated at Princeton Theological Seminary where she received a Master of Divinity and a doctoral degree. She was ordained as an American Baptist minister and an officer of the Progressive National Baptist Convention. In 1978, she became the pastor of Rose of Sharon Baptist Church in Philadelphia, the church of her father.

Hall was also among the first group of preachers of any race in the 20th century who achieved national notoriety. She was a revivalist, which was an unusual achievement for female preachers. Before Hall's death, she held the position of the Martin Luther King Jr. Chair in Social Ethics, serving as an Associate Professor at Boston University School of Theology. Hall explained this in her sermon, titled "Between the Wilderness and a Cliff," which was one of her favorite and best-known sermons. The wilderness and cliff referred to her own life challenges, such as the fight for civil rights, losing her young daughter to a stroke, criticism from the church because of her position, as well as managing health issues and divorce (Simmons & Thomas, 2010). In spite of her early demise, we are fortunate to have Hall's contributions to Black female leadership in the church.

Claudette A. Copeland

Claudette A. Copeland (1952–) was born in Buffalo, New York, on August 17, 1952, to E. Juanita Anderson Day and Charles A. Anderson. At age 18, she was licensed as an evangelist in the Church of God in Christ. Copeland's education consists of a Bachelor's degree in Psychology from the University of Connecticut, a Master's of Divinity in Pastoral Care and Counseling from the Interdenominational Theological Center in Atlanta, Georgia, and a Doctorate of Ministry from United Theological Seminary in Dayton, Ohio (Simmons & Thomas, 2010).

Copeland was ordained in 1979 and became a commissioned officer in the United States Air Force Chaplaincy in 1980. She and her husband, David, were the first African American clergy couple in the history of the U.S. military chaplaincy program. They served the military with distinction before returning to their civilian pastorate. The Copelands are co-founders of the New Creation Christian Fellowship of San Antonio, Texas. They served the church for more than 20 years as pastors. Copeland's focus on the ministry is mission fieldwork, preaching, teaching, and lectures in national and international venues. She has been hailed as one of the most outstanding women preachers in the world (Simmons & Thomas, 2010).

In addition to the aforementioned, Copeland founded COPE Professional services, a consulting firm providing personal effectiveness training in the public sector. She created Destiny Ministries, a national empowerment group for women. She has written several publications and is widely recognized for her ability to apply biblical insights to the complexity of the human condition (Simmons & Thomas, 2010).

Renita Weems

Renita Weems (1954–) grew up in Nashville, Tennessee with her stepmother. Weems remembers her stepmother telling her at the age of 15 that God had hands on her life. It took two decades for her to understand what these words meant. She earned her Bachelor's in Economics from Wellesley College and a Doctorate in Biblical Studies, specializing in Hebrew Bible, at Princeton Theological Seminary in 1989. After earning her bachelor's degree, she began working as a stockbroker. She then served as the William and Camille Cosby Visiting Professor in the Humanities at Spelman College in Atlanta, Georgia. Her publications, writings, and sermons explore women's relationships, spirituality, and wholeness. Weems and her husband, the Reverend Martin Espinosa, served as co-pastors of Ray of Hope Community Church in Nashville, Tennessee. As a lecturer and preacher, Weems utilizes American folk-style preaching and traditional biblical scholarship throughout the United States and internationally (Simmons & Thomas, 2010).

Conclusion

This work features notable Black women who laid a foundation for Black female leaders in the church. Although Black female pastors made great strides over time, some associations refuse to change their rigid views. For instance, the Memphis Baptist Ministerial Association refuses admission to women. While this association includes some of the oldest and most respected leaders of the community, as a group they are determined to retain the status quo (Bradley, 2010). Also, numerous churches accept women as ministers but not as senior pastors. Due to these practices, some Black female leaders have turned to predominantly White churches to find a place in the pulpit. Black female activists seek transformation of such churches and hold that change is overdue.

We celebrate Black female leaders that have mastered their journeys. They remind us that Black women such as those featured in this work rarely give up on quests they feel are worth working towards. We are grateful to the Jerena Lees, the Harriet Tubmans, the Sojourner Truths, and all the Black laywomen, ministers, and evangelists leaders of spirit. To them we give homage.

Bibliography

Bowman, C. (1996). Coping with personal problems. In W. Neighbors & J. S. Jackson (Eds.), *Mental health in Black America*, (pp. 105–123) Thousand Oaks, CA: Sage.

Bradley, B. (2010, July 18). *Dynamic pastor Dr. Gina Stewart leads the way as more women shepherd Black Protestant flocks.* Retrieved April 21, 2010, from the Commercial Appeal: Memphis, TN, http://www.commercialappeal.com/news/2010/jul/18/spreading-the-word/?print=1

Briggs, D. (2009, February 15). *Women fight for leadership in Black churches.* Retrieved April 15, 2009, from the *State Journal Register*, Springfield, IL, http://www.sj-r.com/features/x817675276/Women-fight-for-leadership-in- Black-churches

Carpenter, D. (2001). Black Women in religious institutions: A historical summary from slavery to the 1960s. *Journal of Religious Thought, 7*–27.

Clinton, C. (2005). *Harriet Tubman: The road to freedom.* New York: Little, Brown & Co.

Easter, O. V. (1995). *Nannie Helen Burroughs: Studies in African American history & culture.* New York: Garland Publishing.

Holley, G. (2009, October 3). *Female Pastors: The stained glass ceiling.* Retrieved March 21, 2011, from *NEMS Daily Journal,* http://nems360.com/printer_friendly/3813165

Jackson, R. (1981). *Gifts of power: The writings of Rebecca Jackson, Black visionay, Shaker eldress.* Amherst: University of Massachusetts Press.

Jones, C., & Shorter-Gooden, K. (2003). Can I get a witness? In C. Jones & K. Shorter-Gooden (Eds,), *Shifting: The Double Lives of Black Women in America* (pp. 259–278). New York: HarperCollins.

Lowen, L. (2011). *The role of African American women in the Black Church—Black women and the church.* Retrieved January 19, 2011, from Aboutcom. Women's Issues, http://womensissues.about.com/od/communityconnection/a/ Blackwomenchurc.htm?p=1

Moon, F. F. (2010). Churches. In J. Carney Smith (Ed.), *Encyclopedia of African American popular culture.* Retrieved April 25, 2011, : http:///ebooks.abc-clio.com/reader.aspx?isbn=978031335 7978idB3142C-4556

Murray, P. (Ed.). (1987). *Song in a weary throat: An American pilgrimage.* New York: Harper & Row.

Nichols, B., & Bello, M. (2010, April 21). *Civil rights activist Dorothy Height dies at 98.* Retrieved April 2, 2011, from *USA Today,* http://www.usatoday.com/news/nation/2010-04-20-height-obit_N.htm?csp=34#

Onyuku-Opukiri, F. (2000). Raising the profile of Black women leaders in the community. *International Review of Mission, 89,* 341–342.

Ross, R. E. (2003). *Witnessing and testifying: Black women, religion, and civil rights.* Minneapolis: Augsburg Fortress.

Simmons, M., & Thomas, F. A. (2010). *Preaching with sacred fire: An anthology of African American sermons 1750 to the present.* New York: W. W. Norton & Co.

Stewart, M. W. (1987). *Maria W. Stewart, America's first Black woman political writer, essays and speeches.* Bloomington: Indiana University Press.

Taylor, R. J., Mattis, J., & Chatters, L. M. (1999). Subjective religiosity among African Americans: A synthesis of findings from five national samples. *Journal of Black Psychology, 25*(4): 524–543.

Vaughn, D. B. (2009, August 9). Pauli Murray project. Retrieved March 12, 2011, from Talking Rights: On and About Human Rights at Home and Abroad, http://robinkirk.com/wordpress/?p=280

Vaughn, D. B. (2009, November 11). Pauli Murray project expands. Retrieved April 24, 2011, from the *Herald Sun*, http://www.hearldsun.com/printer_friendly/4437749

Vaughn, D. B. (2010, November 17). Woven exhibit, interwoven life. Retrieved April 24, 2011, from the *Hearld Sun*, http://www.hearldsun.com/printer_friendly/10358108

Wood, L. (2008, March 5). The Black Woman: Backbone of the African American Family? Retrieved April 25, 2011 from *A Better Covenant*, http://blackandreformedministries.wordpress.com/2008/03/05/the-black-woman-backbone-of-the-african-american-family/.

Whitson, M. (1997). Violence against women. *Sexism and sexual harassment: Concerns of African American women of the Christian Methodist Episcopal Church, 3*(4):382–400.

Williams, D. S. (1993). *Sisters in the wilderness: The challenge of womanist God-talk.* New York: Orbis Books.

Wise, J. (2010, October 12). Remembering Pauli Murray: What comes next for activist's childhood home? Retrieved April 15, 2011, from the *Durham News*: 2011.

Chapter Four

African American Mothers Leading Daughters

Virginia Cook Tickles

Research on motherhood in the African American community has evolved over time from a perspective rooted in White America's view of what motherhood is, or should be, to a perspective that considers cultural and historical constructs (Garey, 1995). Mothers serve as daughters' first models of what society expects from young women, thus impacting the way daughters think about their gender and possibilities stemming from it. As role models, motivators, and pathfinders in the eyes of their daughters, mothers understand the value placed upon them as they navigate their own lives, while working to guide and build wholesome lives for their daughters.

Mothers and researchers interested in the implications associated with motherhood agree that motherhood is complex (Adams, 1995; Andersen, 1993; Boyd-Franklin, 1989; Oberman & Josselson, 1996; Ross, 1995). Nancy Chodorow (1998) describes women as producers of future mothers possessing the capabilities and the desire to mother, which thereby facilitates mother-daughter relationships. The mother-daughter role, as transparent as it may appear, is very dynamic. McMahon (1995) describes a "socially and historically variable relationship," while Ferguson (2001) talks about the expectations and meanings of motherhood varying across culture and time. Motherhood is not a monolithic experience (Wade-Gayles, 1984). For example, differences exist in mothering a young daughter versus an adolescent or young adult. The mother's age during the daughter's various phases of childhood to adulthood; socioeconomic status; race; cultural beliefs; and size or make-up of the family structure affect these dynamics and make an analysis of the role complex.

For most African American women, regardless of the relationships formed, family is extremely important (Boyd-Franklin, 1989). Likewise, a rich history of positive values passed down through African American families has yielded much respect for the wisdom and intellect of the mother figure. For many African American mothers, motherhood connects them to their experiences with other mothers, with their children and that of others, with the larger village (or African American community), and with their selves. Collins purports that motherhood serves as a space where African American women express and learn the power of self-definition, self-worth, self-respect, self-reliance, and independence, all leading to self-empowerment (Collins, 1991).

Today, through Black feminist thought and theory, research on motherhood in the African American community dispels many skewed views of Black women (Burgess, 1995), revealing their strengths and their instrumental roles in cultivating the health and survival of their families (Giddings, 1992). A plethora of scholars—Anderson (1993), Billingsley (1992), Collins (1991), Dickerson (1995), Herskovits (1990), and Williams (1991)—study African American motherhood and examine differences across a wide spectrum of variables. However, a common element found across perspectives on motherhood is that mothers serve as vital parts of their families and are often the greatest influences upon children.

As such, many definitions exist to describe leadership in this context. Theorists have proven that leadership styles vary across culture and gender. Elements central to the definition of leadership include: leadership is a process; leadership involves influence; leadership occurs in a group context; and leadership involves goal attainment (Northouse, 2007). The fact that leadership involves influence, supports the premise that mothers are leaders, as they provide the greatest influence on the children and family.

There is much to be told regarding African American mothers in their leadership roles and the influence they have on their daughters. The relationship between a mother and daughter brings with it an infinite number of complexities (Adams, 1995). In most cases, the mother serves as the role model, mentor, nurturer, teacher, provider, and usually has the greatest influence on the young daughter. A daughter often looks up to her mother as the person who models womanhood, the template to compare her growth and maturity, the rubric to set her standards and value systems, and the inspirational source to her personal being. A woman cannot truly explore who she really is without considering the effects her mother or the mother figure has on her life. The mother serves as the blueprint who guides the initial footprints in shaping who that daughter chooses to become.

Much of the research regarding African American mothers and their leadership roles has been ignored or devalued and fails to represent the perspectives of African American women (Collins, 1990). The Black feminist perspective, only recently being given noteworthy attention, provides a platform recognizing Black women as self-defined, self-reliant individuals who confront race, gender, and class oppression and stand in opposition to systems that devalue Black women and their ideals (Collins, 1990). Specifically, standpoint theory asserts that members of oppressed groups hold special knowledge based on their group's unique experiences (Collins, 1990; Harnois, 2010). Because women are not a monolithic group and do not share the same standpoint, feminist scholars such as Sandra Harding, Patricia Hill Collins, Dorothy Smith, and Julia Wood chronicle the varied experiences lived and told by African American women.

Many African American mothers dedicate themselves to socializing their daughters to be strong, confident, educated, and independent women as they develop them for womanhood. With the ever-changing role of African American women in society, especially those with professional careers, elements of these relationships continue to evolve. This essay examines the changing dynamics of an African American mother and her four daughters, their expectations of one another, and the impact of the mother's leadership role in the home and community.

Leadership, in the context of this work, is the process where individuals succeed in attempting to frame and define the reality of others (Smircich & Morgan, 1982). Virginia Young Collins (1915–2011) embodied the spirit of leadership defined by Smircich and Morgan in that she demonstrated enormous success in her effort to shape the lives and roles of those whose lives she touched. Being the eldest of 14 children, wife for more than 50 years (until husband's death), mother of 11, daughter of a Baptist minister, PTA president, community volunteer, and civil rights activist, she exemplifies African American female leadership in America. Born in 1915, she embodied the free spirit that many women have yet to understand in today's world. Throughout her life, she worked to address the plight of Black people worldwide on such issues as negligible educational opportunities, poor health care, economic deprivation, and inappropriate or lack of legal redress.

She traveled extensively throughout the United States and abroad in the interest of human rights, marched with Dr. Martin Luther King Jr. on several occasions, and testified before committees of the U.S. Congress on various affairs related to the struggles of Black people. Becoming increasingly disenchanted with meager gains and slow progress towards the equal and fair treatment of her people, she concluded that the status of African Americans would never change without their believing that they, as a people, deserved reparations and should initiate their own destinies.

Born on March 4, 1915 in the town of Phoenix, Louisiana, on the Mississippi River, Virginia Collins' first tastes of community involvement came from participation in her father's church, which developed her skills as an organizer and active member of an organization. This fostered her participation in various other early organizations, such as the PTA (Parent Teachers Association), the NAACP (National Association for the Advancement of Colored People), the Urban League, the Women's International League for Peace and Freedom, SCLC (Southern Christian Leadership Council), CORE (Congress of Racial Equality), SNCC (Student Nonviolent Coordinating Committee), the League of Women Voters, and more. Her parents being Garveyites, proponents of African Americans migrating back to Africa, Collins embraced alternative ideas of race relations in the U.S. She was an educated woman, a qualified teacher, a certified nurse, and in tune with the community's needs.

Collins interacted with intellectuals, yet remained in touch with common people. In many ways, she embodied the spirit of Robin Hood where she would gain the knowledge and trust of the upper echelon and recycle that knowledge to benefit those with little education. Even so, in all that she accomplished, she serves as a pristine example of an African American mother leading daughters towards understanding and demanding their roles in society.

With four daughters of her own, Virginia Collins, an active leader in many of the issues facing African American women and families, was a different mother to each of her girls. Marilyn, being the eldest, born in 1935, experienced a young, energetic, and vibrant mother with high ideals and lofty goals. She reflects:

> My mother was adamant about Black women proclaiming their strength, [being] uplifting,. . . motivating their men [husbands and sons], and preparing their daughters to play a decisive role in integrating financially, socially, and intellectually with America. . . not as separate entities, but as equal, unique contributors and deserving recipients of a good life. She understood the importance of developing a healthy person, made sure we had nourishing food even through poverty, believed in education, thought it necessary to develop the mind to its full potential, fanatically pushed us to do extensive reading and develop an appreciation for the arts, was a skilled dressmaker [seamstress] and dietician who taught others while working on government projects. . . She was always the domineering figure. However, she made no decisions without my father's approval.

Collins' daughter Antoinette, born in 1941, states:

> Mother was a force to reckon with. . . everyone in the community respected her in that she gave her absolute best effort, not only to her children, but to other children, mothers, and families in the community.

Another daughter, Lydia, born in 1947, shares:

> My mother is a born warrior. . . a warrior for the Lord and her people. Her revolutionary spirit was fueled by the injustices faced by her people in this country,

the USA. Her life successes have been minimized as a result of her involvement with the Republic of New Africa. The RNA was labeled as a terrorist organization by the U.S. government, so everything she did in support of the cause was scrutinized and devalued. Her activities within the RNA were wrought with inaccuracies, embellished, and skewed by those who wished to discredit her work. The phrase she always used, "I loved that which is me," was not so much about her, but her family, friends, and her race. She knew that her mission, calling, and passion required her to take a stand for what she believed, in spite of the consequences.

The youngest born female, Georgia, born in 1951, experienced a determined, focused, and independent mother:

> It made me want to be like her. It also taught me how to be independent and forceful about everything in my life. . . in making things happen in the progression that it should happen. She gave me the substance that I needed to make all these things happen in the right way for my immediate family, be it alone raising my five children, or with the help of the fathers of my children. With or without their help, I was able to take care of business with what she equipped me with through my education, upbringing, and my exposure to things necessary to fulfill or enrich life.

Lydia adds:

> I think [her] participation in the RNA was significant. She helped women become part of the decision making process and take leadership positions. Most of the family thought the ideas of the RNA were too ambitious and warranted strife. Her participation is an example to the community of how a male dominated organization could be influenced and led by a woman. For the young women in the organization, I felt that having mother involved was a good thing because [of] one thing I knew for sure. . . she would change the role of women in that organization and give the male chauvinists direction. They needed her knowledge, strength, and level headedness.

Virginia Young Collins also served as the mother figure to many young women in the African American community of New Orleans, Louisiana. African American women demonstrate motherhood not only to their daughters with whom they give birth, but also through the roles of grandmother, other-mothers, and fictive kin. This has been referred to as *multiple mothering*. In these roles, African American women serve as figures of their own empowerment, strong voices in community activism, and figures of commitment to the African American community (Collins, 1990). Under the new lens of feminist thought and associated theories, African American mothers are found to be resilient, strong, and key components of Black America (Collins, 1990).

Virginia Young Collins embodied the role of the family matriarch while never being in competition with men in the family. Instead, they fully supported her effort and energy. Collins exhibited the energy and spirit of the strong Black mother image, as she was heavily involved in all activities. She fully understood her role as a nucleus in the family structure, evident in the teachings to her daughters. Some of the things she did during her life demonstrated her commitment to this role. In the neighborhood she was a fixture: praising or correcting any children who came in contact with her. Youngsters and adults who had nowhere to go knew they were welcome in her house. If they were hungry, she fed them. If they were thirsty, she gave them drink. If they were tired, she allowed them to rest. If they were depressed, she tried to uplift them. During the Depression and recession years, her house was a regular well-known stop for hoboes. Members of the community and family who remember those years speak out about being afraid of the hoboes. She would always say, "Don't be afraid, these men are just hungry and looking for work."

For her own children, she was a counselor, comforter, and caregiver. She was their motivator who made the unattainable and impossible seem plausible and possible. She made the immovable movable, the insurmountable mountable, and the negative episodes of life bearable and changeable. She was a woman who rarely uttered a word of defeat, a tone of victimization, and was always in control, effective, efficient, compassionate, driven, purposeful, fulfilled, accomplished, and celebrated. Though not perfect in any stretch of the imagination, she had a strong sense of family. She simply knew what it took to make things happen and was willing to go the distance.

She was a mother who learned from her ancestors, listened to stories told by her mother and enslaved grandmother, and lived to witness many generations of mothers transition through life. She clearly understood and fought against and for issues of class, race, and gender, living to watch many of the fruits of her labor materialize. One cannot intelligently believe that African American mothers are of one type, for we are as different in our mothering skills and rearing of our children as we are in the varied shades of our skin. Collins held that we are queens and daughters of queens and our expectations for self must be high in order for us to rise to the occasion.

Her goal was to raise her girls in an ever-changing society. She knew that whether one was a wife and mother, single or widowed mother, businesswoman, church activist, community activist, or some combination thereof, preparation toward self-fulfillment was vital. Collins had the vision to raise her daughters to be able to compete and to be complete no matter what the circumstances and to be true to themselves in their own defined spaces.

Collins held a belief in a higher power as her source of strength, sustainability, and empowerment. Her daughter Lydia notes:

My mother, Virginia Evalena Young Collins was and still is a courageous woman who always put God first in her life. She was a proud woman, strong in her words, strong in showing her love for her family and friends. She also could spew venom that could hit below the belt. In that same breath, she would ask God's forgiveness. She made sure that I had a solid foundation in the Word of God, his power and love, as well as all the tools needed on becoming a woman in this society. . . good morals, character, education, self-sufficiency, the belief that I could do it all.

She also held respect for the family structure, whether traditional (with both parents in traditional roles), single mother, or other-mother. While keeping with society's traditions of male-headed homes, she had a husband who respected her decision-making skills. Unlike many women, she was able to operate outside the boundaries defined by society without spousal backlash. Lydia recalls:

She felt that a woman should. . . be educated, work to help and support her family. She felt a woman should not be solely dependent upon a man for her livelihood, nor should she take a backseat and let him make all the decisions in the family. . . A woman should maintain her independence and strive to balance her role as a woman first, wife, mother, and whatever other ventures she aspired to partake.

Collins advocated educational preparation of self, children, and the community to meet and set goals. Lydia adds:

She gave me all that she had to give and more. My mother inspired me to be creative, love family, support the struggle, be a leader not a follower, demand respect, continue our legacy, keep God in my life, to pursue higher education, [and to] love and read books.

Collins also believed in giving back or staying connected to the community. Marilyn shares:

Like my mother, I still push for education, spiritual, and social development. But I have [also] developed a compassion for those who fall by the wayside. . . I try to intervene individually partly because I became a school teacher, but mostly because of the leadership and motivation of my mother, who felt. . . you are your brother's keeper.

Further, Collins was passionate in endeavors and sought self-fulfillment. Lydia and Antoinette stated:

Lydia: She was and still is a force to deal with. She was a socialite, loved. . . to look good, loved God, [and] had a deep commitment to serve her people.

Antoinette: I fashioned myself to strive for some of the things my mother represented. Like her, I was always fashionable, enjoyed activities that surrounded me with other people, and very expressive. Even though my mother was short in stature, she made up for it in the powers she possessed and her ability to engage, lead, instruct, and influence all classes, races, and educational levels of people.

Collins fought for change on issues of race, gender, and class. Her daughters note:

Marilyn: She oftentimes balked at the ignorance of Black males who. . . embraced the White slave owner mentality and want to enslave us [Black women] mentally, socially and financially and make us subject to them and their masculine domination and authority.

Georgia:. . . We weren't elite. We weren't poor, but we weren't elite. We were working class. She fought the perceptions. She made it clear that I will handle this with you as a Black, a working class Black, whether it was race, class, or gender. She taught us how to fight for that. Schools, voting, jobs, she made us understand why she fought and why we should fight. . .

Conclusion

Interviews with my grandmother and namesake, Virginia Young Collins, my mother and aunts' observations, and the experience of raising daughters of my own leads me to the conclusion that many mothers are natural leaders, teachers, and coaches of their daughters. They lead by example, understand the need to build relationships based on honesty and trust, know the importance of discipline, educate their daughters to learn from and how to deal with issues, and listen to the needs of their daughters as individuals. Oftentimes mistakes are made in an effort to shield, shelter, or protect daughters from the ills of the world. Mothers work within the confines of the family structure and its many dynamics, define suitable paths for their children, and help daughters to avoid making mistakes. The best we can do is to lead by example, to understand the need for individuality, and to allow our faith to determine the direction and role that each woman is destined to play.

As previously defined, leadership is the process where individuals succeed in attempting to frame and define the reality of others (Smircich & Morgan, 1982). Every African American woman who serves as a mother, grandmother, othermother, or fictive kin (Collins, 1990) is a leader in the home, community, and the lives of those they serve. In the article, "I Am My Mother's Daughter: Early Development Influences on Leadership," Adler (2008) presents a unique case history to elucidate the cultural, historic, and societal forces that influence how one becomes a leader and a human being. Adler states:

Each of us has a personal story embedded in a cultural and family history that has shaped us as individuals and has given us our unique and highly personal combination of values, inspiration, and courage—our humanity—that we draw on in our day-to-day and larger leadership efforts. The more clearly we understand the roots of our identity and humanity, the more able we will be to use our strengths and core values to achieve the vision we have for ourselves and the world around us. (p. 13)

This statement supports the observations from family, friends, and significant others of Virginia Evalena Young Collins as they described her leadership efforts in shaping the lives of those around her.

There is little doubt that Virginia Collins was a pillar of strength and a prominent example to women in the community. Everybody respected and loved her, and admired her tenacity, strong beliefs, and her willingness to act on them. Her style of leadership mimicked transformational leadership (McCaslin, 2001) in that she understood that her role as a leader was to reach back and assist in lifting others to higher levels of morality and expectation. Her belief in a higher power for strength, sustainability, and empowerment; respect for the family structure; educational preparation of herself, children, and the community; reciprocity to the community; passion and self-fulfillment; work towards positive changes on issues related to race and gender; and achieving a balanced lifestyle influenced those around her.

To African American mothers like Virginia Young Collins, motherhood is "a base for self-actualization, status in the Black community and a catalyst for social activism" (Collins, 2000, p.176). Through activism, mothers are voices in their own communities—voices for themselves, their families, their children, and others in the community—thus making them leaders of their flock. As emphasized in feminist thought, African American mothers are found to be resilient, strong, and key components of the Black community (Collins, 1990). It is hoped that the information provided here serves as a guide to mothers interested in creating a recipe for empowerment and success in raising their daughters as they navigate through the world facing issues (i.e., sexism and racism) that African American women encounter.

Bibliography

Adams, A. (1995). Maternal bonds: Recent literature on mothering. *Signs: Journal of Women in Culture and Society, 20*(21), 414–427.

Adler, N. J. (2008). I am my mother's daughter: Early developmental influences on leadership, *European J. International Management, 2*(1), 6–21.

Andersen, M. (1993). *Thinking about women: Sociological perspectives on sex and gender.* New York: MacMillan.

Bell-Scott, P., Guy-Sheftall, B., Royster, J. J., Sims-Wood, J., Decosta-Willis, M., & Fultz, L. (Eds.). (1991). *Double stitch: Black women write about mothers and daughters.* Boston: Beacon Press.

Billingsley, A. (1992). *Climbing Jacob's ladder: The enduring legacy of African American families*. New York: Simon & Schuster.

Boyd, J. A. (1993). *In the company of my sisters: Black women and self-esteem*. New York: Penguin Books.

Boyd-Franklin, N. (1989). *Black families in therapy, A multi-systems approach*. New York: Guilford Press.

Burgess, N. (1995). Female-headed households in sociohistorical perspective. In B. Dickerson (Ed.), *African-American single mothers* (pp. 21–36). Thousand Oaks, CA: Sage.

Chodorow, N. (1978). *The reproduction of mothering: Psychoanalysis and the sociology of gender*. Berkeley & Los Angeles: University of California Press.

Chodorow, N. (1998). *The reproduction of mothering: Psychoanalysis and the sociology of gender with a new preface*. Berkeley: University of California Press.

Christian, B. (1985). *Black feminist criticism: Perspectives on Black Women Writers*. New York: Pergamon.

Collins, P. H. (1990). *Black Feminist Thought: Knowledge,Consciousness, and the Politics of Empowerment*. Boston: UnwinHyman, pp. 221–238.

Collins, P. H. (1991). The meaning of motherhood in Black culture and Black mother-daughter relationships. In P. Bell-Scott, P. B. Guy-Sheftall, J. J. Royster, J. Sims-Wood, M. Decosta-Willis, & L. Fultz (Eds.), *Double stitch: Black women write about mothers and daughters* (pp. 42–60). Boston: Beacon Press.

Collins, P. H. (1994). *Black sexual politics: African Americans, gender, and the new racism*. New York: Routledge.

Collins, P. H. (2000). *Black feminist thought: Knowledge, consciousness, and the politics of empowerment*. New York: Routledge.

Collins, P. H. (1997). The meaning of motherhood in Black culture and Black mother-daughter relationships. In M. M Gergen & S. N. Davies (Eds.), *Toward a new psychology of gender* (pp. 325–340). New York: Routledge.

Coltrane, S. (1998). *Gender & families*. Thousand Oaks, CA: Pine Forge Press.

Dickerson, B. J. (Ed.). (1995). *African American single mothers: Understanding their lives and families*. Thousand Oaks, CA: Sage Publications.

Exley, H. (1998). *My daughter my joy: The greatest tributes to daughters that have ever been written*. Hertfordshire, Great Britain: Exley Publications.

Ferguson, S. (Ed.). (2001). *Shifting the center: Understanding contemporary families*. Mountain View, CA: Mayfield Publishing.

Garey, A. (1995). Constructing motherhood on the night shift: "Working mothers" as "stay-at-home moms." *Qualitative sociology, 18*(4), 415–437.

Giddings, P. (1992). Forward. *Climbing Jacob's ladder: The enduring legacy of African-American families*. New York: Simon & Schuster.

Harnois, C. E. (2010). Race, gender and a Black woman's standpoint. *Sociological Forum, 25*(1), 68–85.

Herskovits, M. J. (1990). *The myth of the Negro past*. Boston: Beacon Press.

Hoffnung, M. (1995). Motherhood: Contemporary conflict for women. In J. Freeman (Ed.), *Women: A feminist perspective* 5th ed. (pp. 162–81). Mountain View, CA: Mayfield.

Jenkins, N. L. (2005). Black mothers: Understanding their lives—Centering their experiences. Doctoral dissertation, University of Georgia.

LaBeach, N. (2003). *Choose yourself: A journey towards personal fulfillment for women*. Los Angeles & Atlanta: Volition Enterprises.

Larson, R., & Richards, M. H. (1994). *Divergent realities: The emotional lives of mothers, fathers and adolescents*. New York: Basic Books.

McCaslin, M. L. (2001). The landscape of leadership building relationships. *Journal of Leadership Studies, 8*(2), p. 21+.

McMahon, M. (1995), *Engendering motherhood: Identity and self-transformation in women's lives*. New York: Guilford Press.

Northouse, P. G. (2007). *Leadership, theory and practice*, 4th ed. Thousand Oaks, CA: Sage Publications.

Oberman, Y., & Josselson, R. (1996). Matrix of tensions: A model of mothering. *Psychology of Women Quarterly, 20*, 341–359.

Ross, E. (1995). New thoughts on the "oldest vocation": Mothers and motherhood in recent feminist scholarship. *Signs: Journal of Women in Culture and Society, 20*(2), 397–413.

Smircich, L. & Morgan G. (1982). Leadership: The management of meaning. *Journal of Applied Behavioral Science, 18,* 2.

Thompson, L., & Walker, A. J. (1989). Gender in families: Women and men in marriage, work, and parenthood. *Journal of Marriage and the Family, 51,* 845–871.

Wade-Gayles, G. (1984). The truths of our mother's lives; Mother-daughter relationships in Black women's fiction. *Sage: A Scholarly Journal on Black Women,* (2), 8–12.

Williams, C. W. (1991). *Black teenage mothers: Pregnancy and childrearing from their perspective.* Lexington, MA: Lexington Books.

Wood, J. T. (1993). Gender and moral voice: Moving from women's nature to standpoint epistemology. *Women's Studies in Communication,* Chap. 34.

Part Two

Leadership in Education

Chapter Five

Each One, Teach One

Black Women's Historical Contributions to Education

Ezella McPherson

Historically, Black women served in leadership roles within the household and developed their leadership skills inside and outside of classrooms before and after the Civil War. Historical literature notes that initially Black women were educated for the following purposes: (1) to become better mothers or wives in the home, and (2) to serve as domestic and agricultural workers (Easter, 1992). In normal schools and colleges, Black women trained to become "teachers, nurses, missionary workers, and Sunday School teachers" (Easter, 1992, p. 22). Yet Black women's leadership service as teachers and administrators in private schools remains unexamined in historical literature. In leading private school classrooms, Black women prepared Blacks to move from *second-class* to *first-class citizenship* by obtaining not only an education, but skills to prepare them for careers in the workplace as teachers, business owners, lawyers, health professionals, and other careers.

This chapter demonstrates how Black women served as teachers and leaders in private schools to encourage Blacks to become literate, self-reliant, and financially independent. The work seeks to fill gaps in knowledge on Black female teachers who served as leaders of classrooms and provided Black children and adults with education in the North and South.

Research Focus and Methods

This historical analysis addresses the following question: In what ways did Black female educators serve in leadership roles to uplift the Black community? To answer this question, the analysis utilized primary documents (e.g., academic articles, autobiographies, journals) and secondary data sources (e.g., books). The initial list of Black female educators came from Dorothy Sterling's historical text entitled *We Are Your Sisters: Black Women in the Nineteenth Century* and Gerda Lerner's book, *Black Women in White America: A Documentary History*. Other Black female educators were identified through a library search of relevant descriptors (e.g., Black women educators, Black women and school founders, Black women and history). The normal schools and institutions[1] chosen for this analysis either were (1) founded[2] by Black women, (2) educated Black women in large numbers, or (3) trained Black women to become teachers in the North, southern and border states.[3]

Schools for Blacks Pre–Civil War to *Plessy*

Prior to the Civil War, the majority of Blacks did not attend public schools in the North or South (Lerner, 1973; Easter, 1992). In the South, former slaves founded private schools in southern states, such as Louisiana, Virginia, South Carolina, Texas, Alabama, and Georgia (Anderson, 1988). In the North, few schools educated Blacks. An exception to the rule was a private, predominantly White institution, Oberlin College, founded in 1833 (Perkins, 1987). Oberlin College prided itself on giving the same opportunities to Blacks as Whites and making Blacks feel a part of their community (Evans, 2007). As a result, in 1850, Lucie Stanton Day became the first Black woman to graduate with a bachelor's degree from Oberlin College (Sterling, 1984). Later she taught in Ohio and Mississippi schools. Several Black female Oberlin graduates served as teachers to Blacks in the North and South. Despite these victories, Blacks accounted for less than 1% of Oberlin's 1,200 student population with an enrollment of 32 Black students in 1859.

In the North, another White organization, the Friends of Philadelphia, founded the Institute for Colored Youth in 1837 to educate Blacks in Pennsylvania (Brown, 1926; Hartshorn, 1910). The Institute for Colored Youth also provided students with knowledge and skills through an industrial and liberal arts education to better serve Black communities. In 1852, the Institute for Colored Youth offered a high school education to Black youth in Pennsylvania (Hartshorn, 1910). Graduates of the Institute for Colored Youth became educators as well.

After the Emancipation Proclamation in 1863 and the end of the Civil War in 1865, Blacks continued to attend southern and northern private schools to be-

---

1   For additional information on schools for Blacks see the text *An Era of Progress and Promise, 1863–1910* by W. N. Hartshorn.

2   Some of the school founders were more known than others and had information readily available.

3   The southern and border states include Alabama, Arkansas, Delaware, Florida, Georgia, Kentucky, Louisiana, Maryland, Mississippi, Missouri, North Carolina, Ohio, Oklahoma, Pennsylvania, South Carolina, Tennessee, Texas, Virginia, and West Virginia.

come literate through reading and writing, along with learning arithmetic. During this time, larger private schools opened to train future Black professionals, teachers, and workers in the South (Hartshorn, 1910). During this Reconstruction era, the American Missionary Association acknowledged "that by 1866. . . normal schools and colleges were needed to produce Black teachers" (Wadelington & Knapp, 1999, p. 5). Support from the American Missionary Association meant that Black schools had to instill Christian values in students though a liberal Christian education. Other Black institutions adhered to Christian principles due to their financial donors from Christian denominations.

In 1866, some Northern missionaries from the Methodist Church founded the private institution, Central Tennessee College, to produce Black teachers who later worked in the Texas public schools (e.g., Mattie J. Haywood-White, Bettie Plummer Fields, Novella E. Davis, Lizzie May Green McClellan, Sophia A. Jackson, Naria Key-Fields), as well as in Kentucky and Alabama (e.g., Florence Johnson-Ford) (Hartshorn, 1910). Central Tennessee College also housed Meharry Medical College, which produced more than 50% of the Black physicians in the South. A year later in 1867, Reverend J. Brinton Smith founded the private school, St. Augustine's School, in Raleigh, North Carolina. The purpose of the institution was to prepare Black teachers to educate other Blacks and to prepare men for the ministry within the Episcopal Church. The school also focused on industrial education with coursework in "cooking and sewing for girls, [as well as] carpentry and masonry for young men" (Hartshorn, 1910, p. 253).

Fewer than ten years later in 1873, another private institution, Bennett College, developed in Greensboro, North Carolina, to provide an elementary and secondary school education geared toward training Blacks as teachers (Bennett College, 2009; Guy-Sheftall, 1982). It transitioned from a co-educational institution to an all-female college for Black women in 1926 (Guy-Sheftall, 1982). Currently, the mission of Bennett College centers upon providing undergraduate women with training to become leaders in the workforce and the broader society (Bennett College, 2009). Similar to Bennett College, another women's institution, Spelman Seminary, was founded in 1881 by two White women, Sophia Packard and Harriet Giles. It sought to offer a private school education to Black girls and women in the South, specifically Atlanta, Georgia (Read, 1961). In 1893, Spelman offered a few classes to Black girls and women in high school, a domestic arts school, nursing education, and normal schooling. By 1895, Spelman provided an English curriculum for students interested in literature and writing. Black female graduates of Spelman were better prepared to serve as leaders in the community as teachers, nurses, and missionary teachers (Guy-Sheftall, 1982; Neverdon-Morton, 1989). The first graduates of Spelman, Ella Barksdale, Clara Howard, Lou Mitchell, Adeline Smith, Sallie Waugh, and Ella Williams, taught at various schools in numerous communities (Read, 1961).

Founded only a year after Spelman in 1882, the Virginia Normal and Industrial Institute's mission centered upon educating Blacks in Virginia (Hartshorn, 1910). This private institution trained Blacks to become teachers until it closed in 1902. A Black woman, Della Irving Hayden, taught at the school to prepare Blacks for the workforce (Sterling, 1984). She also served as an instructor in the Virginia public schools for more than 50 years and ultimately founded her own school (Hartshorn, 1910). Another former instructor, Lucey Laney, founded the private school, the Haines Normal and Industrial Institute in 1886 in Augusta, Georgia, to provide Blacks with an industrial education and to train teachers (Lerner, 1973).

Four years later, in 1890, the Girls' Training School became a private school supporting the education of Black girls in Franklinton, North Carolina (Hartshorn, 1910). Similar to the Girl's Training School, the Girls' Industrial School in Morehead, Mississippi, emerged in 1892 through its founder and principal, Miss Sarah L. Emerson. This private school housed six instructors along with 125 students during the year of 1908 (Hartshorn, 1910). Two years later, Emma J. Wilson opened up the Maysville Institute in 1892 to educate Black children in Mayes, South Carolina. This private school became the Maysville Educational and Industrial Institute in 1896. The mission of the school was to provide Black youth with a liberal industrial education. It built students' character through teaching morals, the importance of working, and purchasing property (e.g., farms, homes) (Hartshorn, 1900). By 1908, the school's enrollment reached 530 students (215 males and 315 females) and employed 14 Black teachers (5 male and 9 female). While some students went to school to become ministers, the school offered courses in "carpentry, blacksmithing, tailoring, bootmaking and repairing, farming, sewing, housework, making and laying of bricks, [and] plastering" (Hartshorn, 1910, p. 354).

Before and after the Civil War, Blacks continued to attend private institutions separate from White peers to prepare for the workforce. In 1896, the *Plessy v. Ferguson* (1896) decision declared that *separate was equal*. The *Plessy* decision led to the institution of Jim Crow laws which "forced Blacks into second-class citizenship by enacting black codes and black laws" (Wadelington & Knapp, 1999, p. 18). This legal precedent resulted in Blacks having to use separate facilities from Whites, including restaurants, schools, hospitals, prisons, cemeteries, "water fountains, restrooms, employment, and public transportation" (Wadelington & Knapp, 1999, p. 18). The *Plessy* decision contributed to a rising number of public schools for Blacks in the southern and border states. By 1900, 94 public schools educated Blacks in the southern and border states (Sterling, 1984). Some private schools that educated Blacks during this time became modern day historically Black colleges and universities (HBCUs). HBCUs seek to make college accessible to African American students and to provide "students with a culturally, socially, economically, and politically relevant education" (U.S. Department of Education, Office for Civil Rights, 1991, p. 8). The following highlights specific Black female educators whose teacher training began in private schools or one of the few public schools available to Blacks.

Black Women's Training to Lead the Classroom

In the 19th century, the majority of Black female educators' teacher training occurred in private schools in the South and North. For instance, Sarah Mapps Douglass (born in 1806 in Pennsylvania) learned to read and write through private tutors (Lerner, 1973). Fewer than 20 years later, born a free Black girl in 1823 in Norfolk, Virginia, Mary Smith Kelsey moved in with her Aunt Mary Paine at the tender age of six to obtain an education at a private school in Alexandria, a suburb of the District of Columbia (Lockwood, 1862). There, she learned English, needlework, and dressmaking. She also enjoyed reading the Bible. By age 16, she completed her education and moved back to Norfolk to live with her mother.

Another future Institute for Colored Youth teacher and former slave born in 1837, Fanny Jackson Coppin wanted to acquire an education to meet her goal of giving back to the Black community through teaching (Coppin, 1902). Her dream became a reality at age 14, when she obtained private schooling, followed by attending "a public colored school that was taught by Mrs. Gavitt" (Coppin, 1902, p.11). After passing an examination, she entered Rhode Island State and Normal College, whose curriculum centered on teaching. Upon completion of her coursework at Rhode Island State Normal school, she attended Oberlin College with financial support from family, church, and the institution. Her prior schooling prepared her to teach night classes to Black male soldiers in Ohio during the Civil War (1861–1865). Despite racism on campus, she became the first Black student teacher in the Preparatory Department at Oberlin College and graduated in 1865.

Only a few years later, Emma Brown (a Black girl born in 1843) attended the northern School for Colored Girls, headed by Myrtilla Miner, which used the standard curriculum (e.g., reading, writing, arithmetic) along with science to train Black girls to become teachers in D.C. public schools (Sterlings, 1984). Brown always wanted to attend Oberlin College. Her wish became a reality when she enrolled at Oberlin in 1860. Brown paid for college through funds from teaching, loans from Miss Emily Howland, and Avery funds. At Oberlin College, Emma Brown suffered from headaches caused by the stressors of prejudice and encounters with racist teachers. Her experience reflects the pervasiveness of racism in American society, which affected Black students' learning at predominantly White schools.

Born enslaved in 1848, Susan King Taylor was raised by her grandmother Dolly in Savannah, Georgia (Taylor, 1902). She learned how to read and write through private lessons from a family friend, Mrs. Woodhouse. Mrs. Woodhouse taught 25 to 30 children in her kitchen, which served as the classroom. Taylor stayed at this school for two years and then transitioned to a school headed by Mrs. Mary Beasley to acquire additional educational training. By May 1860, she attended a private school led by a high school student, James Blouis. Her schooling was interrupted due to Blouis being called to serve the Savannah Volunteer Guards. Despite this setback, her prior schooling allowed her to become literate, enabling her to write passes for Blacks to stay out past dark due to the sundown laws.[4]

Another former slave and future teacher born in 1854, Lucey Laney became literate in Macon, Georgia, through a home library and private lessons from her mother's boss (Lerner, 1973). Financial support enabled her to attend and finish her high school studies at Atlanta University in 1873. She was among Atlanta University's (now Clark Atlanta University) first graduating class. Della Irving Hayden was also born a slave in 1854 (Sterling, 1984). At the end of slavery, as a child she entered one of the few public schools open to Blacks in Franklin, Virginia. As an aspiring teacher, she attended the private institution, the Hampton Institute at the age of 18 and graduated in 1877 with a teaching degree.

Similar to Hayden, born in 1859, Anna Julia Cooper was a slave from birth to the early years of childhood in Raleigh, North Carolina (Cooper, 1892). Despite familial poverty, she pursued an education from the private institution, St. Augustine's Normal School and Collegiate Institute in 1868. There, she learned classical coursework and religious studies. Later, she pursued higher education at Oberlin College in 1881 and took coursework in classical studies, math, literature, philosophy, and science. The prior school work prepared her to teach Advanced Algebra at Oberlin between the years of 1882 to 1884. She obtained a Bachelor's of Science degree in mathematics in 1884 and an honorary Master's degree in mathematics from Oberlin in 1888 (Evans, 2007). She completed her final degree, a doctorate in Latin in Paris, France from Sorbonne University in 1925 at age 67 (Evans, 2007).

A former student of Dr. Anna Julia Cooper and future educator, Nannie Helen Burroughs, was born in 1878 (Easter, 1992). Jennie Pointdexter Burroughs wanted a better education for her daughter (Nannie), so they moved from Virginia to Washington, D.C. There, Burroughs attended M. Street High School to pursue business and domestic science studies and graduated in 1896. Burroughs had challenges securing employment as a domestic science instructor in D.C., so she became a domestic worker prior to teaching and ultimately founding a school.

---

4   See the book *Sundown Towns: A Hidden Dimension of American Racism*, by James Loewen for a discussion of the former sundown towns and laws in American society.

The final highlighted educator is school founder Charlotte Hawkins Brown, born in 1883 in Henderson, North Carolina (Constance-Hill, 1977). At the young age of 12, she was one of a few people who developed a kindergarten class to teach youth in Sunday school classes held in her church. In 1888, Brown's family moved from North Carolina to Boston, Massachusetts, then Cambridge, Massachusetts, in 1895 to attend Allston Grammar School, followed by Cambridge English High School and Latin School (Wadelington & Knapp, 1999). She continued her education at Salem Normal School at Salem, North Carolina. Her caring spirit resulted in her feeling personally responsible for educating Blacks as a teacher in a rural school in McLeansville, North Carolina.

The aforementioned evidence from the narratives suggest that the majority of Black female educators' training began in private schools and continued in colleges primarily in the South with the exception of a few institutions like the Institute for Colored Youth, Myrtilla Miner's School for Colored Girls, and Oberlin College. Acquiring an education set the foundation for them to become literate and educate other Blacks through leadership in schools within their communities. The following section describes how some Black women led classrooms to uplift Black communities through promoting literacy in both private and public schools.

Black Women as Leaders of Classrooms

Through leadership as teachers in public and private schools, some Black women played instrumental roles in uplifting Blacks and encouraged progress towards *first-class citizenship* by becoming literate, self-reliant, and financially independent. This section provides narratives of Black women serving as leaders in classrooms throughout the 19th century.

In 1820, a Black woman, Sarah Mapps Douglass, created a private homeschool to educate Black girls in Philadelphia in efforts to limit the illiteracy of Black girls and women (Lerner, 1973). The school was funded by the Philadelphia Female Anti-Slavery Society, an organization in which Douglass was a founder and member.

In 1853, Sarah Mapps Douglass served as a teacher in the Girls Preparatory Department at the Institute for Colored Youth (Coppin, 1902). The Preparatory Department offered elementary school courses and teacher preparation courses for future teachers. For 12 years, a New York Central College at McGrawville graduate, Grace Mapps served as a teacher and head of the Girls High School. Grace Mapps made sure that the Institute for Colored Youth had a strong math curriculum, which included a bookkeeping course implemented through the Institute for Colored Youth's principal, Charles Reason.

Less than six years later in 1859, Emma Brown taught at her own private school in Georgetown to raise funds to pay for her tuition at Oberlin College. Two years later, during the Civil War in 1861, a Black woman named Mary S. Peake (formerly Mary Smith Kelsey) opened a private school in Virginia to teach Black children the power and importance of prayer through spiritual instruction which included teaching prayer, praying with students, and reading hymns (Lockwood, 1862). Besides youth, she taught adults using the Holy Bible in evening classes.

After the Civil War, a Black woman named Susan King opened a private homeschool in Savannah, Georgia, due to Blacks being denied access to public schools in the South (Taylor, 1902). As a teacher, King taught Blacks how to read and write for a dollar per month. She instructed younger Blacks during the day and older Blacks at night. The loss of her husband, Sergeant Edward King, coupled with the opening of a larger school, the Beach Institute, led to King closing her private school in 1868.

At another southern private school, Augustine's Normal School and Collegiate Institute in North Carolina, Anna Julia Cooper taught math, Greek, and Latin between the years of 1871 and 1881 while simultaneously taking care of her family in Raleigh, North Carolina (Johnson, 2000). In 1884, she continued teaching as a professor of modern languages at Wilberforce University, an HBCU in Ohio. In 1887, she became a math and science teacher in Washington, D.C., at the Washington Colored High School, which became M. Street High School in 1891. Upon departing from M. Street High School in 1906, she taught Blacks at another HBCU, Lincoln University in Jefferson City, Missouri, for four years. More important, during her tenure as an instructor, she advocated for Black girls and women to pursue higher education in order to be of service to other Blacks in the community, serve as good wives to their husbands, and become economically independent.

Similarly, Lucey Laney served as a teacher in Atlanta's public schools for Black youth from 1873 to 1883 (Loewenberg & Bogin, 1976). She was interested in the education of Black youth, especially girls who could be trained to uplift the Blacks through engaging in teaching. As an educator and school leader, she was among the first to create kindergarten classes in Augusta, Georgia. The kindergarten classes enabled Black students to learn at an earlier age and further prepare them for the next grade level. Only seven years later, in 1890, the Chandler Normal School, funded by the American Missionary Association and headed by Principal Fanny J. Webster, provided an education to promote the literacy of Black students in Lexington, Kentucky (Hartshorn, 1910). In 1908, the school had an enrollment of 312 students who were taught by 11 instructors.

As teachers and leaders of classrooms, Black women sought to reduce illiteracy in African American communities through teaching other Blacks. Through education, Blacks had the potential to move towards first-class citizenship by working to earn higher wages to take care of their families. More important, through education Blacks could further provide schooling for their children to produce a future generation of workers, teachers, doctors, and lawyers to uplift Black communities. To further understand the growth in knowledge through education, the following discusses Black women's leadership roles outside of the classroom.

Black Women in Leadership beyond the Classroom

Outside of the classroom, some Black women served in leadership positions to educate Blacks in the military, as well as school principals and presidents of colleges. Beginning with the Civil War era, Black female educators' narratives of leading outside of classrooms are described in this section.

In 1862, Susan King Taylor traveled from Savannah, Georgia, with her uncle's family at age 14 (Taylor, 1902). In Savannah, per the request of Captain Whitmore, she taught 40 Black children to read and write in the day and adults at night on one of Georgia's Sea Islands, St. Simon's Island. Per the request of General Hunter, Captain C. T. Trowbridge recruited soldiers from Simon's Island to enlist troops in August 1862. This led the soldiers and King to travel to Beaufort, South Carolina, during October of 1862. While in Beaufort, the troops resided at Camp Saxton where Susan King Taylor taught soldiers how to read and write.

Beyond the military, Black women headed academic departments and held administrative positions in schools. For instance, after teaching for several years as a principal, Emma Brown lead the John F. Cook School in D.C. and became a principal at Summer School (Sterling, 1984). In another northern school, the Institute for Colored Youth, Grace Mapps headed the Girls' High School (Perkins, 1987). The future termination of Grace Mapps led to Fanny Jackson Coppin's appointment at the Institute for Colored Youth in 1865. Coppin worked at the Institute for Colored Youth from 1865 to 1902 (Perkins, 1987). During Coppin's first year of teaching at the Institute for Colored Youth, Black girls' enrollment increased from 42 to 80. Through teaching, she became appointed principal of the Female Department in 1869 for the Institute for Colored Youth (Perkins, 1987). As one of the first Black female graduates of Oberlin College holding a bachelor's degree, Mary Patterson worked alongside Coppin in the Female Department (Brown, 1926)

Upon finding out about Coppin's new principal appointment, Mary Patterson departed from the Institute for Colored Youth to serve in a leadership role as the principal of Preparatory High School (later renamed Dunbar High School) (Sterling, 1984). Frazelia Campbell became the assistant principal of the Institute for Colored Youth Girl's High School. During this time, Coppin continued to increase the number of incoming Black students and decrease the dropout rate of pupils. In addition to increasing student enrollment as a principal, Coppin eliminated corporal punishment as a form of discipline at the Institute for Colored Youth. Through Fanny Jackson Coppin's school leadership, more Black girls graduated with teaching degrees. At the Institute for Colored Youth, African American girls' and women's advanced education allowed them to fight for better educational opportunities for other Blacks. Today, Cheyney University of Pennsylvania (formerly the Institute for Colored Youth and the first HBCU) continues to provide higher education to people of African descent (Perkins, 1987).

Other Black women held leadership positions in the North. For instance, after teaching for 15 years, Anna Julia Cooper became the principal of M. Street High School in 1902 (Washington, 1988). There, Cooper disciplined her students while teaching them to believe in themselves and hold racial pride. At M. Street High School, she encouraged Black students to pursue higher education after high school. As a result, some of her former students attended private colleges, including Brown University, Harvard University, Dartmouth College, Oberlin College, and Yale University (Washington, 1988).

While some Black women educated military troops, other Black women contributed to disciplinary policies, curriculum development, recruitment, and retention of Black students in schools. In these administrative roles, Black women not only changed the structure of schools, but also encouraged Blacks to pursue a college education.

Black Women School Founders after *Plessy*

As leaders of classrooms and educational administration, it is no coincidence that some Black women founded schools to educate Blacks in order to prepare them for the workforce after the 1896 Plessy decision. In 1897, with the support of private donors, a Tuskegee Institute graduate named Elizabeth E. Wright "opened up stairs over an old store-house, with no bells, chairs, or benches" in Denmark, South Carolina, with only two instructors and 14 students (Hartshorn, 1910, p. 347). In less than a year, the enrollment significantly increased to 250 students. The school's curriculum emphasized agricultural studies in 16 different areas and spiritual instruction (e.g., reading biblical scriptures, singing hymns, praying). Students were also required to attend church services on Sundays. By 1908, the school had 22 instructors and 320 students.

Less than three years later, in 1902, Charlotte Hawkins Brown opened up a private school in North Carolina with support from donors to promote literacy of Blacks, especially Black girls and women (Hartshorn, 1910; Reynolds, 2002). A year later in 1903, the school became the Alice Freeman Palmer Memorial Institute to honor Alice Palmer Freeman's financial support of the school after her untimely death. The elementary curriculum focused on reading, writing, arithmetic, drawing, and hygiene (Wadelington & Knapp, 1999). Students beyond elementary school took general education classes and other courses, including geography, English literature, agriculture, and history. If a student aspired to attend college, he/she enrolled in education, government, and language courses. Other students took vocational courses providing them with knowledge and skills to prepare them for the agricultural industry beginning in 1908. The agricultural and manual training program's curriculum consisted of home economics, agriculture, and industrial arts classes.

Della Irving Hayden also opened up a school, Franklin Normal and Industrial Institute, in 1904 for Black children in Virginia as "many schools that gave black youngsters the education denied them elsewhere" (Sterling, 1984, p. 379). She financed the school through church donations. The small school had three teachers who occupied one of four classrooms. In her first month of teaching, she taught 20 students from Monday to Friday in a "room 15 by 20 feet. . . [She] bought two dozen chairs, got a blackboard, stove, table and broom" (p. 379). Despite limited resources, the 40 graduates of Franklin Normal and Industrial Institute became teachers, business consultants, and college graduates. More recently known as Hayden High School, it prepared Blacks for college until the 1980s.

In 1904, Mary McLeod Bethune founded the Daytona Literary and Industrial School for Negro Girls in Florida (Thomas-McCluskey, 1991). Bethune's school consisted of three departments: the English Department, the Industrial, and the Biblical Department (Thomas-McCluskey, 1991; Smith, 2001). She taught all of the courses at her school, from the basics of reading, writing, and arithmetic to home economics, domestic work, and religious studies. Mary McLeod-Bethune's industrial curriculum trained Black girls and women for traditional domestic work positions. Several years later, she hoped to teach Black girls and women to be more economically independent. The Daytona Literary and Industrial School expanded by offering high school and college courses to prepare Black women for professions in business administration, teaching, and nursing. Daytona Literary and Industrial School's changes in curriculum led to the educational and career advancement of many Black girls and women by providing them with educational opportunities to further prepare them for the workforce and become economically independent. Today, Bethune-Cookman University (formerly the Daytona Literary and Industrial School) continues to educate Blacks to prepare them for the workforce in American society in liberal arts and teacher education in Daytona Beach, Florida (Bethune-Cookman University, n.d.).

Similarly, a former student of Anna Julia Cooper at M. Street High School, Nannie Helen Burroughs always dreamed of starting her own school for colored girls (Easter, 1992). In 1909, she opened the National Training School for Women and Girls (NTSWG) in Washington, D.C. The purpose of NTSWG was to "give a training of *head, hand, and heart* and develop a definite and active social interest in the spiritual and moral forces that make for human welfare" (Easter, 1992, p. 84). NTSWG offered junior high and junior college curricula in dressmaking, printing, sewing, missionary work, music, and Black history. It was known as the school that taught the three B's: the Holy Bible, bathtub, and the broom. In 1918, NTSWG expanded its programs to include a normal school to train teachers and a beauty school. Fewer than 10 years later, in 1926, NTSWG opened a trade school. NTSWG's trade school offered classes from domestic arts and sciences, nursing, and public health to management, power machine operation, and social services. Graduates of this school became domestic workers, teachers, technicians, or worked in the health professions. Currently, this elementary school (now Nannie Helen Burroughs School) provides a private education to male and female students in Washington, D.C. (Nannie Helen Burroughs School, n.d.).

Like her student, Burroughs, Dr. Anna Julia Cooper served in a leadership role at the collegiate level as president of Frelinghuysen University in Washington, D.C., from 1930 to 1942 (Bhan & Lemert, 1998). Frelinghuysen University served working-class students and employed Blacks. When the school had financial challenges, Dr. Anna Julia Cooper opened up an annex called the Hannah Stanley Opportunity School, named in honor of her mother, Hannah Stanley Haywood. The Hannah Stanley Opportunity School's mission was to educate low-income Black children and adults in hopes of encouraging them to pursue coursework leading to a trade or earn a college degree to prepare them for the workforce. The curriculum focused on reading, writing, and arithmetic.

Lessons Learned: Black Female Educators' Legacies

Black women have historically served as leaders in their communities, not only as mothers and wives, but also as teachers, administrators, and school founders. In schools, Black women believed in the educational talents of Black students and encouraged the growth and development of those talents. Through teaching, Black women served as leaders in the workforce and provided Blacks access to educational opportunities in public and private schools so they could become self-sufficient, self-reliant, and financially independent. By founding schools, Black women provided a space for Black students to learn in a segregated society and become educators, leaders, and professionals, as they pursued higher education in American society. Today, some of these schools remain as historical sites and educational institutions promoting the continued education of Black Americans. The legacies of Black female educators and leaders promise to prompt continued inquiry into the current state of Black women's leadership at the primary, secondary, and postsecondary levels of education, as well as their limited presence in these academic spaces (Cooper, 2006; Dowdy-Kilgore, 2008; Evans, 2007).

Bibliography

Anderson, J. D. (1988). *The education of Blacks in the South, 1860–1935*. Chapel Hill: University of North Carolina Press.

Bennett College. (2009). Bennett College for Women Fact Book 2008–2009. Retrieved from www.bennett.edu.

Bethune-Cookman University. (n.d.). History. Retrieved from http://www.cookman.edu/

Bhan, E., & Lemert, C. (1998). The voice of Anna Julia Cooper. New York: Rowman & Littlefield Publishers.

Brown, H. Q. (1926). Homespun heroines and other women of distinction. Xenia, OH: Aldine Publishing Co.

Brown, C. H. (1941). The correct thing to do, to say, to wear. Sedalia, NC: Charlotte Hawkins Brown.

Constance-Hill, M. (1977). Lengthening shadow of a woman: A biography of Charlotte Hawkins Brown. Hicksville, NY: Exposition Press.

Cooper, A. J. (1892). A voice from the South. Xenia, OH: Aldine Printing Office.

Cooper, T. L. (2006). The sista' network: African American women faculty successfully negotiating the road to tenure. Boston: Anker Publishing.

Coppin, F. J. (1913). Reminiscences of school life, and hints on teaching. Philadelphia: A.M.E. Book Concern.

Dowdy-Kilgour, J. (2008). PhD stories: Conversations with my sisters. Cresskill, NJ: Hampton Press.

Easter, O. V. (1992). Nannie Helen Burroughs and her contributions to the adult education of African-American women. Unpublished doctoral dissertation. DeKalb, Northern Illinois University.

Evans, S. Y. (2007). Black women in the Ivory Tower, 1850–1954: An intellectual history. Gainesville: University Press of Florida.

Guy-Sheftall, B. (1982). Black women in higher education: Spelman and Bennett College revisited. Journal of Negro Education, 51(3), 278–287.

Hartshorn, W. N. (1910). An era of progress and promise, 1863–1910. Boston: Priscilla Publishing.

Hayden High School. (n.d.). Hayden High School remembrances. Retrieved from http://www.franklinsafety.com/haydenhighschool/index.html

Johnson, K. (2000). Uplifting the women and the race: The educational philosophies and social activism of Anna Julia Cooper and Nannie Helen Burroughs. New York: Garland Publishing.

Lerner, G. (1973). Black women in White America: A documentary history. New York: Vintage Books.

Lockwood, L. (1892). Mary S. Peake: The colored teacher at Fortress Monroe. Boston: American Tract Society.

Loewenberg, B. B. J., & Bogin, R. (1976). Black women in nineteenth century American life: Their words, their thoughts, their feelings. University Park: Pennsylvania State University Press.

McPherson, E. (2011). Moving from separate, to equal, to equitable schooling: Revisiting school desegregation policies. Urban Education, 46(3), 465–483. doi: 10.1177/0042085910377431

Nannie Helen Burroughs School. (n.d.). Nannie Helen Burroughs, Inc. Retrieved from http://www.nhburroughs.org/

Neverdon-Morton, C. (1989). Afro-American women of the south and the advancement of the race, 1895–1925. Knoxville: University of Tennessee Press.

Perkins, L. M. (1987). Fanny Jackson Coppin and the Institute for Colored Youth 1865–1902. New York: Garland Publishing.

Plessy v. Ferguson, 163 U.S. 537 (1896).

Read, F. M. (1961). Story of Spelman College. Princeton, NJ: Princeton University Press.

Reynolds, K. C. (2002). Charlotte Hawkins Brown and the Palmer Institute. In A. R. Sadovik and S. F. Semel (Eds.), Founding mothers and others: Women educational leaders during the Progressive Era (pp. 7–17). New York: Palgrave.

Smith, E. M., & Thomas-McCluskey, A. (2001). Mary McLeod Bethune: Building a better world essays and selected documents. Bloomington: Indiana University Press.

Sterling, D. (1984). We are your sisters: Black Women in the nineteenth century. New York: W. W. Norton & Co.

Taylor, S. K. (1902). Reminisces of my life in camp with the 33rd U.S. Colored Troops late 1st South Carolina volunteers: A Black woman's memoirs. New York: Markus Wiener Publishing.

Thomas-McCluskey, A. (1991). Mary McLeod Bethune and the education of African American girls in the South, 1904–1923. Unpublished doctoral dissertation. Bloomington, Indiana University.

U.S. Department of Education, Office for Civil Rights. (1991). Historically Black colleges and universities and higher education desegregation. Washington, DC: U.S. Department of Education. Retrieved from http://www.ed.gov/about/offices/list/ocr/docs/hq9511.html

Wadelington, C. W., & Knapp, R. F. (1999). *Charlotte Hawkins Brown & Palmer Memorial Institute: What one young African American woman could do*. Chapel Hill: University of North Carolina Press.

Washington, M. H. (1988). Introduction. In H. L. Gates II (Ed.), *A voice from the South* (pp. xxvii–liv). New York: Oxford University Press.

Chapter Six

Black Women's Historical Leadership in African American Home Education

Rhonda Hudson and Dannielle Joy Davis

I f one considers home education as an intentional refusal of, as well as an alternative to, education established and mandated by dominant society, then it unquestionably has a long history among African Americans. Home education practices date back to slavery, when learning how to read and write could often only be taught in secrecy (Gaither, 2008). Historical documentation reveals that enslavement of African Americans during the colonial era forced them to seek various ways to become educated. During colonial times, young enslaved children were sometimes allowed a home education in exchange for hard labor or homemade crafts. Yet even upon receiving an education, they were still expected to exhibit docile, subservient behavior (Gaither, 2008).

Despite the oppressive conditions of home education, enslaved African Americans voluntarily embraced home-schooling activities for various reasons. Throughout the colonial period and the Civil War, if home education was used by Whites to conform to American society, it was employed by African Americans to counter domination (Gaither, 2008). For the duration of the three decades before the Civil War, African Americans lived in a society where several states passed anti-literacy laws forbidding them—whether free or enslaved—to learn how to read and write.

Despite dangers and difficulties, African Americans continued to participate in secret forms of home education to learn the skills of reading and writing (Anderson, 1988). Several free African Americans sent their children away to family members who lived in the North to learn to read and write. Others engaged in secret or underground educational activities, normally in home environments (Gaither, 2008). In some states where learning to read and write was illegal for Blacks, enslaved African American children would disguise their school books and sneak into the homes of free African American women, avoiding the police and other Whites, in order to learn to read and write. After learning activities ended, the children would sneak back to their homes (Gaither, 2008). Slaves also traded food and money for information on the alphabet and words with White children (Gaither, 2008). In addition, some slave children often learned to read by asking White children what they learned at school each day in exchange for gifts, such as marbles. After secretive learning with slave owners' children or wives, slave-to-slave transfer of learning often took place. Much of these lessons took place on Sundays while the slave owners and their families were at church (Gaither, 2008). During colonial times and beyond, the participation in secret forms of home education was indeed a way of life for African Americans.

Later, some years before the Civil War, many African Americans looked to public schools for their education. Several hoped it would bring freedom and prosperity during segregation, while others believed public education held them back (Gaither, 2008). Inequity of educational funding, resources, and overcrowded schools were primary reasons behind African American home education during segregation (Gaither, 2008). Historical research demonstrates that African American parents heavily participated in their children's education, particularly during segregation (Fields-Smith, 2005). During segregation, home education among African Americans primarily were collaborations between parents, other concerned adults, as well as trusting African American educators (Gaither, 2008). Parents conducted learning activities at home to support what was learned in the African American schools (Gaither, 2008). Today, this form of home education is often referred to as supplemental home schooling.

After the Civil War, African American parents continued to pursue education, often under severe conditions in which White leaders did not consider educational equality a priority (Gaither, 2008). Home education would continue to be a necessity for Blacks due to continued injustices. Despite the fall of de jure segregation, African American parents have dealt with de facto segregation: tracking within schools; issues of social and cultural differences between homes and schools; and low expectations from teachers (Fields-Smith, 2005).

Many of the issues contributing to African Americans' participation in home education changed little after emancipation, desegregation, or after the famous *Brown v. the Board of Education* Supreme Court decision. An assumption held by advocates of *Brown v. the Board of Education* was that equality in access would also grant equality of outcomes for African Americans. Yet the education of African American students versus White peers in public schools has statistically proven less than equal. (Taylor, 2005). Throughout the 20th century, in efforts to oppose the inequalities in public education, certain African American families held their children out of the public schools and instructed them at home (Gaither, 2008). Later, during the 1990s, home education became more mainstream.

One of the first parents to organize African American or minority home education was Donna Nichols-White. She and her husband, Clifford, didn't allow any of their three children to attend public schools (Gaither, 2008). According to Gaither (2008), there were many reasons for this family to participate in home education. The three main reasons included their desire to enjoy family life, the less than acceptable academic expectations of public schools, and last but not least, the horrific statistics that illustrated poor academic performance among African American children in public schools (Gaither, 2008). This prompted Ms. Nichols-White to reach out to others who also taught their children at home by starting the first magazine published by and for minority home educators. *Drinking Gourd* magazine, which was named after an old Negro spiritual, regularly described how public schools did not prepare African Americans or other minority children for success (Gaither, 2008). This ignited a national movement that united minority home educators via national organizations. Participation in home education among African Americans has increased year after year since.

No movement takes place without some controversy. During the 1990s, other national home education organizations held conferences guided by the early "Christian" American principles (Gaither, 2008). This caused many African Americans to be skeptical of the home education movement due to slavery, long-term oppression, and the racism that White Christians often promoted. Uncertainty about motives behind this movement continued throughout the 1990s for some African Americans (Gaither, 2008). Yet, home education continued to grow rapidly among the group.

Those forming national minority home education organizations during recent years often cite a study by Dr. Brian Ray's National Home Education Research Institute (NHERI), which reported no achievement gap among African American and White children who participated in home education (Gaither, 2008). Ray held that African American children who participated in home education scored in the 87th percentile in reading and the 77th percentile in math, which he claims highly exceeds the ratings of African Americans attending public schools and is equal to White children attending these schools (Gaither, 2008). This study implied that African Americans specifically are in need of home education and would highly benefit from participating. The study, like others, has its limitations and only represents a small segment of the country. Yet it offers insight from which future studies might draw upon in further assessing the academic achievement of African American versus White students participating in home education.

Our nation's past comprises many unsung African Americans who participated in home education. However, only a small number are highlighted in history. Robert Moton and his mother illustrate early Black women's roles in leading via educating their children at home. Born in 1867, Moton's mother worked on a plantation where she was the head cook, while his father headed the plantation field hands (Moton, 1920). Although they were free, it was illegal for African Americans to learn to read and write. Hence, his literate mother took caution while teaching him these skills (Moton, 1920). For many years, Mrs. Moton hid from the plantation family that she was literate as she taught her son. Though subsequently discovered by the slave owner's wife, she was pleased with the discovery of the Motons being literate (Moton, 1920). Thereafter, Moton was sent to study at a free school for African Americans directed by a former officer of the Confederate Army (Du Bois, 1940). In 1885, Moton was an 18–year-old student at the Hampton Institute (Du Bois, 1940). After graduating in 1890, he became the school's commandant in charge of military discipline, holding this post for 25 years. During his tenure at Hampton Institute, he traveled to cities in the North persuading philanthropists to contribute money to the predominantly Black college (Du Bois, 1940). Moton ultimately left Hampton Institute in 1915 to replace Booker T. Washington and become the president of Tuskegee Institute (Du Bois, 1940).

Moton's mother represents one of many unsung Black women who provided home education for the advancement of their families and the race (Anderson, 1988). Ms. Moton's leadership as a home educator serves as a strong example of these historical contributions Black women made upon their families, communities, and our nation as a whole. Black women's roles in African American home education have remained consistent from the colonial era until now. This history, along with the increasing participation of African Americans in home education, may inform future studies of home education as a form of supplemental education for parents. Numerous women, such as the second author's mother and other female relatives, have worked to defy academic odds and have taken leadership roles in their children's educations through either traditional or supplemental homeschooling. As opposed to leaving their children in the hands of failing schools, they became the primary educators of their offspring who ultimately reaped the benefits of this form of schooling. Home education holds great promise of continuing to contribute to closing the academic achievement gap between Black and White students in the United States and beyond.

Bibliography

Anderson, J. (1988). *The education of Blacks in the South, 1860–1935.* Chapel Hill: University of North Carolina Press.

Du Bois, W. E. B. (1940). Moton of Hampton and Tuskegee. *Phylon (1940–1956), 1*(4), 344–302.

Fields-Smith, C. (2005). African American parents before and after *Brown. Journal of Curriculum and Supervision, 20*(2), 129–135.

Gaither, M. (2008). *Homeschool: An American history.* New York: Palgrave Macmillan.

Moton, R. (1920). *Finding a way out: An autobiography.* New York: Doubleday, Page & Co.

Taylor, V. (2005). Behind the trend: Increases in homeschooling among African American families. In B. Cooper, *Homeschooling in full view: A reader* (pp. 121–133). Charlotte, NC: Information Age Publishing.

Chapter Seven

Black Women as Educational Leaders

Emotional Neutrality and Psychic Duality

Talia R. Esnard, Laurette Bristol, and Launcelot Brown

Introduction

Over the past decade, many debates surrounded stereotypical understandings of how men and women operate in educational leadership[1] (Ouston, 1993; Rhode, 2003; Coleman & Campbell-Stephens, 2010). As sociocognitive assessments, Rhode (2003) asserted that these gender stereotypes influence "beliefs, behaviors and self-concept at both conscious and unconscious levels, and perceptions of leadership ability are inescapably affected by these stereotypes" (p. 8). More recently, Hoyt (2007) espoused that "substantial empirical evidence revealed that gender stereotypes can significantly alter the perception and evaluation of female leaders and directly affect women in or aspiring to leadership roles" (p. 307). Yet, "the relationship between sex-role stereotypes and leadership. . . has not fully been defined" (Hoyt, p. 307), particularly in developing countries like the Caribbean. Thus, concerns over how women acquire and respond to these stereotypes in their practices of educational leadership remain the subject of intense debate in educational leadership literature and an empirical gap in the Caribbean. Two questions that one may logically ask therefore are (1) How do gender stereotypes framed within stratified and structural processes affect the perceptions and experiences of women in educational leadership in Trinidad and Tobago, and (2) How do these women respond to these stereotypes in the formation of their professional identi-

---

1   Educational leadership is a visionary construct, which Bush (2007) defined as "a process of influence based on clear values and beliefs and leading to a vision for the school" (p. 403).

ties? This paper attempts to contribute to this debate in the educational leadership literature through the phenomenological exploration of the understandings and experiences of educational leadership for six early career (i.e., less than five years) primary school women principals in Trinidad and Tobago.

The structure of this paper is therefore twofold. First, we discuss the importance of the intersection of gender, religion, and age stereotypes through the perceptions and experiences of women as educational leaders. Second, we examine the link between these stratified complexities, the position of *emotional neutrality*, and the eventual emergence of a *psychic duality* (e.g., affectivity vs. authority) as reflected in their professional identities.[2] By so doing, the major contention of the paper is that social stereotypes that govern understandings of women as educational leaders are rooted in stratified and structured systems of social interaction. These stratified and structured systems that were internalized by these stereotypes engender positions of *emotional neutrality* and *psychic duality*, which emerges from their conscious and unconscious responses to these social stereotypes.

Structure of the Education System in Trinidad and Tobago

The twin island Republic of Trinidad and Tobago is the most southerly of the West Indian islands. It is a multiethnic, multireligious society with an estimated total population of 1.3 million people (CSO, 2010). In relation to its age structure, 45.2% of the population is under 25 years of age. Mandating all educational policies is the Ministry of Education (MOE), which is the central authority in charge of the education system. For administrative purposes, the country is divided into eight educational districts each of which is headed by a school supervisor III (SS III), assisted by school supervisors IIs (SSIIs) responsible for secondary schools and school supervisor Is responsible for primary schools. There is also early childhood care and education, which is a separate department in the MOE.

The system comprises four levels: (1) early childhood care and education (3–4 year olds), (2) primary education (5–11/12 years), (3) secondary education (12–16/17 years), and (4) the tertiary level, which consists of all postsecondary education and training. There are 484 public primary schools. Of this number, 30% are government-funded and -managed nonreligious schools. The remaining 70% are government-funded schools but managed by denominational boards representing the Christian, Hindu, and Muslim religions (MOE, 2001).

A major legislative agreement that incorporated the role of the church in the public education system is the Concordat of 1960. The Concordat is an agreement between the church and the state in which the church is given assurance that

---

2   For the purpose of this research, *professional identity* is the subjective self-conceptualisation associated with the work role adopted (McGowen & Hart, 1990) and relates to how people compare and differentiate themselves (attitudes, values, knowledge, beliefs, and skills that are shared with others within a professional group) from other professional groups (Haslam et al., 2000).

allows for the preservation and character of their schools. In this agreement, the church—through its denominational boards—is responsible for one-third of the cost of the building and maintenance of the school buildings and facilities, and it recruits and selects principals and teaching faculty for their schools. The MOE, based on the recommendations of the denominational boards, appoints and dismisses principals and teachers through the Teaching Service Commission (TSC) and is responsible for the payment of all salaries.

In many ways, the Concordat of 1960 has been beneficial to the country. While there was a long history of free access to denominational primary schools, the agreement opened a number of formerly denominational private secondary schools, giving the public unprecedented access to secondary education through national government examinations. However, the agreement also solidified the pivotal role of the church in the selection process of principals for their schools. The implication, therefore, is adherence to the teaching and values of the church plays as critical a role as leadership characteristics in the final decision as to whom is selected as principal.

Policy and Educational Leadership in Trinidad and Tobago

In Trinidad and Tobago, there is no official or documented definition of what is educational leadership (Brown & Conrad, 2007). In this context, reference to principals is used interchangeably with reference to educational leaders and principals are "left with the task of individually defining their roles with regards to the functioning of their schools and meeting the expectations of the public and the Ministry of Education [MOE]" (Brown & Conrad, 2007, p. 185).

Outside of these subjective and individualistic understandings, what remains are dual unofficial understandings of educational leadership as rational and as transformational; a dual understanding that emerged from the implementation of postindependent legislative and educational policy reforms adopted by the state since the 1960s. More specifically, the unchanged 1966 Education Act promoted rational models of educational leadership. However, the Education Plan of 1985–1990, the 1993–2003 Educational Policy Paper, and the MOE Strategic Plan 2002–2006 all encouraged transformational leadership. As such, within this myriad of educational policies, one of the major shifts in educational planning over the period was the movement from traditional, rational-legal emphases of leadership to considerations of school-based management (SBM) as part of this transformational thrust. In that regard, the 1993–2003 Education Policy Paper and onward mandated the expansion, reorganization, and phased decentralization of the education system (where schools became one of the primary units of decision making), the implementation of the SBM approach, and the introduction of a revised system for principal selection. In terms of the selection process, the 1993–2003 Education Policy Paper marked a movement away from the use of seniority to the use of expertise gained through expanding accredited professional development programs.

Collectively, these educational policies promoted transformational understandings of educational leadership, which for London (1997) functioned dialectically as related to sociopolitical, economic struggles and the conflict and expectation of transformational leadership that they bring. This became the burden of educational leaders and, by extension, the education system. What emerged is a paradox where educational policy reform was juxtaposed against the constraints of (1) institutional bureaucracy, (2) institutional pluralism,[3] (3) the ideological peculiarities of state as well as the church as protected through the Concordat and (4) the related rational or task-based emphases of the unchanged Education Act.

Realistically, educational expansion and the reorganization of the education system altered traditional male domination within the highest echelons of the education system in Trinidad and Tobago. In fact, recent educational statistics from the MOE show that for the period 2001–2009, there has been a general increase of 10% in the number of women filling vacant posts for primary school principals in Trinidad and Tobago, compared to men who declined by 10%. Table 7.1 below shows the increasing representation of female principals in primary schools of Trinidad and Tobago.

Academic Year	Male N (%)	Female N (%)	Total
2001–2002	194 (43)	255 (57)	449
2002–2003	196 (42)	269 (58)	465
2003–2004	194 (41)	283 (59)	477
2004–2005	191 (51)	186 (49)	377
2005–2006	171 (36)	303 (64)	474
2006–2007	160 (34)	317 (66)	477
2007–2008	157 (33)	317 (67)	474
2008–2009	155 (33)	321 (67)	476
TOTAL	**1,418**	**2,251**	**3,669**

Table 7.1 Sex Distributions of Principals in Government and Government-assisted Primary Schools in Trinidad and Tobago (Source: MOE, 2001–2009)

3   Institutional pluralism is a concept first popularized by M. G. Smith (1965), which focuses on the diverse ethnic beliefs and practices at an institutional level in a multicultural society.

Similar trends also apply to the case of vice principals of government-assisted and government primary schools in Trinidad and Tobago as shown in Table 7.2. Here, the number of female vice-principals also increased from 69% to 79% over the same period.

Academic Year	Male N (%)	Female N (%)	Total
2001–2002	50 (31)	110 (69)	160
2002–2003	43 (30)	100 (70)	143
2003–2004	37 (27)	99 (73)	136
2004–2005	31 (24)	97 (76)	128
2005–2006	28 (26)	79 (74)	107
2006–2007	31 (27)	83 (73)	114
2007–2008	26 (24)	82 (76)	108
2008–2009	23 (21)	86 (79)	109
Total	**269**	**736**	**1,005**

Table 7.2 Sex Distributions of Vice-Principals in Government and Government-assisted Primary Schools in Trinidad and Tobago (Source: MOE, 2001–2009)

Thus, the data show the increasing predominance of women as primary school principals in Trinidad and Tobago and illustrate, based on the trends, that the increasing domination of women as principals in primary schools is likely to continue in the near future.

Theoretical Framework

One consensus in the literature on gender stereotypes and educational leadership is that "educational leadership lies in baggage of the past" (Hill-Somers & Ragland, 1995, p. 6) and "resonates deeply with wider cultural mythology: our experiences of history, religion and politics" (Sinclair, 1998, p. 27). Thus, as part of advancing a more in-depth theoretical understanding of the underlining processes and stereotypes that shape educational leadership, the study embraces a constructed leadership theory.

Conceptually, Sinclair (1998) stated that leadership can best be understood as a phenomenon constructed in the minds and eyes of the audience (p. 176). Thus, constructed leadership theory points to the powerful interplay of race, class, gender, and religion as *archetypes of leadership*, which derive from "embedded cultural stories and icons and continue to pervade the supposedly objective assessment of leadership potential in our organizations" (p. 32). Additionally, for Sinclair arche-types of leadership unconsciously and consciously shape personal and professional identities.

In the case of the former, this notion of archetypes of leadership can be linked to what Lorber (1994) identified as the process, structure, and stratified basis of gender stereotypes. In terms of the process, Lorber presented gender as a complex element of social differentiation, values, and norms learned through socializa-tion, which produces a gendered identity and colored notions of gender roles in various societal institutions. At the theoretical and empirical levels, some Carib-bean scholars have challenged structural-functional discourses of Black Caribbean women in which the historical reference to *matrifocality*[4] silences their authority, consciousness, and autonomy (Lazarus-Black, 2001; Sutton & Makiesky-Barrow, 2001). As a structure, gender stereotypes divide economic activity in such a way that it privileges men, legitimates those in authority, and organizes sexuality and emotional life (Lorber, 1994). In the case of the Caribbean, it is clear that while the changing value and policy systems challenge the historical marginalization of women, the separation of men and women into different economic activity remains (Lynch, 1995) and expressions of sexuality continue to favor men over women (Chevannes, 2002). As a stratification system, Lorber (1994) argued that gender ranks men and women of the same race and class; a process that depends on differential evaluation. Here, the "complexities of race-based and gender-based assumptions permeate other leadership arenas outside of politics, including school leadership" (Reed & Evans, 2008, p. 487). In some cases, this is also accompa-nied by entrenched beliefs that educational leadership should be based on gender role expectations and harnessed by religious beliefs (Reed & Evans; Coleman & Campbell-Stephens, 2010; Fincham, 2010). In these studies, however, many au-thors suggest that although gender, race, and age complicate leadership percep-tions and experiences, gender plays a greater role in regard to negative experiences (Wrushen & Sherman, 2008).

In the case of the latter, this inherent postmodern perspective permits one to observe how the dominant notion of leadership as masculine shapes women's professional identities (Coleman, 2003; Crow, 2006). Thus, Sinclair (1998, p. 175) declared that "for women in leadership roles, there has been no discernible reinforcing relationship between being a leader and being a woman." While her early work challenged the narrow expressions of masculinity as the basis of un-derstanding leadership, it also linked these archetypes of leadership to "women('s) conscious and unconscious use of strategies to conceal their gender and sexuality, to camouflage, to blend rather than stand out" (Sinclair, p. 175). This is a direct

---

4   In this definition, R. T. Smith (1973, p. 25) sees matrifocality as a situation in which "it is women in their roles as mothers who come to be the focus of relationships."

result of collectively experienced expectations, "beliefs and feelings of a group of people, which are rarely articulated and sometimes unconscious" (Sinclair, p. 31).

Thus, collectively the notion of archetypes of leadership represents societal constructs (Hill-Somers & Ragland, 1995) that capture "the early [stratified] experiences that emerge from collective, constructed and unconscious dimensions of leadership" (Sinclair, 1998, p. 176). These provide powerful templates of what is, and how leadership should be understood and practiced. In this context, the use of the concept of archetypes of leadership and the related focus on aspects of gender, age, and religion present a valuable theoretical construct that allow us to examine the relevance of these archetypes as these stereotypes become self-perpetuating (Strachan, Akao, Kilavanwa, & Warsal, 2010) in their *perceptions* or *expressions of leadership.* Additionally, the theory highlights the conscious and unconscious responses of women and ways in which these processes create a new or unique type of leadership, that is, one that is based on *emotional neutrality* and *psychic duality* in their *performance of leadership* for six Black[5] early career primary school principals in Trinidad.

Women in Leadership: *Emotional Neutrality* and *Psychic Duality*

One of the most contentious issues in Western literature on educational leadership is the debate on leadership styles of female versus male principals (Rhode, 2003; Seyfarth, 2008). In the discussion, gender stereotypes label women as weak, *emotional,* caring, indecisive, creative, subjective, informal, frivolous, and not suited for educational leadership (Ouston, 1993). Gender stereotypes, on the other hand, label men as aggressive, decisive, competitive, objective, formal, and *rational* in leadership positions (Gray, 1993). In terms of educational leadership styles, Hoyt (2007) stated that robust research across settings revealed that "women lead in a more democratic, or participative manner than men" and that "women were devalued compared to men when they led in masculine manner (autocratic or directive), when they occupied typically masculine roles" (pp. 266–67). Such research suggests that differences expressed are based on cross-pressures in which women must "be masculine and tough, but as women they should not be too manly in their leadership" (Hoyt, p. 277). In such cases, Wharton and Erickson (1993) suggest that when persons are faced with conflicting role expectations, they tend to mask their emotions or display some degree of "emotional neutrality" where their emotions are expected to be muted and any excessive display discouraged (p. 467). This is related to internalized notions of gender role expectation, the cognitive evaluations of social-contextual situated differences (Brody & Hall, 1993) and the "association of authority with an unemotional persona" (Wharton & Erickson, p. 467).

5   For the purpose of this study, this is defined as peoples of African descent.

Thus, concerns over whether women respond (be it cognitively, behaviourally, and affectively) to these socially constructed notions of women as leaders and whether, in these cases, these responses are contextual remain the subject of intense debate in educational leadership literature. Some researchers also contend that women do respond to these social constructs and, in such cases, expectations of women as educational leaders lead to the development of unique integrated strategies (Rhode, 2003). In such contexts (Powell & Butterfield, 1984; cited by Butterfield & Grinnell, 1999), the internalization of these stereotypes in the leadership styles of women becomes androgynous (establishing a duality) rather than masculine or feminine. This integration of feminine and masculine styles points to an understanding of this process as a split or an emerging duality, which presents unique styles of educational leadership in their performances and expressions of gender.

As part of this discussion, this paper explores the related and underexplored concept of psychic duality and its possible relevance to the understanding of how these stereotypes affect the professional identities of women as educational leaders. In one of his earliest explorations of psychic duality as expressive, Du Bois (1897) spoke of the collective psyches of peoples of African descent as being torn between competing cultural dictates as a result of their encounter with the West. More specifically, Du Bois stated that:

> It is a peculiar sensation, this double-consciousness, this sense of always looking at one's self through the eyes of others, of measuring one's soul by the tape of a world that looks on in amused contempt and pity. One ever feels his two-ness—an American, a Negro; two souls, two thoughts; two unreconciled strivings; two warring ideals in one dark body, whose dogged strength alone keeps it from being torn asunder. (pp. 194–95)

This double consciousness is seen as a universal phenomenon in which Blacks resist the pressures to submerge the essence of Black identity but face the problem of warring Black ideals, a tension, which suggests that their racial identity is transcendental rather than phenotypical in nature. Similarly, Fanon (1968) argued that via a history of colonialized inferiority, Blacks have a split psyche: one with their fellow Black people and the other with White people in which they behave differently within Black- and White-dominated contexts based on their consciousness of "being for others."

In her performative model, Butler (1990) also referred to the notion of psychic duality as a process in which individuals learn, rehearse their stereotypes, and regurgitate these in his or her conscious and unconscious everyday acts and gestures. Thus, Butler argued that:

Acts, gestures and desire produce the effect of an internal core or substance, but produce this on the surface of the body, through the play of signifying absences that suggest, but never reveal, the organizing principle of identity as a cause. Such acts, gestures, enactments, generally constructed, are performative in the sense that the essence of the identity that they otherwise purport to express becomes a fabrication manufactured and sustained through corporeal signs and discursive means. (pp. 336–37)

From this point of view, gender is a learned performance that functions to create an illusion of truth in the understandings of the individual, thereby engendering the reproduction of performances deemed consistent with that, which is expected to be masculine or feminine. By extension, using Butler's schema, this performance becomes a charade; a direct result of the internal conflict related to whether and how they reproduce social expectations surrounding understandings of themselves as women.

Methodology

The purpose of this study was to gain a greater understanding of the perceptions and lived experiences of early career Black women as educational leaders. As such, the study utilized a phenomenological research design or method of inquiry (Van Manen, 1990) that embraced the "constructivist and interpretative view of human consciousness" (Willis, 2001, p. 14). As a form of interpretative phenomenology, it focused on the narratives and the "underlying meaning of the experience and emphasize the intentionality of consciousness where experiences contain both the outward appearance and inward consciousness based on memory, image, and meaning" (Creswell, 1998, p. 52). In this approach, the intentionality of consciousness centers on an individual's perception of an object (or phenomenon) and its reality, based on the conscious awareness of it and the meaning of the experience to the individual. The use of an interpretative phenomenological research design allowed for the exploration of major themes surrounding the development of expressed meanings and experiences of educational leadership for early career Black female principals in Trinidad and Tobago.

Given the focus of the study, we used a combination of purposive and snowball sampling. In order to do this, we used professional and personal contacts to identify the first principal for interviewing and, subsequently, used these contacts and the initial principal interviewed to "identify or put the researchers in touch with others who qualify for inclusion and these in turn, identify yet others, hence the small sample" (Cohen, Manion, & Morrison, 2008, p. 116). We interviewed six Black early career female principals in individual sessions for an average of 45 minutes. Their years of teaching experience prior to the assumption of duties as principals (P1) ranged from 14 to 39 years with only two participants having fewer than 20 years of experience. The time in their current positions as principals ranged from less than one year to just over four years. Their school populations ranged from 45 to 900 students with 10 to 40 teachers on staff, depending on the size of the school. Three of these principals were between the ages of 35 to 55 with the other three between the ages of 50 to 55.

As a way of voicing the experiences of women as educational leaders, we collected data using semi-structured interviews with open-ended questions, a strategy that allowed for depth, expressions of meanings, and the flow of conversations between researchers and participants (Reissman, 1993). Researchers developed questions to allow principals to speak about their perceptions, experiences, challenges, successes, and their views on societal expectations of women in positions of educational leadership. Interviews were transcribed, manually coded, and analyzed on an on-going, open-ended, inductive basis (Reissman) where analytic memos (Maxwell, 1996) were written throughout the data collection stage as a way of establishing patterns in the data. Here, researchers searched for inherent meanings of specific statements and themes in relation to their reference to critical incidents in professional and gender-based experiences (Creswell, 1998; Marshall & Rossman, 1999).

Findings

In order to understand the essence of educational leadership experiences, we explored the archetypes of educational leadership in their collective, constructed, conscious, and unconscious perceptions of their experiences. Two main themes emerged in this analysis: expressions of leadership as stratified (gender, age, and leadership; religion and leadership) and leadership as performed (leadership styles).

Stratified Leadership: The Importance of Gender and Age

Theoretically, gender serves as one the most visible and conscious stratified representations of the archetypes of leadership. In their expressions of educational leadership, the findings revealed that women questioned constructed notions of femininity and stereotypical associations of women within the private space of the home. They highlighted the tensions that it created for them as they attempted to strike some balance in the formation of their professional identities. For instance, Principal F expressed that "as a woman in leadership in Trinidad & Tobago. . . people associate you with house and rearing children still in 2011." However, Principal T illuminated the tensions related to work and family balance and the performance of her womanly duties. She commented that:

> [my son] has exams shortly, and I have to give him my time now. . . I find that sometimes being very hard on me, because of the demands of the job. . . as a female and as a mother with a family. . . that is my challenge.

Sinclair (1998, p. 175) postulated that "there has been no discernible reinforcing relationship between being a leader and being a woman." Thus, Principal V elaborated on the tensions of being a woman, a wife, and a principal when she stated that:

> It's tough because you are sort of under the microscope with everybody and the men are looking to see what this woman can do. . . My husband is recently retired and he sets up his face every morning I leave to go [as if to say]. "You abandoned me." So as a woman I have to be able to straddle all those horses. I have to be a leader for men. . . my own women. . . for my family and. . . make all my roles work.

Gender as a process remains another critical element of these archetypes of leadership. According to Sinclair (1998) overt behaviors that are consistent with constructed notions of femininity draw attention to and additional examination of women in educational leadership. Within this context, two principals also spoke about the additional examination of their private and sexual life. Principal A commented that "they look at you, they look at how you dress, they look at what you say, they look at how you discipline, even the teachers as well." Similarly, Principal S revealed that:

> dating and teaching. . . is hell. My social life has suffered greatly. . . after the first set of rumors, my friend did not want to come [here]. . . and I don't like that. Now if I were a guy and my house is full of girls and guys every weekend, there would be no question. They [are] just having a good time, but as a female you are always under scrutiny.

Furthermore, when age, as another stratified element of archetype of leadership, interacts with gender, women are faced with unique and complicated challenges of educational leadership. As such, Principal S stated that the misconception of an educational leader as someone of mature age further complicated the interplay of gender and age. Thus, as a young woman in her 30s, she became the target of great personal and social analysis. Additionally, Principal A stated that:

> the majority of them (95% of staff) were older than me, so [they] got the impression that [I was] a young girl. That is what they told [me]. . . [They would say,] well she is a young girl, how [did] she reach [this position]? that was the impression.

Furthermore, Principal T said, "I got the respect. . . but they were very wary of me because of my youth." Similarly, Principal S shared:

> I feel that I. . . still have to prove that I can do it because. . . I am a women still in my 30s. . . there will always be those who say, "well she is so young she has no experience," why did they put her there?" so I always constantly feel like I have to do everything right so as not to come under criticism."

The dominant understanding of leadership as masculine remains another structural element of the archetypes of leadership. The findings revealed that many principals were also conscious and critical of the privileges associated with masculinity and how these transfer into spaces of educational leadership. Thus, Principal F commented that the notion of leadership as masculine encourages greater response from staff. Principal V also noted the dominance and understanding of the men's club within educational leadership. Principal V posited:

> It's a gender thing. A male principal can walk across by [X bar] and sit and have a drink with the boys. . . If this female principal does that, alot of eyes [*sic*] will talk and word will reach MOE."

In contexts like these (Kanter, 1977; cited by Hoyt, 2007), "women experience significant pressure as their highly visible performance is scrutinized and they are perceived through gender-based lenses" (p. 278).

Thus, in spite of the grievances with these gender role expectation imbalances, these women consciously responded to the social construction of leadership as masculine through their adoption of a position of emotional neutrality or masking of emotions, a trait that is perceived as consistent with masculine leadership. Principal A said, "I tend to not get emotional, because once you're emotional, [you] make the wrong decisions. So your challenge here is to not get emotional and to do what is right." Indeed, "being seen as a woman diminishes one's leadership" (Sinclair, 1998, p. 175). Thus, many of these principals saw the display of emotions as a sign of weakness and the display of strength as a critical response to perceived notions of themselves as educational leaders. In defining her notion of strength as leadership competence, Principal T explained, "They must see you as a strong person, who knows what you are about." Other principals used the language of strength to describe a show of commitment, objectivity, persistence, and resistance from crying. Recent research indicated that "women become significantly more masculine; for example, becoming more assertive and valuing leadership and power more as job attributes, without losing their femininity" (Twenge, 2001; cited by Hoyt, 2007, p. 281).

Stratified Leadership: The Importance of Religion
Religion provides yet another stratified and structured element of these archetypes of leadership. Strachan and colleagues (2010, p. 70) saw "religion has a powerful influence on how women practice their leadership." Here the notion of servitude as a religious trait provides a powerful explanation for the experiences of educational leadership. Thus, Principal S commented: "I think being a good leader means that you have to be a very good servant we look at servant leadership very seriously." In terms of religion as a process, many of these principals expressed concern over the religious scrutiny to which potential female educational leaders

are subjected. In particular, Principal S revealed that in her interview for principalship, "The [interviewer] asked me. . . 'are you one of those young 30 somethings who is going to get pregnant out of wedlock?' But [if] I do while holding this post I would come under some heavy artillery fire." She also commented that principals must live a religious lifestyle, one different from that tolerated for men particularly in rural coastal villages. She stated:

> a friend of mine who is also a [new] principal,. . . she was going through a divorce when someone in the village called [the board regarding her circumstance] the board did not know that she was going through a divorce because when she was interviewed by the Board she and her husband were still on good terms, their marriage had not began to dissolve. . . [the Board] called her in and raked her over the coals.

As a result of these tensions, the women also held a double consciousness in their position on religion. That is, they were consciously critical of the ways in which it controls their access to and experiences in educational leadership, yet they were dependent on the fundamental belief systems as a source of comfort for dealing with the challenges of women as educational leaders. Thus, many of these women used notions of Christianity to help them cope with their tensions. Principal F said, "I always say the Holy Spirit you see that little prayer the Holy Spirit prayer it works right." Principal S said, "You pray that you are doing the right thing, oh you pray a lot in this job! You pray constantly." Principal V said that "you find alot of women just. . . hope and pray."

Leadership as Performance: Leadership Styles

This psychic duality was also evident in their leadership styles. In the case of this study, many of the principals saw authoritative masculine leadership as problematic and advocated the need for relational or distributed styles of leadership. However, in their performances of educational leadership practices, these women attempted to demonstrate and demand some element of authority and respect from all stakeholders involved. In one case, Principal V said:

> There was not much collaboration prior to my entry. Things were just told to you. . . so then I started to share with teachers. . . and I think the staff started to come around.

However, although she came in with intentions to practice a relational style of leadership, she also said that she used a more authoritative leadership style. She shared:

> My husband says "you are in the right profession: you always want to give people advice and boss them around." I am not bossing them around. . . and [I] advocate the need for relational and shared leadership from principals.

In the literature, the expectation is that "women tended to display a democratic and participatory style" (McGee-Banks, 2007, p. 315) and were more task oriented than male peers. However, there are men who practice democratic styles of leadership and women who exercise autocratic styles of leadership. Principal T said, "Regardless of what is happening around you, you must give respect where respect is due. You must respect my office." As such, like many of the other principals, Principal A uses the language of authority and respect to suggest that it is necessary for effective leadership. She suggested, "You had to gain respect. . . even though some of them still don't give you the respect that you need."

However, these women also developed a psychic duality as they also drew on their internalized notions of femininity in the use of relationships and promotion of teamwork (usually associated with women) in the formation of their professional identities. In that regard, Principal A commented that "you had to build relationships." Other principals also supported the need for shared, relational, moral, and spiritual leadership while maintaining one's position of authority in their professional roles claiming that it works. Additionally, these women also expressed the need for personal attachment, respect, sensitivity, caring, and even love in leadership practices. Thus, Principal S said that being "there to listen to them, that has been the most significant thing for me as a leader." Principal F said:

> [If] teachers are happy, they love you, you are good. Anyone my age who has been teaching from that time and still in it, it is out of the love, devotion, care for children, especially when you have children of your own. . . that gets you more into it.

In sum, these women were all conscious and critical of the stratified systems of gender, race, and religion, as well as the ways in which they complicate their experiences in educational leadership. Brody, Vissa, and Weathers (2010) argued that principals do not enter into professional preparation programs without knowledge of what constitutes good or bad leadership. As a response to these stereotypes, women attempted to be emotionally neutral. However, what emerged out of this response was an unconscious psychic duality in which they harnessed a unique leadership style that embraced both masculine and feminine notions of educational leaders.

Discussion and Implications

The purpose of this study was to gain a greater understanding of the perceptions and lived experiences of early career Black women as educational leaders in Trinidad and Tobago. Overall, the findings provided theoretical and empirical support for the constructed theory of leadership. First, it showed the relevance of gender, age, and religion as theoretical and empirical elements of these archetypes of leadership and the ways in which these stereotypes shaped their professional identities. Thus, further research should explore the ways in which women internalize these stereotypes and the critical instances of socialization they draw upon as part of exploring the depth and breadth of these archetypes among other social groups. Second, the study provides support for the theoretical preposition that dominant notions of masculine leadership shape a psychic duality among these women in their expressions and performances of educational leadership. As such, these women made conscious efforts to mask internalized notions of themselves as emotional—a process that resulted in unconscious duality in both their expressions and performances of educational leadership. They assumed a unique quasi-masculine, more integrated leadership style in which they focused on the display of leadership strength while they also engendered spiritual, relational, and shared leadership styles usually associated with women. Thus, further research should be directed toward a deeper understanding of the structure versus agency element of professional development and in particular research allowing for the interrogation of their own practices and that of others.

The study had four limitations. First, the purposive selection of principals was restricted to early career Black female principals and thus does not allow for generalizations. However, in spite of this, the information gained from this study is useful to knowledge building and the understanding of women as educational leaders. Second, the sole use of semi-structured interviews during the data collection stage did not allow for cross-validation of interview data. Third, the use of snowballing as a technique for sample selection allowed for some bias in the sample as most principals interviewed were from denominational schools. Last, the small sample did not include principals from other religious, private, and state schools.

Conclusion

A phenomenological examination of the perceptions and experiences of the educational leadership of six Black early professionals revealed that the stratified and structured nature of their organizational cultures shaped a position of emotional neutrality and psychic duality in the development of their professional identities. Within this dual psyche, they attempted to balance the role acquisition process with expressions and performances that were consistent with masculine notions of leadership while camouflaging their internalized notions of femininity. They embraced the expectations of these gendered understanding of themselves and unconsciously reproduced "the sayings, doings and relatings of educational leadership" (Coleman, 2003; Kemmis & Grootenboer, 2008). These conflicting roles thus created a unique reality, style, and professional identity for these women. Thus, the essence of being early career Black women in educational leadership was a continuous struggle of defining and negotiating their professional roles and, by extension, identities.

Biography

Brody, L., & Hall, J. (1993). Gender and emotion. In M. Lewis & Havilland, J. (Eds.), *Handbook of emotions* (pp. 447–460), New York: Guilford Press.

Brody, L., Vissa, J., & Weathers, J. (2010). School leaders' professional socialization: The contribution of focused observations. *Journal of Research on Educational Leadership, 5*(14), 611–651.

Brown, L., & Conrad, A. D. (2007). School leadership in Trinidad and Tobago: The challenge of context. *Comparative Education Review, 51*(2), 181–201.

Bush, T. (2007). Educational leadership and management: Theory, policy and practice. *South African Journal of Education, 27*(3) 391–406.

Butler, J. (1990). *Gender trouble: Feminism and the subversion of identity.* New York: Routledge.

Butterfield, A. D., & Grinnell, J. P. (1999). "Re-Viewing" gender, leadership, and managerial behaviour. In G. N. Powell (Ed.), *Handbook of gender and work* (pp. 223–238). Thousand Oaks, CA: Sage.

Central Statistical Office (CSO). (2010). *Review of the economy.* Port-of-Spain, Trinidad, and Tobago: Ministry of Finance and Planning: Author.

Chevannes, B. (2002). Gender and adult sexuality. In Patricia Mohammed (Ed.), *Gendered realities: Essays in Caribbean thought* (pp. 486–494). Mona, Jamaica: University of the West Indies Press.

Cohen, L., Manion, L., & Morrison, K. (2008). *Research methods in education* (6th ed.). New York: Routledge.

Coleman, M. (2003). Gender and leadership style: The self-perceptions of secondary head teachers. *Management in Education, 17*(1), 29–33.

Coleman, M. (2005). Gender and secondary school leadership. *International Studies in Educational Administration, 33*(2), 29–33.

Coleman, M., & Campbell-Stephens, R. (2010). Perceptions of career progress: The experiences of Black and Minority ethnic school leaders. *School Leadership and Management, 30*(1), 35–49.

Creswell, W. J. (1998). *Qualitative inquiry and research design: Choosing among five traditions.* Thousand Oaks, CA: Sage.

Crow, M. G. (2006). Complexity and the beginning principal in the United States: Perspectives on socialization. *Journal of Educational Administration, 44*(4), 310–325.

Du Bois, W. E. B. (1897). Strivings of the Negro people. *Atlanta Monthly, 70,* 194–198.

Fanon, F. (1968). *Black skin, White masks.* London: MacGibbon & Kee.

Fincham, D. (2010). Head teachers in Catholic schools: Challenges of leadership. *International Studies in Catholic Education, 2*(1), 64–79.

Government of Trinidad and Tobago (GOTT). (1960). *The Concordat of 1960.* Port-of-Spain: Ministry of Education.

Government of Trinidad and Tobago (GOTT). (1966). *Laws of Trinidad and Tobago: Education Act, Chapter 39: 01.* Port-of-Spain: Trinidad and Tobago.

Government of Trinidad and Tobago (GOTT). (1968). *Ministry of Education: Draft Education Plan.* Port-of-Spain: Ministry of Education.

Government of Trinidad and Tobago (GOTT). (1985). *Ministry of Education: Educational Plan, 1985–1990.* Port-of-Spain: Ministry of Education.

Government of Trinidad and Tobago (GOTT). (1993). *Ministry of Education: Education Policy Paper 1993–2003.* Port-of-Spain: Ministry of Education.

Gray, H. L. (1993). Gender issues in management training. In J. Ozga (Ed.), *Women in educational management* (pp. 106–115). Buckingham: Open University Press.

Haslam, S. A., Powell, C., & Turner, J. C. (2000). Social identity, self-categorization, and work motivation: Rethinking the contribution of the group to positive and sustainable organisational outcomes. *Applied Psychology: An International Review, 49,* 319–339.

Hill-Somers, M., & Ragland, J. C. (1995). *Women as educational leaders: Opening windows and pushing ceilings.* Thousand Oaks, CA: Corwin Press.

Hoyt, L. C. (2007). Women and leadership. In Peter Northouse (Ed.), *Leadership: Theory and practice* (4th ed.). (pp. 265–300). Thousand Oaks, CA: Sage.

Kemmis, S., & Grootenboer, P. (2008). Situating praxis in practice: Practice architectures and the cultural, social and material conditions for practice. In S. Kemmis & T. J. Smith (Eds.), *Enabling praxis: Challenges for education*, Vol. 1. (pp. 37–62). Rotterdam: SENSE Publishers.

Lazarus-Black, M. (2001). My mother never fathered me: Rethinking kinship and the governing of families. In R. Reddock & C. Barrow (Eds.), *Caribbean sociology* (pp. 389–402). Kingston: Jamaica: Ian Randle Publishers.

London, A. N. (1997). Educational planning and its implementation in Trinidad and Tobago. *Comparative Education Review, 41*(3), 314–330.

Lorber, J. (1994). *Paradoxes of gender.* New Haven, CT: Yale University Press.

Lynch, R. (1995). *Gender segregation in the Barbadian labour market: 1946–1980.* Mona Jamaica: Consortium Graduate School of Social Sciences, University of the West Indies Press.

Marshall, C., & Rossman, G. B. (1999). *Designing qualitative research* (3rd ed.). Thousand Oaks, CA: Sage.

Maxwell, J. A. (1996). *Qualitative research design: An interactive approach.* Thousand Oaks, CA: Sage.

McGee-Banks, A. C. (2007). Gender and race as factors in educational leadership and administration. In *The Jossey-Bass reader on educational leadership* (2nd ed.). (pp. 299–338). San Francisco: Jossey-Bass.

McGowen, K. R., & Hart, L. E. (1990). Still different after all these years: Gender differences in professional identity formation. *Professional Psychology: Research and Practice, 21,* 118–123.

Ministry of Education of Trinidad and Tobago (MOE). (2001). *Summary of public primary schools in Trinidad and Tobago.* Port-of-Spain, Trinidad and Tobago.

Ouston, J. (Ed.). (1993). *Women in educational management.* Philadelphia: Open University Press.

Reed, L., & Evans, E. A. (2008). What you see is [not always] what you get: Dispelling race and gender leadership assumptions. *International Journal of Qualitative Studies in Education, 21*(5), 487–499.

Reissman, C. K. (1993). *Narrative analysis.* Newsbury Park, CA: Sage.

Rhode, D. (2003). *The difference "difference" makes: Women and leadership.* Stanford, CA: Stanford University Press.

Seyfrath, J. (2008). *Human resource leadership for effective schools.* Boston: Pearson Educational.

Sinclair, A. (1998). *Doing leadership differently: Gender, power and sexuality in a changing business culture.* Melbourne, Australia: Melbourne University Press.

Smith, R. T. (1973). The matrifocal family. In J. Goody (Ed.), *The character of kinship* (pp. 121–144). Cambridge: Cambridge University Press.

Strachan, J., Akao, S., Kilavanwa, B., & Warsal, D. (2010). You have to be a servant of all: Melanesian women's educational leadership experiences. *School Leadership and Management, 30*(1), 65–76.

Sutton, C., & Makiesky-Barrow, S. (2001). Social inequality and sexual status in Barbados. In R. Reddock & C. Barrow (Eds.), *Caribbean Sociology* (pp. 371–388). Kingston, Jamaica: Ian Randle Publishers.

Van Manen, M. (1990). *Researching lived experience: Human science for an action sensitive research.* Albany: State University of New York Press.

Wharton, S. A., & Erickson, R. J. (1993). Managing emotions on the job and at home: Understanding the consequences of multiple emotional roles. *Academy of Management Review, 18*(3), 457–486.

Willis, P. (2001). The "things themselves" in phenomenology. *Indo-Pacific Journal of Phenomenology, 1,* 1–16.

Wrushen-Rivers, B., & Sherman, W. H. (2008). Women secondary school principals: Multicultural voices from the field. *International Journal of Qualitative Studies in Education, 21*(5), 457–469.

Chapter Eight

Sisters of the Academy

Cultivating Leadership and Collaboration among Black Women

Dannielle Joy Davis, Virginia Cook Tickles,
Montressa Washington, Ifeoma Amah,
and Monika Hudson

Women of African descent continue to be underrepresented and marginalized in predominantly White postsecondary settings (Davis & Sutherland, 2008; Holmes et al., 2007; Holmes, 2003). The double minority status of being both Black and female often renders members of this group "isolated, underutilized, and. . . demoralized" (Carroll, 1982, p. 115). Sisters of the Academy Institute works to counter this marginalization via embracing and celebrating this population, while integrating them into academe. Professional integration and engagement promises to move academe toward racial parity within the professoriate. This chapter features the history and current work of Sisters of the Academy (SOTA), an organization centered upon the professional development and advancement of Black female faculty and leaders in higher education.

The History of Sisters of the Academy

Sisters of the Academy Institute was founded on March 7, 2001, by seven graduate students at Florida State University: Dr. Anna L. Green, President Emeritus, Dr. Adria Belk, Dr. Tamara Bertrand Jones, Cindy Gipson, Dr. LeKita Scott Dawkins, Dr. Amanda Turner, and Dr. Rheeda Walker-Obasi.

Reitumeste Obakeng Mabokela and Anna L. Green's edited book, *Sisters of the Academy: Emergent Black Women Scholars in Higher Education* (2001), sparked the idea to create the organization, thereby taking insights and experiences expressed in the book to the level of practice. The founders of SOTA believed their needs and concerns related to being graduate students in master's and PhD programs at predominantly White institutions were not being met. They knew it was their responsibility to create the supportive environment needed to complete their programs of study. The founders were already friends, but realized they needed this extra layer of support to successfully graduate. As stated by SOTA's first president, Anna Green, "We had professors' support, we had. . . leadership's support, (and) we had minority support (in that) there were minority faculty and staff that could provide for us. (Yet), we were missing a camaraderie of sisterhood."

While forming the organization, the founders of SOTA faced challenges such as attracting members and criticism from sources inside and outside of academia as to why there was need for the organization. Founders of SOTA received questions such as, "Why create an organization specifically for African American women?" "Why are you excluding others?" and "Is this just another clique or a sorority?"

Despite these criticisms, SOTA membership has grown to well over 100 members. Women not only join SOTA as members, but also eagerly seek leadership positions. SOTA members believe in the ideals set forth by the founders. SOTA members want to see the organization grow and are instrumental in its growth and progress. Many believe that membership has its privileges in that their professional and personal networks have grown, they have honed their research and writing skills, and they are provided refereed venues to publish papers and contribute to various writing projects.

In terms of SOTA's future, Green envisions an institution well known for supporting African American women in higher education via their work as scholars in academia. She wants SOTA to be known for its programs such as the Research BootCamp, the Writing Retreat, the Grantsmanship Seminar, and to be rewarded for its collaboration with government and other institutions committed to SOTA's mission. Green envisions SOTA hosting conferences, similar to the Academy of Management or the American Educational Research Association, where it would bring together African American female scholars from around the world to share research, present papers, and contribute to their fields.

Featured Programs

Sisters of the Academy (SOTA) Institute aims to build a substantial platform centered on programmatic activities promoting the success of Black women in higher education (Davis & Sutherland, 2008). Via its programs, the organization provides mentoring opportunities for members and outreach to the communities within the United States and throughout the diaspora.

During the inception of the organization, a group of newly minted Black female PhDs envisioned developing programs that provided safe and supportive spaces for members to actively and collaboratively engage in academic research and writing. Through this vision, three programs were established: (1) the Research BootCamp™, (2) the Writing Retreat, and (3) the Intensive Grantmanship Seminar. These programs have assisted faculty, doctoral students, and administrators with identifying, clarifying, developing, and maintaining the knowledge, skills, and values necessary for successful teaching, scholarly inquiry, and community service.

The Research BootCamp is an intensive one-week summer program open to Black women in various academic disciplines and leadership positions in higher education. The initiative was established in 2005 and is hosted by a four-year university every two years. Participants have options to be housed in apartment-style, on-campus housing, or off-campus housing. In order to ensure that all individuals' needs are met, there are three levels of participation which include: (1) junior, pretenured faculty and higher education administrators in the academy, (2) level 1 doctoral students preparing research or a dissertation proposal, and (3) level 2 doctoral students who have successfully defended research proposals and are in the data-collection stage. The competitive application process for each level is open to both SOTA members and nonmembers.

The purpose of Research BootCamp is to further develop participants' research agenda and professional networks. Senior scholars facilitate workshops designed to enhance the research skills, writing productivity, as well as personal development of doctoral candidates, administrators, and junior scholars (Davis & Sutherland, 2008). Students also work with senior scholars to conceptualize and design key components of their research proposals and dissertations. Administrators and junior scholars are assisted in developing manuscripts for publication and clarifying future research agenda and career goals. In addition, participants are paired with mentors and colleagues to aid them with their continuous development as scholars (Davis & Sutherland, 2008). These mentoring relationships allow participants to receive personalized attention and address challenges faced as Black female graduate students, academics, and administrative professionals.

The Writing Retreat, a biennial program that emerged from the Research BootCamp in 2008, is an opportunity for SOTA members and other Black women within the academy to spend two to three days receiving support and mentorship on their writing in a collegial space. Specifically, they obtain assistance on writing projects, such as proposals, dissertations, manuscripts, and articles. While the first writing retreat occurred in the spring of 2008 with institutional support from a small public university on the east coast, the following retreat happened virtually via telecommunication. During the retreat, participants were placed in writing circles with four other women holding similar research interests. Through the guidance of a facilitator, the women collaboratively worked toward creating drafts of their publications and engaged in presentation activities. The intended outcome of the Writing Retreat for participants centered upon completing their writing projects through the support of writing circle members and other retreat attendees, as well as networking with other sisters at various levels.

While discussions of funding opportunities occur during the Research BootCamp, SOTA members can also participate in the Intensive Grantmanship Seminar. Through this seminar, participants are paired with mentors and meet with representatives from various funding sources through workshops, plenary sessions, roundtable discussions, and collaborative proposal writing. The goal of the seminar is to help doctoral students, postdoctoral fellows, junior or senior faculty, and administrators learn information about: (1) public and private funding sources, (2) the grant writing and submission process, (3) transforming ideas into practical, fundable research, (4) developing technical writing skills, (5) the budget development process, and (6) building professional networks with funding program officials. SOTA has partnered with funding agencies interested in hosting workshops and collaborating with members of the organization.

The Influence of Sisters of the Academy

An organization that seeks to bring about change for African American women, Sisters of the Academy is a critical entity in today's society. Creating such an organization required action focused upon forming a community of practice, intellectual exchange, and generative learning. Few organizations exist with the commitment, structure, and fortitude that SOTA holds with the ability to influence participants, institutions, and communities that are historically underserved.

Sisters of the Academy influences the lives of many African American women in academia. In its signature program, the Research BootCamp (held in 2005, 2007, 2009, and 2011) SOTA successfully assisted its doctoral participants through coaching and mentoring them as they navigated the process of researching, writing, and defending their dissertations. Junior faculty are also coached in the areas of strengthening their scholarship and preparing for tenure and promotion. Many participants have since been promoted in their fields of expertise. One participant shares her journey:

> SOTA was a godsend in my doctoral journey, the single most influential entity outside of the institution. I came to the Research BootCamp with essentially nothing but an idea and I left the BootCamp with a finished proposal, lifetime mentors, and wonderful friends. The workshops were invaluable, especially the section on methods. I learned more about methods that one week, than I had in a full semester [at my university]. SOTA was amazing. The women were genuine, non-threatening, and had high expectations of us. . . They lifted us and we delivered. SOTA was fundamental to my success. I felt like I had gone to the mountaintop by finding this new circle of women who understood me

and the journey, who were able to assist me in a way that was culturally relevant and gender specific, using a model of empowerment that works. I needed the support, the community, and the validation from people like me who had been there and had delivered. Having so many senior Black women who believed in us, who cared, changed everything. I would not be where I am had it not been for SOTA. SOTA not only provided me with the skills to complete my dissertation, but also gave me survival strategies that I use every day and a circle of scholarly sisters who truly have blessed my life. (Dr. Queen Takiyah Amin, 2009 BootCamp Participant)

SOTA's Writing Retreat debuted at Western Connecticut University, which served as the organization's host in 2008. It provided a setting for African American female scholars at all levels to create writing circles, connecting them to other academic women for collaboration, research, and publication purposes. The retreat admitted more than 25 participants, who participated in 10 writing circles. The second retreat utilized technology for a virtual writing retreat experience. One participant of SOTA's Writing Retreat and Research BootCamp shares her experience:

Being a member of SOTA has helped me maintain my thin thread of sanity during this hellacious experience called [the] Ph.D. process. I first joined SOTA three years ago when I participated in the Writing Retreat. I was overwhelmed by all of the love—genuine love—the women showed. Until that point, I really believed I was the only Black woman in the academy experiencing frequent moments of isolation, aggravation, and frustration. I walked away from the Writing Retreat with new mentors and friends that have become some of my best relationships. I never thought my Writing Retreat experience could be topped until I participated in the Research BootCamp in 2009. The support, guidance, and knowledge I gained that week helped me successfully complete my comprehensive exams. I'm most impressed with the consistency of sisterly love the SOTA sisters provide. The support, guidance, and love don't end when the Writing Retreats or BootCamps end. SOTA is a lifelong experience. It's been comforting for me to know that on the days when I have one foot off the ledge ready to jump off the PhD cliff, I can call a SOTA sister to talk me back onto solid ground. SOTA has impacted higher education by consistently producing highly qualified and educated Black women professors, researchers, and administrators." (Breea Willingham, 2008 Writing Retreat and 2009 Research BootCamp Participant)

SOTA has positively impacted the academic community. Because of the success of its programs, and through word of mouth from individuals sharing their experiences with colleagues, family, and friends, membership has grown from 30 members in 2001 to approximately 150 in 2011. Currently, members come from 16 states, and 30 universities. Through membership and participation in events, many members have built professional relationships with one another, have authored and co-authored books, journal articles, and other publications, and have presented group presentations at many conferences within the academic community. SOTA has redefined the way accomplished African American female academicians and leaders view their roles in the academic culture and has provided an avenue for them to give back to other women in the professoriate. It challenges its members by helping them tap into individual gifts, while building and expanding their repertoire of knowledge and experience.

> I came to SOTA during the Writing Retreat to expand my research agenda outside the institutional setting. Working outside of academia, I wasn't as connected to the information and the resources. I was paving my own way in educational research. What I left with was the knowledge that I was on the right track with a new love and commitment towards utilizing my skills, ideas, and energy towards helping other African American women achieve their goals. I love the work that SOTA does and the way they step out in the forefront to uplift so many other African American women. (Virginia Cook Tickles, 2008 Writing Retreat Participant)

SOTA also influences the broader African American community. Every event that SOTA hosts includes a community outreach project, demonstrating commitment to the importance of leaving footprints in the community to show our appreciation and desire for positive change. For instance, SOTA provided baskets of toiletries to a homeless shelter in Auburn, Alabama, during the 2003 Research BootCamp at Auburn University; created a mentoring project for approximately 25 middle school girls in rural Lowndes County, Alabama (KEMET Academy), during the 2007 Research BootCamp at Auburn University; and held a Literacy Project Book Drive resulting in more than 450 donated books to George Washington Carver Elementary school in Tuskegee, Alabama, at the 2009 Research BootCamp at Auburn University. In 2010, the Literacy Project managed to collect more than 550 books. In 2011, the project not only managed to supply books to a local school, but also to an adjacent community center. The book drive in Tallahassee, Florida, provided R. Frank Nelms Middle School 6th graders and the Character Center Summer Program with more than 350 books. This project took place at the 2011 Research BootCamp at Florida State University. Research has indicated that while print materials are crucial to reducing illiteracy, almost two-thirds of low-income families nationally have no age-appropriate reading materials in their homes for youth. Therefore, the long-range impacts of the SOTA Literacy Project are significant given that the inability to read is directly linked to higher rates of poverty, unemployment, and incarceration.

SOTA has also reached out via mentoring efforts. Through the mentoring project with KEMET (Knowledge and Excellence in Mathematics, Equilibrium, and Technology) Academy, SOTA mentors high school and middle school African American students. In addition, during the Writing Retreat in 2008, SOTA members paired with middle school girls as part of a long-term professional mentoring effort.

Thus, SOTA has influenced elementary, middle, and high school students via mentorship, encouraging postsecondary attainment, and improving literacy outcomes. It also has helped a community to provide assistance to the homeless and provide other forms of community outreach. A mother and her daughter, a SOTA protégée, comment on how SOTA has influenced their lives:

> In addition to her educational achievement, one of my most pressing goals for my daughter is for her to be a humanitarian. The women of SOTA have helped me to realize this goal by inspiring her to not only excel academically, but to also reach out and bridge the gap [so] others can excel and achieve their goals. SOTA has influenced her to become a balanced individual who gives back to her community and the world. (Parent of SOTA Protégée)

> SOTA has caused me to believe in myself. Just seeing other Black women pursuing their dreams has helped me to know that I [don't] have an excuse. I too can achieve greatness and make a positive impact on society. (SOTA Protégée)

Without a doubt SOTA has had a profound influence on those whose paths it has crossed. It enriches the lives of many women pursuing their scholarly goals and connects them to others like themselves, while forming nurturing, professional circles. SOTA uplifts their spirits, makes them fearless in reaching their goals, and helps them understand their purposes as they excel to new heights while remembering to reach back and lift others. SOTA strengthens institutions by assisting participating women in attaining their Ph.D.s, in the promotion and tenure processes, with publication, and their teaching. The organization touches the lives of young girls through mentoring them in setting goals, embracing challenges and change, and learning to climb and build others in their journey. It has influenced the African American and broader professional communities through outreach efforts, partnerships, and collaborations. SOTA has changed the paradigm of African American women via dispelling negative myths and raising the bar of this group as an organization.

The Future of SOTA

No organization can make use of its full potential without vision, strategies, and a framework for the future. While SOTA has been successful in its undertakings, continued vigilance toward improving its effectiveness includes creating a continuous influx of new members and ideas. Members of Sisters of the Academy hold the dual roles of educational catalysts and community leaders. SOTA's business lies in understanding the needs of Black women in multiple contexts, while using its skills and expertise to serve the broader community. SOTA exemplifies "a network of individuals who share a passion about a topic and who deepen their knowledge and expertise by interacting with each other on an ongoing basis" (Wenger, McDermott, & Snyder 2002, p. 4). Thus, the future of SOTA depends greatly on the ability to continuously collaborate and merge diverse perspectives toward common goals.

At the crux of SOTA's future lies its goal of generative learning. Generative learning refers to "value driven learning that seeks what is alive, compelling, and energizing and that expresses a willingness to see radical possibilities beyond the boundaries of current thinking" (Allee, 2003, p. 262). SOTA members "think outside of the box." SOTA understands the need to be creative in thought, innovative in implementation, and motivated in helping others meet their goals. The future of this dynamic scholarly sisterhood renders SOTA at the center of possibility and academic exchange in higher education.

Though SOTA has a strong success rate serving African American women seeking dissertation support, it seeks to further influence the graduation rates of Black female doctoral aspirants and foster the scholarship of Black female professors. SOTA understands that as African American women, we have a voice that is often silenced. The Sisters of the Academy recognize strength in numbers, varied skill sets, interests, strong professional relationships, and collaboration. The organization looks forward to continued success and making its mark on history as one of the first American organizations centered upon the success of Black female scholars and postsecondary leaders.

Bibliography

Allee, V. (2003). *The future of knowledge: Increasing prosperity through value networks*. Boston: Butterworth-Heineman Publisher.

Carroll, C. M. (1982). Three's a crowd: The dilemma of the Black woman in higher education. In G. T. Hull, P. B Scott, & B. Smith (Eds.), *All the women are White, all the Blacks are men, but some of us are brave* (pp. 115–128). Old Westbury, NY: Feminist Press.

Davis, D. J., & Sutherland, J. (2008). Expanding access through doctoral education: Perspectives from two participants of the Sisters of the Academy Research Boot Camp. *Journal of College Student Development, 49*(6), 606–608.

Holmes, S. L. (2003). Black female administrators speak out: Narratives on race and gender higher education. *National Association of Student Affairs Professionals, 6*, 45–63.

Holmes, S. L., Land, L. D., & Hinton-Hudson, V. D. (2007). Race still matters: Considerations for mentoring Black women in academe. *Negro Educational Review, 58*(1–2), 105–129.

Mabokela, R. O., & Green, A. L. (Eds.) (2001). *Sisters of the academy: Emergent Black women scholars in higher education*. Sterling, VA: Stylus Publishers.

Wenger, E. C., McDermott, R., & Snyder, W. C. (2002). *Cultivating communities of practice: A guide to managing knowledge*. Cambridge, MA: Harvard Business School Press.

Chapter Nine

The Leadership of First Lady Michelle Obama

Perceptions of Black Female College Students

Cassandra Chaney

A good leader inspires people to have confidence in the leader, a great leader inspires people to have confidence in themselves. —Unknown

As I watched the inauguration of the nation's 44th president, the feminist in me could not help but think about the kind of impact that the nation's first Black First Lady, Michelle Obama, would have on the nation. In contrast to her husband, whose racial heritage was Black and White, Michelle was a Black woman born of two Black parents, who *looked Black*. This statement is not to minimize the intellect, experience, determination, and focus that helped Barack Obama secure the presidency but rather to highlight the willingness of America to embrace a Black woman who did not perpetuate many of the negative stereotypes that are characteristic of Black women in the media or represent the usual Eurocentric standard of attractiveness. Due to her high level of visibility, my position is that Michelle Obama is a leader, and as such, she has demonstrated several aspects of leadership in her life. In order to determine how Michelle Obama is perceived by Blacks, I focused on how Black women between 18–25 years of age understand her. Attention was given to Black women in this age group as they are emerging adults (Arnett, 2010) and are thus on the brink of entering their first jobs, establishing their professional careers, and starting their own families. In other words, these Black women are currently where Michelle Obama was approximately two decades ago. Thus, the perspectives of these young Black women are worthy of attention.

There are three reasons why this topic is important. First, there are considerably more college-educated Black women than Black men. According to the *Journal of Blacks in Higher Education*, in spite of the increase in the number of Black men who graduate from college (over the past 15 years Black men have improved their graduation rate from 28% to 35%), Black women still outpace Black men in regards to college completions (http://www.jbhe.com/features/50_blackstudent_gradrates.html). Since these women have improved their college completion rate from 34% in 1990 to 46% in 2005, it behooves researchers to better understand the types of leadership that motivate these young women to succeed. Second, the increasing number of Black women who have successfully secured positions in business (Brown et al., 2006; Campbell, 1982), education (Brown-Glaude, 2010; Chisholm, 2001; Crewe, 2009; McCluskey, 1994; Mogadime, 2008; Murtadha & Watts, 2005), and politics (DeLany & Rogers, 2004; Rogers, 2005) begs scholars to examine how young Black women define leadership, as well as the qualities that good leaders possess. Third, and most important, as the aforementioned quote acknowledges, by using First Lady Michelle Obama as the focus, we can understand how young Black, college-educated women's perceptions regarding this historical African American figure can encourage these women to have confidence in themselves, inspire others, and carve a path that will bring their life plans to fruition.

Review of Literature

Before I highlight the work of past scholars in regards to Black women and leadership, I believe that it is important to define the word *leadership*. According to *Webster's New Dictionary of the English Language* (2001), leadership means to "direct the operations, activity, or performance of." Essentially, this definition recognizes the position of leaders (e.g., they set an example for those that follow) as well as the characteristics that leaders must possess to motivate others to follow their example. This definition will be important as I frame this discussion for it suggests that the ability of a leader to direct others is related to how the leader is perceived by others. In the section that follows, I provide a historical and contemporary overview of the ways that Black women have successfully combated racial and gender discrimination by serving as role models, thus supporting other Black women as they earn positions of leadership.

Historical Role Models

Although we are more than a decade into the new millennium, we must acknowledge that contemporary Black women leaders would not exist if it were not for past models of strong leadership that "directed the performance" of the former (Webster's, 2001). In the early 20th century, African American author

Mary McCloud Bethune struggled to educate herself and took the lead in educating free slaves (McCluskey, 1994). Years later, her mentee, Dorothy Irene Height, assumed the position as chair of the National Council of Negro Women (NCNW). In addition to her social activism, Height worked to eliminate much of the sexism and racism that stifled the abilities of Black women. According to Height, much of her early life was influenced by women's clubs, most notably the National Association of Colored Women's Clubs of which her mentor, Mary McLeod Bethune, was president. Height chronicled her encounters with racism in her memoir *Open Wide the Freedom Gates* and her leadership role in NCNW, and she firmly believed in the power of women to support and nurture one another in their quest for leadership (Crewe, 2009). As a group, Black women have become leaders and catalysts for change and have followed the leadership model provided by Bethune several decades earlier. For example, during the Greensboro, North Carolina, student-led sit-in protests at Bennett College in February 1960, Black women were instrumental in raising the social consciousness of both men and women in the Black community as well as solidifying the civil rights efforts of various organizations throughout the nation (Flowers, 2005). The desire for Black women to elevate their communities can also be seen in the educational realm.

More than 70 years ago, noted historian Carter G. Woodson argued in his classic text *The Mis-Education of the Negro* that Black educational leaders must overcome several barriers in order to effectively serve the African American community. By creating schools where none existed, struggling against the perpetuation of unequal educational environments, and building viable alternative schools, African American female educators worked diligently to "uplift the race." Thus, through their organization and development of institutions to mitigate the harsh realities of Black life, many Black women were responsible for the positive changes within school administration, leadership, reform, and change (Murtadha & Watts, 2005). Thus, it is important to note that perhaps one of the greatest successes for Black women—both historically and contemporaneously—has been the unfailing nurturance and support of other Black women.

Contemporary Role Models

More recent scholarship in the area of Black women and leadership has highlighted the salience of Black women supporting one another in various contexts. More than two decades ago, Campbell (1982) qualitatively examined the plight of Black women who sought decision-making administrative positions in the United States. Although many Black women who seek these positions face a host of barriers to their success (e.g., racism, sexism), an increasing number of them have secured positions in administration through sponsors who have nurtured their knowledge and skills and have thus helped them ascend through the ranks (Campbell, 1982). Chisholm's (2001) qualitative study in this area found that in spite of the multitude of practices that associate leadership and competence with masculinity, rationality, and Whiteness, and that work to lever women out of their positions, Black women drew on a range of personal and social resources to deal with the stresses and strains of working in educational administration. Essentially, Black women drew strength from a belief in the collective strength and capability of women rooted in maternal feminism (Chisholm). Therefore, it is important for Black women to remain committed to one another, support the voices of one another, and look to one another as role models (Browne, 2002).

In addition to the opportunities that have been denied them due to their race, Black women in the corporate world oftentimes face gender discrimination that limits their advancement. To combat the negative effects of racism and sexism in their professional aspirations, the first Black women college graduates successfully organized themselves, built on their individual and collective strengths, and encouraged one another to succeed (Perkins, 1990). Thus, the courage demonstrated by Bethune and the Black women leaders of the Bennett College sit-in protest of 1960 paved the way for Janice Bryant Howroyd to become the CEO of Act 1 Group, Ursula M. Burns to become corporate senior vice president of Xerox Corp, and Amy Ellis-Simon to become the first African American woman to become a managing director of Merrill Lynch (Brown et al., 2006).

Although a fictional account of a Black woman's experience in the legal academy has been provided (Washington, 2009), the real-life experiences of 22 African American women who hold elected offices within America and the male-dominated government in Chicago, Illinois, reiterate how these women are oftentimes bombarded with practices that are steeped in racism and sexism. Thus, in addition to highlighting the politics of contemporary women in politics, such as former U.S. Senator Carol Moseley Braun, former Chicago Alderwoman Anna Langford, Chicago Commissioner Bobbi Steele, and Chicago Alderwoman Dorothy Tiliman.

Society must learn what these women can teach others as they negotiate through the biases of the dominant culture to achieve leadership roles (DeLany & Rogers, 2004). Since the African American woman "has been called upon to create herself without model or precedent" (Carroll, 1982, p. 126), attention will now be given to the theoretical framework that guides this study.

Black Feminist Thought

This study will highlight the "voices" of college-educated Black women in the emerging stage of adulthood and will thus use Black feminist theory as a theoretical lens by which to accomplish this. This lens will highlight the perspectives of women who have historically occupied marginal positions in higher education (Howard-Hamilton, 2003). In the book *Racial and Ethnic Diversity in Higher Education*, Black feminist scholar Patricia Hill Collins called for the importance of ideas "produced by Black women that clarify a standpoint of and for Black women" (2002, p. 468). There are three key assumptions in Black feminist thought: (1) Although others have documented the stories of Black women, the framework is shaped and produced by the experiences Black women have encountered in their lives. (2) Although the stories and experiences of each woman are unique, there are intersections of experiences between and among Black women. (3) Although commonalities do exist among Black women, the diversity of class, religion, age, and sexual orientation of Black women as a group are multiple contexts from which their experiences can be revealed and understood. Thus, Collins' Black feminist theory provides "a deeper context and meaning for African American women who have been searching for a voice within rather than one heard from the outside."

Significance of the Current Study

There are three reasons why this study is important. First, this study focuses on First Lady Michelle Obama. Although recent research has examined how Black, college-educated men and women perceive the marital relationship of the Obamas (Chikowore, 2009), considerably more scholarly (Finkenbine, 2009; Harlow, 2009; Ifill, 2009; Street, 2009) and nonscholarly (Coles, 2009) attention has been given to President Barack Obama. As a Black feminist scholar, I find this fundamentally problematic as the ascendance of President Obama could not have occurred without the support of his wife. In numerous interviews, the president himself attests to this fact. Therefore, I strongly believe that more attention should be given to First Lady Michelle Obama because, although her husband receives a tremendous amount of national and international attention, she is an extremely visible, educated, articulate, and accomplished presence in her own right.

Second, this study specifically focuses on Black college women in the "emerging adulthood" stage of their lives and is important as the perceptions of this unique group of women can reveal the characteristics of First Lady Michelle Obama's leadership that currently informs how they navigate the world as well as the future decisions they will make as they establish their careers and families. Since women have found it increasingly more difficult to successfully balance their lives as administrators, wives, mothers, and caretakers, Loder's (2005) work illuminated key commonalities and differences in how 31 Black and White women administrators from different generations and racial-ethnic identities negotiate work-family conflicts. The findings in this intergenerational study found that women in the "older" generation, or those born prior to the Civil Rights and women's movements, tended to prioritize family above professional pursuits more so than women in the "younger" generation, or those born after the aforementioned times. With respect to race-ethnicity, Black administrators relied on extended women kinship ties for child care and household support whereas White administrators primarily sought spousal support. Since the point in life in which an individual finds herself is directly related to how she sees the world, this study purposefully examines women in the "emerging adulthood" (Arnett, 2010) phase of their lives, thereby recognizing the relationship between how they perceive First Lady Michelle Obama as well as the ways in which they seek to emulate her as they transition from college to the outside world.

Last, and most important, this study utilizes a qualitative approach to validate the voices of Black women, and no studies to date have bridged the Black literature and emerging adulthood literatures in this way. Although a burgeoning body of scholarship has encouraged the use of multimethod, ethnographic approaches to better understand the experiences of Black women (King & Ferguson, 2001), more is certainly needed as Black women are considerably more prone to experience racism, sexism, classism, loneliness, microaggressions, marginality syndrome, and the status of outsider within (Collins, 1990, 1998, 2002; Robinson & Howard-Hamilton, 2000). Since the voices of Black women are more likely to be ignored, minimized, or rejected (Collins, 1990, 1998, 2002), this study allows these young women to share *what is important to them*.

The Current Study

This qualitative study will examine how Black women in the emerging stage of adulthood perceive the leadership of First Lady Michelle Obama. Given the historical salience of the current administration (the first self-identified Black U.S. president and Black First Lady in U.S. history), no studies to date have examined how Black women conceptualize leadership. This study is based on the following questions: (1) When you think of the word *leadership*, what do you think of? (2) What qualities must a good leader possess? (3) First Lady Michelle Obama has led the nation's efforts in reducing childhood obesity. In your opinion, what makes her qualified to assume this position? Describe these qualities. (4) In what ways does First Lady Michelle Obama demonstrate leadership in her life? (5) In what areas of your life would you like to lead like First Lady Michelle Obama?

There are two major limitations with the aforementioned research. For one, the aforementioned studies primarily concentrate on Black women who are no longer in the emerging adulthood stage (Brown et al., 2006; Campbell, 1982; Chisholm, 2001; Crewe, 2009; Loder, 2005; McCluskey, 1994; Murtadha & Watts, 2005; Rogers, 2005) of life. Thus, their experiences in acquiring positions of leadership after completing their college educations may be generationally different from the women in this study. Therefore, the aforementioned studies fail to bridge the emerging adulthood and Black literature in a qualitative way. Second, with few exceptions (Chikowore, 2009), no study to date has systematically examined the perceptions of African American women in the "emerging adulthood" (Arnett, 2010) stage of life or connected these perceptions to the nation's first Black First Lady. This study will fill this gap in the research by qualitatively analyzing college Black women's written narratives regarding the leadership of First Lady Michelle Obama.

Methodology

Sample

Thirty-one Black women participated in the study. Because I was interested in obtaining the perspectives of women in the emerging adulthood phase of life, a purposeful age sample was implemented. The participants were recruited from two universities in the southern region of the United States. In addition to contacting students that I knew fit the selection criteria, a professor at a local university advised students in one of her introductory classes regarding the goal of the study. The students were advised that I was interested in how they perceived the leadership of First Lady Michelle Obama. After completing the necessary consent and demographic forms, participants were asked to respond to the five questions that were foundational to this study. The women in this study represented a diverse selection of majors: business management (3 women), child and family studies (3 women), child development, childcare development/secondary education, criminal justice (2 women), elementary education, environmental management systems, film production, fine arts, mass communications, nursing (8 women), office information systems, pre-dentistry, pre-radiology technician, radiology technician (2 women), physical therapy, psychology, and ultrasound technician.

The age of the participants ranged from 18 to 25 years. The mean age was 19 years and ten women (32.5%) were 18 years old; eight women (25.8%) were 19 years old; one woman (3.2%) was 20 years old; seven women (22.5%) were 21 years old; one woman (3.2%) was 23 years old; three women (9.6%) were 24 years old; and one woman (3.2%) was 25 years old. The average level of education was 14.2 years. Eighteen (58.0%) women were freshmen; six women (19.3%) were sophomores; one woman (3.2%) was a junior; four women (13.0%) were seniors; and two women (6.5%) were recent graduates. As related to the type of environment in which the participants were reared: 16 women (51.6%) were reared in two-parent families; 12 women (38.7%) were reared in single-mother households; 2 women (6.5%) were reared by a legal guardian; and 1 woman (3.2%) was reared by both a single mother and legal guardian. All of the women were single, never married. Although the majority of the women in the study did not have children (90.3%), three women had at least one child between the ages of 9 months and 4 years old.

In regards to religion, although three women did not disclose this information, 7 women (22.5%) identified as None; 8 women (25.8%) identified as Catholic; 10 women (32.2%) identified as Baptist; 2 women (6.4%) identified as Non-Denominational; and 1 woman (3.2%) identified as Methodist. In regards to annual income, while one woman (3.2%) had an annual income in the $50,000–$59,999 range; another (3.2%) in the $30,000–$39,999 range; and two (6.4%) in the $20,000–$29,999 range, the overwhelming majority of the women in this study (87.2%) had annual incomes below $10,000. The identity of all women was protected by pseudonyms.

Research Design

To identify the themes that emerged from the written interviews, all narrative responses were content analyzed using grounded theory and an open-coding process (Holsti, 1969; Strauss & Corbin, 1990; Taylor & Bogdan, 1998), and themes were identified from the narratives. In order to clearly abstract themes from the written responses, words and phrases were the units of analysis. Specifically, coding involved examining all responses, keeping track of emerging themes, assigning words and symbols to each coding category, and examining how the themes presented are specifically related to the questions of interest (Strauss & Corbin, 1990). When the respondent used several words or phrases to respond to a question, these responses were collapsed into a major theme that was comprehensive and encompassed the views provided by the women.

To assess the reliability of the coding system, a list of all codes and their definitions along with the written responses was given to an outsider who then coded the transcripts based on this predetermined list of codes. The outside coder was selected due to their extensive experience with coding and analyzing narrative data. After a 99% coding reliability rate was established between the researcher and the outside coder, it was determined that the themes presented in this study were valid, reliable, and directly related to the questions of interest.

Results

This section of the chapter will focus on the narrative responses by the young Black women who participated in this study. In regard to the first research question, these women generally associated leadership with (a) *Leading and/or Organizing Others*; (b) *Being a good Role Model*; (c) *Demonstrating High Moral Character* (e.g., fairness, justice, intelligence, compassion, honesty, integrity, god-oriented); and (d) *Being Responsible*. In regard to the second research question, these young women believed that a good leader must possess certain extrinsic and intrinsic qualities that set her apart from others, impel others to follow her example, and make her qualified to lead. In regard to the third research question, (a) *Her Posi-*

tion as First Lady; (b) *Her Role as a Wife, Mother, and Positive Role Model*; and (c) *Her National Focus on Reducing Childhood Obesity* make First Lady Michelle Obama highly qualified to lead the nation's efforts in reducing childhood obesity. In regard to the fourth research question, First Lady Michelle Obama demonstrates leadership in the domains of (a) *Work*; (b) *Family*; (c) *Successfully Balancing Work and Family*; (d) *Being a Positive Role Model and Influence;* and (e) *Altruism*. In regards to the last research question, these young women would like to lead like First Lady Michelle Obama in the realms of balancing work and family life, positive community influence and involvement, and establishing and/or meeting personal goals. The subsequent paragraphs will highlight narratives that supported these findings.

Theme 1: How Young Black College-educated Women Define Leadership

Qualitative analyses of the written responses revealed that these young women define leadership in relation to four broad areas: (1) Leading and/or Organizing Others; (2) Being a Good Role Model; (3) Demonstrating High Moral Character (e.g., fairness, justice, intelligence, compassion, honesty, integrity, god-oriented); and (4) Being Responsible. *Leading and/or Organizing Others* refers to the ability of leaders to successfully guide others in a particular direction. *Being a Good Role Model* refers to the ability of a leader to be a good example that others seek to emulate. *Demonstrating High Moral Character* refers to ideal moral standards of human behavior. *Being Responsible* refers to the ability of leaders to be conscious of the responsibility that they have for themselves and others when making decisions. In the paragraphs that follow, I provide examples that support each of these themes.

Leading and/or Organizing Others

Thirteen (42%) young women defined leadership with the ability to successfully lead others. Déjà, a 19–year-old freshman in criminal justice wrote: "Leading someone." Judy, an 18–year-old freshman in fine arts had a similar view: "Being a guider." Raven, a 21–year-old junior in business management defined leadership in terms of "someone who has the ability to lead and guide." Another young woman described leadership as an activity that the leader should be skilled at developing in various contexts. Tiara, a 22–year-old graduating senior described leadership in this way: "When I think of the word leadership, I immediately think of people, organizing, and working various types of events and meetings." In support of Tiara's assessment of leadership, Thelma, a 21–year-old sophomore in elementary education focused on the process by which leaders accomplish their tasks ("A leader can run things smoothly"). Another young woman believed that leaders are inherently good. Celeste, a 19–year-old sophomore in childcare development/secondary education shared her view in this way: "Leadership means to be a good person that is able to stand up and take charge and be responsible." For Patricia, a 19–year-old sophomore in business management, a leader is "Someone who takes charge." For Constance, a 24–year-old freshman in nursing, a leader must also be able to cooperate with others: "Someone that is in charge and that can work well with others." For Helena, a 24–year-old sophomore majoring in office information systems: "I think of someone that can lead and do a good job in the position that they are going for." In a slight departure from the narratives that have been already featured, Erica, an 18–year-old freshman in ultrasound technician, leadership means leading people on a path that will be beneficial for them. She shared her thoughts in this way: "Someone who can lead people on the right path." In addition to leading individuals on "the right path," Janet, an 18–year-old freshman in criminal justice highlighted the altruistic nature of leaders as they are: "Being able to help others." In addition to guiding others, Michaela, a 20–year-old freshman in radiology technology believes that the leader is fair and just in his or her actions: "Someone who does the right actions by others and who can guide people." In addition to guiding and assisting others, another young woman believed that a leader must put aside their differences in order to successfully work with others. This was the view opined by Dwanna, a 25–year-old freshman in radiology technician when she wrote: "To be able to deal with people no matter what your personal opinion is against them."

Being a Good Role Model

Seven (22.5%) young women believed that leaders should be positive examples that others can look to. Shanice, an 18–year-old freshman in child development believed a leader is "A person you can trust and look up to." Alexis, a 21–year-old freshman in film production: "Somebody that is a good role model and is very good at being in control." Interestingly, Jada's, an 18–year-old freshman in nursing, comment is also identical to Alexis': "Taking control and being a role model." The importance of being a role model was reiterated by Agnes, a 21–year-old sophomore in nursing ("A leader and being a role model"); Halle, an 18–year-old freshman in nursing: "Someone who gives an example of the right things to do!" and Monica, a 19–year-old freshman in nursing: "Someone who is trying to lead by example." Interestingly, Denise, a 19–year-old freshman in nursing simply provided historical and contemporary names that she associated with being positive role models, namely: "Martin Luther King, Barack Obama, Michelle Obama."

Demonstrating High Moral Character

Seven (22.5%) young women believed that leaders should, in addition to possessing other qualities, demonstrate exemplary character. For these women, character was evident in the values, beliefs, and behaviors of leaders. Charlita, a 23–year-old sophomore in nursing, said: "Someone of great character, god-oriented, and can take and give out orders." India, an 18–year-old freshman in nursing shared: "Someone that is understanding and understands what it takes to be a leader. . . a hard worker that gets the job done." Aliyah, a 22–year-old graduating senior in environmental management systems, addressed the ethical considerations that good leaders possess. She said: "Possessing qualities that help someone to be an effective leader. I think of ideals like fairness, justice, intelligence, and compassion." Another 22–year-old child and families studies senior by the name of Kiara described leadership in this way: "Leadership means honesty and integrity. One being a servant of the people and keeping ethics at the forefront of everything you do. A leader must serve and be a servant." In addition to serving others, another woman provided the name of a historical figure to illustrate that leaders must never falter under the weight of criticism. To support this, Nina, an 18–year-old freshman in psychology wrote: "Martin Luther King Jr. and what he did for Black people and a person who is not afraid of rejection." In a slight departure from Nina's comment, Asia, a 22–year-old graduating senior in child and family studies believed that true leaders motivate her to do her best. She used the following words to express her viewpoint: "I think of someone who can earn my respect by their actions. Someone that motivates me to do my best. Someone who is as fair as they can be and not afraid to admit when they are wrong. This person tries to make good decisions by knowing what is right and what is wrong." Capris, a 24–year-old freshman in pre-radiology technician believed that strong leadership can stand the test of time. She used the following words to express her view: "I think of foundations. Good leadership is determined by a strong foundation. It can withstand time."

Being Responsible

Four (12.9%) young women used the word *responsible* to describe what leadership meant to them. Sharon, an 18–year-old freshman in physical therapy wrote: "When I think of the word "leadership," I think of a responsible, well-educated person who will guide others to be leaders." Toni, an 18–year-old freshman in pre-dentistry stated: "I think of being responsible for who you are leading and leading them into the right path." However, in addition to being responsible, for Antonia, a 19–year-old freshman in nursing, leaders are dedicated and ambitious: "I think of a responsible, dedicated, ambitious person." Meghan, a 19–year-old freshman in mass communications used the following words to express what responsibility means to her: "When I hear the word leadership I think of someone taking responsibility for certain topics that other people wouldn't. Someone that will fight to get other's voices heard."

Theme 2: The Qualities That a Good Leader Must Possess

Overall, these young women believed that a good leader is able to balance personal ambition with compassion, professionalism, fairness, confidence, focus, and a sincere interest in the welfare of others. Specifically, these women described these characteristics in terms of several intrinsic and extrinsic qualities that a good leader develops over time. Extrinsic qualities were those that are evident to observers, while intrinsic qualities were based on those that the leader develops within.

Extrinsic Qualities

Sixteen (51.6%) young women used a list of overlapping and mutually exclusive terms to denote the qualities that a good leader must possess. For the most part, these qualities centered on being a good role model, being responsible, kind, and having good people skills. While Agnes, a 21–year-old sophomore in nursing used the word *leadership* as a summation of these characteristics, Patricia, a 19–year-old sophomore in business management used the phrase *Organization and experience* to share her view. According to Raven a 21–year-old junior in business management, "A good leader must be confident, committed, open to change, be self-knowledgeable, and lead by example." For Alexis, a 21–year-old freshman in film production, a good leader must always be committed to "getting things done right and on time and being a role model to the young." Jada, an 18–year-old freshman in nursing: "Respectful, polite, and caring." For three women, these extrinsic qualities centered on being a responsible individual. Shanice, an 18–year-old freshman in child development: "Being a responsible person." Janet, an 18–year-old freshman in criminal justice: "Being responsible and confident." Antonia, a 19–year-old freshman in nursing: "Responsible, dedicated, and ambitious."

In addition, other women in the study believed that people with good people skills naturally impel others to follow their example. An important point to note is that 10 (22.5%) young women believed that an effective leader must have the ability to successfully get along with a large array of individuals. This was the case for Dwanna, a 25–year-old freshman majoring in radiology technician who shared: "She has great people skills." To support the "people skills" comment provided by Dwanna, Charlita, a 23–year-old sophomore in nursing, offered additional qualities that a good leader must possess: "Kind, caring, goal-oriented, people skills, and a people person." Other women did not directly mention the term *people skills*, however they provided adjectives that, if implemented, would work for good relations with others. For example, Judy, an 18–year-old freshman in fine arts firmly believes leaders must be "respectful, kind, and responsible." Lending further support to Judy's view, Halle, an 18–year-old freshman in nursing believed good leaders must have "charisma, responsibility, loyalty, dedication, and commitment." Constance, a 24–year-old freshman in nursing, believed: "You must be able to follow first!" While Sharon, an 18–year-old freshman in physical therapy believed that a good leader answers to a higher moral code than what is usual: "Good leaders should lead by example and show people wrong from right. They should also be a positive influence." Erica, an 18–year-old freshman in ultrasound technician also believed that good leaders should: "Be kind, nice, caring, and a good listener, and very good with people." On the other hand, India believed hard work and focus to be the pinnacle of good leadership: "Being a hard worker, patient, determined, trustworthy, and focused." Helena, an 18–year old freshman in nursing shared: "The qualities a good leader must have is to be on time and work as a team with one another."

Intrinsic Qualities

Thirteen (41.9%) young women provided internal qualities that a good leader must first develop within *before* she leads others. In general, these qualities were predicated on honesty, integrity, determination, courage, and seeking the best interests of others. For many women, good leadership was predicated on honesty. According to Patricia, good leaders have "good character and are honest." The importance of honesty was supported by Déjà, a 19–year-old freshman in criminal justice, who believed honesty to be essential to good leadership: "Honesty and loyalty." The importance of honesty was seconded by Toni, an 18–year-old freshman in predentistry: "By being honest, accessible, a good listener, helpful, and respectful." According to Kiara, a 21–year-old senior in child and family studies, a good leader must have "integrity, honesty, [and be willing to provide] service to and for others." For Asia, another 21–year-old recent graduate in the same field, good leaders must also possess certain intrinsic qualities that make it possible for them to lead others. She states: "Qualities that a good leader must possess are being respectful, honest, be good with people, be an eloquent speaker, motivator, earnest, compassionate, and a good person."

Providing further clarification regarding what Asia referred to as "a good person," Aliyah, a 21–year-old recent graduate in environmental management systems used these words to express her thoughts: "A good leader has to be fair, compassionate, empathetic, respectful, tactful, clear communicator, responsible, driven and cooperate well with others." According to Tiara, a 21–year-old senior in child and family studies, a good leader possesses several characteristics that greatly increase the likelihood that they will be successful. Tiara expressed herself in this way: "A good leader must possess a positive and good work ethic, honesty, and timeliness. He or she must also be professional, be open-minded, have patience and understanding, and have the ability to work well with others in group situations."

For several women, determination and drive are the catalysts that propel good leaders to succeed. For Denise, a 19–year-old freshman in nursing, a good leader must be: "Focused, determined, trustworthy, and a high-achiever." For another young woman, a good leader should balance drive, faith, and mental acuity. Meghan, a 19–year-old freshman in mass communications, shared: "The leader needs to possess drive, determination, faith, [have] a good spirit, and [be] quick-minded." Helena, a 24–year-old sophomore majoring in office information systems also believed that drive and determination are foundational to a leader's success: "Drive, ambition, determination, good listener, one who has everyone's best interest at heart." For Nina, an 18–year-old freshman in psychology: "Strength, leadership, dedication, patience." Interestingly, for one woman this drive should encourage leaders to take charge in the lives of others, particularly when it will benefit them. For Monica, a 19–year-old freshman in nursing: "A good leader should push/motivate people to do the thing that is right for them." For Capris, a 24–year-old freshman in pre-radiology technician: "A good leader must possess knowledge, courage, tenacity, make good decisions, be driven, and be loyal."

Theme 3: What Makes First Lady Michelle Obama Qualified to Lead

Although her husband is the commander-in-chief, the young women in this study regard First Lady Michelle Obama as a leader in her own right. Essentially, these young women were quite aware that her First Lady status gives her a platform that can draw attention to issues in the country and lead to the greater good of society. According to these young women, three things make First Lady Michelle Obama qualified to lead: (1) *Her Position as First Lady*; (2) *Her Role as a Wife, Mother, and Positive Role Model*; and (3) *Her National Focus on Reducing Childhood Obesity*.

Her Position as First Lady

Ten (32.2%) young women believed that Michelle Obama's position as first lady of the United States makes her qualified to be an effective leader. This fact was simply stated by Denise when she shared: "She's the first lady of the United States." Déjà: "Her position and being a leader that has high standards." Erica regarded the first lady as "very focused on it [leadership] and she is determined." For Patricia, Obama's "concerted efforts and concern, and diligence in making change" make her a qualified leader. Other women believed Mrs. Obama's formal education and world travels make her particularly suited for leadership. Charlita shared her view in this way: "Because she educates herself on each task she takes and applies it to everyday life to help everyone." On the other hand, Sharon believed that the many people that Obama has met in her world travels has made her particularly sensitive, which thus makes her a qualified leader. Sharon expressed herself in this way: "She qualifies because she has been all over the world and she knows that people are concerned about health." Continuing with the world travel theme introduced by Sharon, Nina also believed that the assistance that Obama shows for people around the world is demonstrative of her leadership: "She helps people around the world even with her busy lifestyle." Toni: "She sets a great example." India: "Michelle Obama has the power to make a change and difference to help others." On the other hand, Kiara showed that she recognized this when she said: "Being the First Lady has automatically propelled her in a leadership position. So, while all eyes are on her she can make a great contribution to society."

When asked about the qualities that make Obama qualified to lead others, Tiara shared this extended narrative:

> First of all, she is the first lady. She is a person of high status that has the resources and respect of many people in order to actually make a difference. People will listen to her not only because of her status, but also because of the way she comes across. She is a very well-spoken, educated, stylish, and overall a very likeable person.

Her Role as a Wife, Mother, and Positive Role Model

Six (19.3%) young women believed that First Lady Michelle Obama's roles as wife, mother, and positive example for many make her qualified to lead. Dwanna believed that since Obama is a mother, it is incumbent that she be a good role model as well: "Because she [Obama] has daughters. She has to be a good role model too." In addition well-mannered children are a resounding testament to the leadership skills of their mother. So, for Judy: "She [Obama] is a great example because she has well-mannered kids." Another young woman believed that although First Lady Michelle Obama's role as wife and mother are important, she was compelled to lead in order to provide a positive example for others. This view was shared by Meghan when she wrote: "She [Obama] has two children of her own and she's the president's wife. So I think that she needed to do this [lead others] because it is something positive and America looks up to her." Like Meghan, Janet also believed that Obama's status as a role model makes her a qualified leader: "She [Obama] is qualified to assume the position because she is a great role model." Alexis: "She is eager and willing to help. She is a positive role model for the young people and she is a very caring person." Antonia: "She is very caring and determined to get things done and be a positive example for others."

Her National Focus on Reducing Childhood Obesity

Seven (22.5%) young women believed that the national platform of First Lady Michelle Obama makes her a qualified leader. For Halle, Obama demonstrates leadership "by supporting and advertising healthy eating habits." In line with this, Patricia acknowledged: "She's [Obama] in good shape." Another young woman was touched by the fact that the first lady saw a need to reduce childhood obesity and responded to this call. Shanice explains: "Michelle took the time out of her life to help kids who were in need. This shows that she is a good leader." While another young woman acknowledged the first lady's education may not be directly related to nutrition, her motherhood status and active lifestyle make her qualified to address childhood obesity. Regarding this, Aliyah said:

> I honestly don't know if she's qualified to do so. I'm not sure if she has a degree in nutrition or something related to childhood obesity. However as a parent of two girls she probably has learned about child health and exercise requirements. I think she played sports growing up so she knows things about fitness.

Monica: "She has seen all of these children that are overweight and she has worked hard to change that." Capris: "First Lady Michelle Obama's passion makes her qualified for this position. Her passion will fuel her campaign for reducing childhood obesity." Helena: "A person who has been through obesity themselves or has known someone who has, you may try to help anyone you can with obesity." For Asia: "The First Lady is qualified to assume this position because she has a huge influence on American families. She is a mother as well. I also believed her background and education in public policy helps her position. These qualities make her qualified to assume her position." According to Raven: "The First Lady cares about the children's weight because she knows what health risk that they can get if they are not healthy. She wants to make sure that they are living healthier."

Theme 4: How First Lady Michelle Obama Demonstrates Leadership in Her Life

In general, these young women believed that Michelle Obama's position as first lady of the United States is the hallmark of leadership. Furthermore, they believed that this historical figure demonstrates strong leadership in both her professional and family life. In particular, the narratives of these women revealed that they perceive Obama as demonstrating leadership in the domains of work, family, successfully balancing work and family, being a positive role model and influence, and altruism.

Work Life

Ten (32.2%) young women believed that Michelle Obama's professional life is evidence of her leadership. According to Toni, Obama does this "by taking accountability and responsibility." Building on the comment provided by Toni, Agnes highlighted the personal attention that Obama gives to those in need ("She visits people in need"). Alexis drew attention to Mrs. Obama's accountability and responsibility extending to overseeing the White House in her husband's absence. Alexis remarked: "She's a role model and she handles the White House while her husband is away." Another young woman drew attention to the national platform to reduce childhood obesity that Mrs. Obama is heading. Denise expressed herself in this way: "I've seen her on the news talking about reducing childhood obesity with the *Beyoncé* song." Another woman was so inspired by the confidence by which Obama performs her work that she deems her worthy of emulation. Raven provided the following source of inspiration: "The First Lady is very confident in what she does and says. She is committed to all different kinds of organizations. She leads by example and that makes me want to do it also."

Family Life

Seven (22.5%) of the women believed Michelle Obama's family life is a living testament to her success and exceptional leadership. When describing how First Lady Michelle Obama exemplifies leadership in her life, Judy, an 18–year-old freshman in fine arts simply stated: "With her family." Aliyah shared, "She is raising two girls." Charlita: "With her children and helping other women around the world." Consistent with the motherhood role provided by Aliyah, Kiara also recognized First Lady Obama's role as a supportive wife. Kiara shared: "First she is supportive of her husband and two girls. Leaders must demonstrate by example first." Halle further reiterated the importance of Obama's support for her husband and positive example to many: "[She] keeps her husband and kids on the right path while being a role model to many." Thelma, a 21–year-old sophomore in elementary education: "She stands by her husband and supports his every decision." In this respect, Capris, a 24–year-old preradiology technician shared: "She demonstrates leadership within her family first as a mother and wife. Her integrity is apparent in the way she carries herself. She is outspoken and strong in her decisions and supporting our president."

Work and Family Life

Four (12.9%) of the women believed Michelle Obama's successful balance of her work and family life is a living testament to her success and exceptional leadership. While the aforementioned women focused categorized Obama's daily activities based on her work or family lives, other women in the study recognized both as an important demonstration of First Lady Obama's leadership in her own life. For example, Patricia shared: "She [Obama] helps her husband and others." Erica recognized: "A good mother, she helps her husband, and wants to reduce the rate of obesity." Tiara used the following words to express herself:

> She works with various organizations and charities to help make a difference in people's lives. She is always very professional and she works very well with people. Since fighting childhood obesity is her main stance, when her children's pediatrician informed her that her children were at risk for being overweight, she immediately began implementing healthier choices for her family. This was a great way to demonstrate how she practices what she preaches.

In addition to "practicing what she preaches," the first lady cares for her children, is a spokeswoman for a major television network, has a particular standard of conduct, presents well, and is confident. These qualities were highlighted by Asia:

> The First Lady demonstrated leadership in her life by taking care of her children and by keeping them physically fit. She also works as a spokesman on Disney channel to promote healthy living. She carries herself with self-respect and pride in the way she dresses and the way she advocates about the things she cares about. She seems confident in her work.

Being a Positive Role Model and Influence

While Jada noted that "she has done things that no other has done," another young woman felt that Obama's love for people is what makes leadership strong. Helena: "She demonstrates that she loves people and being a positive role model." Nina: "She does things without Obama's consent and sticks with it!" Monica believed: "First Lady Michelle Obama demonstrates leadership by always having a positive attitude about things and eating healthy." Sharon: "She demonstrates good leadership by being a positive influence on everyone and by the way she presents herself as a woman." Dwanna: "She is always dressed to impress, and she is very well spoken." One young woman by the name of Helena offered that First Lady Michelle Obama's leadership is a strong motivator to help create the person that she is currently and will yet become. Helena used the following words to express herself: "To be the person I am. Also to be something more than what I thought I could be."

Altruism

Five (16.1%) of the women believed the first lady's commitment to helping those outside of her immediate household is further proof of her demonstrative leadership. Déjà recognized: "[She lends others] a helping hand." Shanice expressed: "Michelle helps people who are in need." In addition, Michaela provided this comment: "By trying to reach out to others." Antonia, on the other hand, was impressed by the first lady's efforts to help the environment. She offered: "Helping the world go green." Last, one young woman recognized that worldwide change does not occur suddenly and that several small steps make change possible. This was the point that India was trying to make when she penned the following: "She is trying to make a difference and change the world and it takes small steps to better the lives of others."

Theme 5: Areas in Life Young Black College-educated Women Would Like to Lead Like First Lady Michelle Obama

Perhaps the most prominent theme voiced by the young Black women in this study is their desire to emulate the level of strength, passion, and poise that First Lady Michelle Obama exemplifies. But in addition to these qualities, the women identified ways that they can now and in the future emulate the example provided by our nation's first lady.

Balancing Work and Family Life

Eight (25.8%) women would like to balance work and family like First Lady Michelle Obama. While Halle simply used the word "Family" to show the importance of family for her, Meghan made this personal by speaking of her own prospective family of origin when she stated, "As far as when I start my family." Further, Thelma expressed the desire to be "family-oriented." Interestingly, even after their families are established, these women seek to successfully balance their work and home lives as expressed by Nina: "Balancing life. . . school and work." Déjà: "By helping my husband." For Asia, the first lady is an anchor that keeps her family stable and secure as well as an advocate for issues that are important to her. Asia expressed the ways that she would like to lead like our nation's first lady in this way: "I would like to lead my family like she anchors her family. I would also like to have the strength to talk about and advocate the issues I feel passionate about."

While another young woman believes that family is her priority, she would like to extend her "gifts and talents" to others. This was the perspective of Kiara, who shared the following: "By example, taking care of my family first. . . then leading by example to reach out and help others in society with the gifts and talents that I have been given as an individual."

Like Asia, there are several ways that Tiara would like to lead like Obama in her own life. Interestingly, she has already demonstrated some of these and is currently working on others. She described these areas in these words:

> First of all, I am very passionate about childhood obesity myself. I've lost 44 pounds and still have a long way to go. However, I have definitely been leading by example. My friends and families have all been making healthier choices because of me. Also, I would like to have my own after school program and summer camp that targets overweight children and teach them about caring for their bodies. In addition to this, I would like to be able to present myself more professionally so I can network and have many resources and contacts to better help the audiences I am passionate about.

Positive Community Influence and Involvement

Almost half of the women (13 women or 41.9%) regarded Michelle Obama's success as a catalyst for their own success. Patricia was so inspired by Obama's level of community involvement she wrote: "I want to help others also." Like Parris, Toni plans to do this "By leading individuals." Judy shared that she plans to "Set an example." For Denise, this means "being a person that young girls can look up to. Extending the comments provided by Parris, Antonia mentioned that she "would like to have an opportunity to make a difference in the world." Sharon: "I would like to become a positive influence on people and convince them to do the right thing." Erica: "I want to help make a change like she is." Alexis: "I would like to be a positive role model to the young and try to save lives like her." Jada: "Taking time to make a difference with kids." Shanice: "I would like to help abused children." Monica: "I would like to lend a helping hand to all the people that need help, like people that are without a home and also make this environment a clean place." Capris: "I would love to impact my community like Michelle Obama. I would also like to use my voice and help others." Raven: "I would like to lead like the First Lady at the age I am now. Because you can teach someone so many things they might not understand." Furthermore, Obama's advocacy efforts were something that Patricia would like to emulate: "I would like to have a positive attitude, be a role model, [engage in active] community involvement, and be a women's advocate." Helena: "In regard to leadership, helpfulness, making an impact, and just being myself."

Establishing and/or Meeting Personal Goals

Seven (22.5%) of the women saw Michelle Obama's success as a catalyst for their own success. Essentially, they believed that if she could successfully meet her goals, they could also. Although their goals were different, they spoke to the various ways that these women planned to change their lives for the good. For example, India's personal goal is "To finish my education." When responding to this question, Aliyah said "responsible and confident." In order to keep her independence, Dwanna's goal is to imitate "the way she [First Lady Obama] carries herself." Michaela admired the attitude by which Obama goes through her work and plans to emulate Obama by "always having a positive attitude." In regard to her future career goals, Constance "would like to be the manager of nurses and just be successful!" Charlita wraps up this section by offering us a beautifully summary of the composite nature of the nation's first Black first lady when she penned the following: "In all aspects of life, she is an excellent role model, and I want to be just like her!"

Discussion

This chapter offered the perspectives of college-educated Black women regarding the leadership of First Lady Michelle Obama. The findings presented herein clearly suggest that these women perceive this historical figure as an individual who is strong, qualified, and a worthy example to emulate in their current and future lives. Results in the current study have made a substantial contribution to the current scholarship by bridging the Black studies and emerging adulthood literature in a nuanced way. More directly, this study accomplished this by clarifying the "standpoint of and for Black women that clarify a standpoint of and for Black women" (Collins, 2002, p. 468).

However, before the findings are discussed, the limitations of this study should be noted. For one, the sample size (although large for a qualitative study) make it difficult to determine whether a larger number of college-educated Black women would have offered the same or similar views. Thus, future research should seek the perspectives of a more diverse group of Black women. Also, the women in this study represented two universities in the southern region of the United States, and thereby, the findings in this study cannot be generalized to Black, college-educated women from other universities in the South, or other regions of the United States. Thus, Black women who represent different ages, marital and parental statuses, geographic regions, educations, religions, socioeconomic levels, and degree of political activism may reveal more varied themes than the ones presented in this study. Furthermore, as the majority of these women (87%) had annual incomes below $10,000, the current sample lacked socioeconomic diversity. Furthermore, since most of these women did not have children (90.3%), one must also be cautious when extending the findings of this study to Black, college-educated women within this age group that has children. However, in spite of these limitations, this study is the first to initiate scholarly dialogue regarding how a unique subset of Black women perceives the leadership of First Lady Michelle Obama. The study's findings suggest that First Lady Michelle Obama is a historically salient role model that is worthy of emulation for contemporary Black women.

What do these findings tell us about how college-educated Black women perceive First Lady Michelle Obama? I believe that these young women teach us five things. For one, although they are in the emerging adulthood stage (Arnett, 2010), these young women have a clear understanding of what good leadership involves. Since most of these women have just begun voting or have been voting for just a few years, the questions posed regarding leadership offered a valuable exercise that helped them think about and crystalize the qualities of leaders that are most salient to them.

In addition, the narratives of these women provide insight into how they expect their leaders to preside over them. While leadership involves the ability to lead and organize others in a responsible way, it also necessitates that one be a role model and demonstrate high moral standards of fairness, justice, intelligence, compassion, honesty, integrity, and be oriented toward God. Furthermore, and as related to the aforementioned point, these women place just as much weight on intrinsic qualities as they do on the extrinsic ones, or those that are visible as the former are more likely to make her leadership more effective and motivate others to follow her example.

Furthermore, Michelle Obama's position as first lady, her role as a wife, mother, and positive role model speak to the multifaceted life of this historical figure.

Added to this, by demonstrating leadership in the domains of work, family, work-life balance, and being a positive role model and influence and helping those in need, the first lady demonstrates that she takes seriously her position as well as her responsibility to lead other young Black women on the right path.

Finally, although these young women are currently at the point of their lives that First Lady Michelle Obama was two decades ago, they believe that they can now make a positive difference in the lives of others and solidify their future plans as wives, mothers, and community activists. In a recently published paper (Chaney, 2011), I examined how 15 Black women between the ages of 18– and 55–years-old conceptualize what it means to be a woman. In particular, I was interested in how these women qualitatively defined womanhood, how they practiced womanhood, and how the ways that Black women understand and perceive womanhood influence the choices they make regarding marriage and motherhood. Specifically, these women defined womanhood in terms of *feminine attitudes* (strength, sensitivity, and sensuality) and *feminine behaviors* (familial care, physical appearance, and self-respect), which they considered to be important aspects of domestic leadership. While the young women featured in this chapter were more likely to highlight their professional aspirations and current and future community involvement, women in both groups viewed family as a necessary component of leadership.

Directions for Future Research

There are three ways that future studies can expound upon the findings that have been presented here. First, future studies would benefit from implementing a life course perspective (Arnett, 2010) in regard to the narratives highlighted herein. Essentially, this would mean eliciting the narratives of these same women in a decade to determine the parallel between their "idealized" and "actual" lives, the challenges they currently face as well as how they cope with these challenges. Second, future studies would also benefit from examining what motivates Black women in this age group to become actively involved in their communities. By allowing Black women to serve in realms that hold the most meaning for them, this will allow them to develop their voice (Collins, 1990, 1998, 2002; King & Ferguson, 2001; Robinson & Howard-Hamilton, 2000), become skilled with working with diverse people, and increase their self-efficacy as they transition from college to the world of work. Last, since Black women are more likely to experience racism, sexism, classism, loneliness, microaggressions, marginality syndrome, and the status of outsider within (Collins, 1990, 1998, 2002; Pârlea-Buzatu, 2011; Robinson & Howard-Hamilton, 2000), it would behoove therapists to understand how these women deal with the challenges to their success.

Conclusion

In all aspects of life, she is an excellent role model, and I want to be just like her! (Charlita, a 23–year-old sophomore in nursing)

At this point in the chapter, I would like to end with the aforementioned quote. Clearly, the findings of this study provide undeniable proof that young, Black, college-educated women in the emerging adulthood (Arnett, 2010) stage of their lives regard First Lady Michelle Obama as a role model worth emulating. In addition to her physical presentation, intelligence, professionalism, confidence, determination, altruism, and concern for the nation's children, Obama is an anchor for her family and presents an ideal by which young women on the brink of establishing their own families can successfully balance their work and home lives. Although these women may not be aware of the many obstacles that the first lady had to overcome to secure her current position, they are motivated to live their lives in the most productive ways possible. Essentially, these women perceive First Lady Michelle Obama as a valid template for success in all aspects of life, now and in the future.

Bibliography

Arnett, J. J. (2010). *Adolescence and emerging adulthood: A cultural approach* (4th ed.). Upper Saddle River, NJ: Pearson Prentice Hall.

Brown, C. M., Lundy, T., Carbon, H. B., Robinson, T. M., & McRae, S. (2006). 50 most powerful Black women in business. *Black Enterprise, 36*(7), 124–144.

Browne, J. (2002). Black women succeeding on the shoulders of Black women. *New York Amsterdam News, 93*(17), 8.

Brown-Glaude, W. R. (2010). But some of us are brave: Black women faculty transforming the academy. *Signs: Journal of Women in Culture & Society, 35*(4), 801–809.

Campbell, V. (1982). Making it despite double discrimination. *Educational Leadership, 39*(5), 337.

Carroll, C. M. (1982). Three's a crowd: The dilemma of the Black woman in higher education. In G. T. Hull, P. B. Scott, & B. Smith (Eds.), *All the women are White, all the Blacks are men, but some of us are brave: Black women's studies.* New York: Feminist Press.

CEOs, members of Congress, educators roll out project to develop Black women leaders. (2010). *New York Amsterdam News, 101*(20), 32–40.

Chaney, C. (2011). The character of womanhood: How African-American women's perceptions of womanhood influence motherhood and marriage. *Ethnicities.*

Chikowore, T. (2009). Media coverage of Barack and Michelle Obama's relationship: African American perceptions of Black love in the media. Master's Thesis. Johns Hopkins University, Baltimore, MD.

Chisholm, L. (2001). Gender and leadership in South African educational administration. *Gender & Education, 13*(4), 387–399. doi:10.1080/09540250120081742

Coles, H. (2009, February). Real love: What we all crave. . . what Barack and Michelle have. *Ebony, 54*(4), 64–69.

Collins, P. H. (1990). *Black feminist thought: Knowledge, consciousness, and the politics of empowerment.* Boston: Unwin Hyman.

Collins, P. H. (1998). *Fighting words: Black women and the search for justice.* Minneapolis: University of Minnesota Press.

Collins, P. H. (2002). Learning from the outsider within: The sociological significance of Black feminist thought. In C. S. Turner, A. L. Antonio, M. Garcia, B. V. Laden, A. Nora, & C. Presley (Eds.), *Racial and ethnic diversity in higher education.* Boston: Pearson Custom Publishing.

Crewe, S. (2009). Dorothy Irene Height: Profile of a giant in pursuit of equal justice for Black women. *Affilia: Journal of Women & Social Work, 24*(2), 199–205.

DeLany, J., & Rogers, E. (2004). Black women's leadership and learning: From politics to Afritics in the context of community. *Convergence, 37*(2), 91–106.

Finkenbine, R. (2009). The idea of a Black president. *OAH Newsletter, 37*(1), 15.

Flowers, D. B. (2005). The launching of the student sit-in movement: The role of Black women at Bennett College. *Journal of African American History, 90*(1/2), 52–63.

Harlow, R. (2009). Barack Obama and the (in)significance of his presidential campaign. *Journal of African American Studies, 13*(2), 164–175.

Hill, S. A. (2005). *Black intimacies: A gender perspective on families and relationships.* Walnut Creek, CA: Alta Mira Press.

Holsti, O. R. (1969). *Content analysis for the social sciences and humanities.* Reading, MA: Addison-Wesley Publishing Co.

Howard-Hamilton, M. F. (2003). Theoretical frameworks for African American women. *New Directions for Student Services,* (104), 19–27.

Ifill, G. (2009). *The breakthrough: Politics and race in the age of Obama.* New York: Doubleday.

Jones, M. H. (1978). Black political empowerment in Atlanta: Myth and reality. *The ANNALS of the American Academy of Political and Social Science, 439*(1), 90–117.

Journal of Blacks in Higher Education. (2006). Retrieved from http://www.jbhe.com/features/50_blackstudent_gradrates.html

King, T. C., & Ferguson, S. (2001). Charting ourselves: Leadership development with Black professional women. *NWSA Journal, 13*(2), 123.

Loder, T. L. (2005). Women administrators negotiate work-family conflicts in changing times: An intergenerational perspective. *Educational Administration Quarterly, 41*(5), 741–776. doi:10.1177/0013161X04273847

McAdams, D. (1989). The biographical consequences of activism. *American Sociological Review, 54*(5), 744–760.

McCluskey, A. (1994). Multiple consciousness in the leadership of Mary McLeod Bethune. *NWSA Journal, 6*(1), 69.

Mogadime, D. (2008). Racial differential experiences of employment equity for women teachers: One teacher's narrative of resistance and struggle. *Journal of Black Studies, 39*(1), 85–108.

Murtadha, K., & Watts, D. (2005). Linking the struggle for education and social justice: Historical perspectives of African American leadership in schools. *Educational Administration Quarterly, 41*(4), 591–608. doi:10.1177/0013161X04274271

Pârlea-Buzatu, D. (2011). The social psychology of work: Career development of professional women. *Contemporary Readings in Law & Social Justice, 2*(2), 331–336.

Payton, C. R. (1985). Addressing the special needs of minority women. In N. J. Evans (Ed.), *Facilitating the development of women.* New Directions for Student Services, no. 29. San Francisco: Jossey-Bass.

Perkins, L. M. (1990). The National Association of College Women: Vanguard of Black women's leadership and education. *Journal of Education, 172*(3), 65.

Robinson, T. L., & Howard-Hamilton, M. F. (2000). *The convergence of race, ethnicity, and gender: Multiple identities in counseling.* Upper Saddle River, NJ: Merrill/Prentice Hall.

Rogers, E. E. (2005). Afritics from margin to center: Theorizing the politics of African American women as political leaders. *Journal of Black Studies, 35*(6), 701–714. doi:10.1177/0021934704268438

Smith, W. A., Altbach, P. G., & Lomotey, K. *The racial crisis in American higher education: Continuing challenges for the twenty-first century.* Albany: State University of New York Press, 2002.

Solorzano, D., Ceja, M., & Yosso, T. (2000). Critical race theory, racial microaggressions, and campus racial climate: The experiences of African American college students. *Journal of Negro Education, 69*(1–2), 60–73.

Strauss, A., & Corbin, J. (1990). *Basics of qualitative research: Grounded theory, procedures, and techniques.* Newbury Park, CA: Sage Publications.

Street, P. L. (2009). *Barack Obama and the future of American politics.* Boulder: Paradigm Publishers.

Taylor, S. J., & Bogdan, R. (1998). *Introduction to qualitative research methods: A guidebook and resource* (3rd ed.). New York: John Wiley & Sons.

Thompson, J. (2009). Celebrating First Lady Michelle Obama in pictures/Celebrating President Barack Obama in pictures/Celebrating the inauguration of Barack Obama in pictures. *School Library Journal, 55*(12), 99.

Washington, D. (2009). The anatomy of a "pantsuit": Performance, proxy and presence for women of color in legal education. *Hamline Journal of Public Law & Policy, 30*(2), 605–626.

Chapter Ten

"If They Don't Make a Place for Us, We Should Make a Place for Ourselves"

African American Women and Nursing at State Community College

Ishwanzya D. Rivers

Women changed the two-year college while the two-year college changed women.[1] In the United States, women of color are confronted with multiple challenges that limit access to opportunities and threaten their educational and economic success. African American women, particularly, provide a unique opportunity for examining how marginalized race, class, and gender statuses intersect and are acted on institutionally to place individuals at risk for economic and educational failure.[2] Black women also represent the opportunity to showcase how marginalized groups are able to utilize educational institutions as a means of etching out an alternate social reality. African American women possess an individual, yet collective, standpoint that warrants additional research to provide information about their unique presence in higher education. In examining the intersecting oppression of race, class, and gender on African American women in the United States, this study looks at the ways in which women of color, particularly African American women in the East St. Louis metropolitan area, utilized the nursing program at State Community College as a means of economic and social mobility and as a means of simultaneously deconstructing and reconstructing their lived realities. The city of East St. Louis and State Community College represented a unique geographical and institutional opportunity to study how women, particu-

---

1   The quote comes from John H. Frye, "Women in the Two-Year College, 1900 to 1970," *New Directions for Community Colleges* 89 (Spring 1995): 5.

2   The terms *African American* and *Black* will be used interchangeably to refer to women of African descent within the United States.

larly African American women, have utilized the community college as a means of transcending economic and educational barriers compounded by the intersections of race, gender, and in the case of East St. Louis residents, class.

East St. Louis, Illinois, with a 97.7% African American population is nestled between the Mississippi River on the west and the coal bluffs on the east. Residents boast of the city being home to such greats as Jackie Joyner-Kersee, Miles Davis, and Donald McHenry to name a few, yet today the city is home only to the Casino Queen and an ever-shrinking tax base and population. A sense of loss currently personifies the overall characteristic and demeanor of the city of East St. Louis. East St. Louis' identity, once tied to industry and profit, suffered a tremendous loss when factories closed and the industrial market fled the area. Once a thriving home to glass makers, meat-packing factories, and other industrial companies, East St. Louis withered into one of the nation's poorest cities accelerated by a decline in the number of factories and the exodus of middle-class Whites and Blacks in the 1960s (Theising, 2003). The 1960s ushered in skyrocketing unemployment, increasing taxes, declining municipal services, growing deficits, bank redlining, and blockbusting for East St. Louis (Reardon, 1997). The loss of population and business resulted in a city without a sufficient economic base to establish a community college, which the residents saw as a viable option in establishing educational and economic opportunities for East St. Louis residents. East St. Louis' inability to provide financial support for the establishment of a local community college resulted in the establishment, by Illinois legislation, of East St. Louis State Community College, funded 100% by the state of Illinois (Reardon, 1997).

In fashioning the community college into a tool to break the intersecting links of race, class, and gender oppression, Black women's experiences in the community college become equally important to study. Their experiences and struggles are essentially void in studies on the educational experiences of community college students. Major texts on community colleges and community college students also fail to adequately address the diversity among women community college students. The narrative of State Community College's nursing program offers an alternate outcome and goal of community colleges from those who would argue that two-year nursing programs are actually a detriment to the African American nurse. Scholars (Gamble, 1995; Hine, 1989; Love, 2009) argue that the rise of two-year nursing programs led to fewer Black nurses being available to assume future leadership roles or occupy influential positions in the profession, institutions of higher education, or branches of government because a bachelor's of science in nursing (BSN) or master's degree is often needed for these positions. What these studies, while recognizing the discriminatory nature of credentials and standards within the nursing profession, fail to realize is that associate degree nursing programs offer students of color, males, older women, and those individuals shut out of four-year colleges and universities an opportunity to become nurses at a cheaper cost, in fewer years, and often in supportive environments.

Karen Flynn (2003) and Evelyn Barbee (1993) argue that racism within nursing is often overlooked and downright denied by interested parties on the premise that the inherent qualities of nursing, such as caring and nurturing, make it impossible for nursing to be discriminatory and prejudicial. Barbee further contends that "the contradictions between caring, a principle part of the identity of nursing, and racism make it difficult for nurses to acknowledge racial prejudice in the profession" (1993, p. 346). In recognizing the disconnect between nonracist ideology and racist practices, this chapter utilizes Black feminist thought to frame an examination of how Black women carved out a space for themselves in a profession that sought to deny them opportunities and in an institution many argue limits opportunities for individuals of color.

Theoretical Framework

The combined forces of racism, sexism, and classism result in a society that traditionally fails to provide Black women with the opportunity to realize and fulfill their human potential, while a feminist lens places African American women and their numerous experiences in the center. The premise of Black feminist thought centers on the empowerment of Black women and the assertion of their voices as central to their experiences while also recognizing and supporting coalitions with other social justice efforts. Black women social theories have traditionally been utilized as a way of "escaping from, surviving in, and/or opposing prevailing social and economic injustice and oppression" (Collins, 2000, p. 5). Historically the image and identity of the Black woman has been defined through the ideology of an oppressive and discriminatory society. Collins states, "Because the authority to define societal values is a major instrument of power, elite groups, in exercising power, manipulate ideas about Black womanhood. They do so by exploiting already existing symbols, or creating new ones. Maintaining images of U.S. Black women as the 'Other' provides ideological justification for race, gender, and class oppression" (pp. 69–70). Schools, the news media, and government agencies constitute important sites for reproducing these controlling images. It is in the face of these realities that Black women have often used these very places (e.g., educational institutions) to create and construct social images that empower Black women. Black women have often resisted oppression from race, gender, and class by creating images of self-definition, self-reliance, and independence. With the advent of nursing as a profession and nurse training programs including two-year programs in community colleges, Black women were able to utilize this profession and career trajectory as a means of directing, controlling, and devising a path to professional achievement.

"Black women's lives are a series of negotiations that aim to reconcile the contradictions separating our own internally defined images of self as African-American women with our objectification as the 'Other'" (Collins, 2000, p. 99). African American nurses continually struggled against images constructed of their ability and skill in the nursing profession. Often faced with a professional image that labeled them as "inferior and other," and rendered them invisible, Black nurses painstakingly constructed an image that through a display of their skill and ability they hoped would portray the opposite of popular discriminatory thought. Black nurses worked twice as hard in helping and caring for their communities, setting up educational institutions, and working within a discriminatory and segregated system (Hine, 2005; Mosley, 1992).

From the mid-to-late 19th century through the mid-20th century, the history of Black women in nursing and nursing education in the United States has been documented to mark milestones in the health sciences legacy, while the impact that nursing has had on the success and aspirations of women, and Black women particularly, has been largely ignored. As there is particular importance in giving voice to Black women, Black women fashioned the nursing profession into a speech box through which their demands for inclusion, the removal of barriers, equal rights, equal pay, and quality education could be heard. Although African American women have been rendered invisible and insignificant in the histories of the American nursing profession, nursing was envisioned as a way to improve the social status of the African American race, particularly African American women (Barbee, 1993, 1994; Hine, 1989).

Literature Review

The literature review is helpful for laying a foundational understanding of Black women's involvement in nursing as a profession. This study utilizes existing literature to comprehend the role of the community college in providing nurse training and opportunities, the impact of East St. Louis class dynamics on educational opportunities for area residents, as well as the development of State Community College's nursing program. Yet there is also space to contribute to the discourse of Black women in nursing as it relates to the pursuit of becoming registered nurses (RNs) through the community college.

Black Women in Nursing

The historical development of Black women in nursing is aligned with societal discrimination and oppression. Black women engaged in a constant struggle to acquire nursing education, to end economic discrimination, and to win professional acceptance. White nurses relied on constructions of "Whiteness," and "womanhood" to define the parameters of professionalization in the field thus inhibiting

Black women's access to available opportunities for "professional" women. Black women, nonetheless, viewed nursing as "one of the best possible avenues for aspiring Black women possessed of few other means to achieve the moral status, self-fulfillment, and economic autonomy so fervently desired" (Hine, 1989, p. xviii). While Black women worked to reconstruct nursing into a profession that would be beneficial for their economic and intellectual well-being, they were often plagued by incidents of inferior education, discrimination in the job market, and a lack of training and professionalization opportunities (Mosley, 1992, p. 54).

Black women became nurses for a variety of reasons. According to Darlene Clark Hine (1989), a powerful combination of parental prodding, head-on collisions with racial discrimination, and the desire to reduce suffering encouraged many Black women to consider a nursing career. Personal and familial influences were undoubtedly important motivations; still the lack of choices and opportunities played a more decisive role in channeling Black women into nursing. The majority of Black women did not have ample employment or educational opportunities. Because of their sex and race, the larger society provided little for and expected less of them; so, they utilized nursing as means of change. Also for many African American women, nursing was the most accessible of all the professions especially during the early part of the 20th century (Barbee, 1994; Carnegie, 2005; Clinton, 1993; Davis, 1999; Hine, 1989). Thus, nursing provided a comparatively open gateway through which young Black women of working-poor backgrounds could cross toward dignified employment, and a middle-class lifestyle, while rendering much-needed services to their people.

Nursing has been and continues to be a particularly important skilled occupation for Black women. "Nursing became a means of upward mobility and a method by which these women could address the myriad of health problems in the Black community" (Barbee, 1993, p. 354). The lure of the middle-class identity attracted people of all backgrounds into the nursing profession but especially women as they worked to distance themselves from gendered positions in society that resulted in lowered pay and ensuing poverty, like the work of domestics (Gilbert, 1998). As a result of nursing's historical background and its relegation to a low-class, low-stature position, many researchers (Buchanan, 1999; Chambliss, 1996; Corley & Mauksch, 1988; Freidman, 1990) question the validity of nursing as a true profession and doubt its ability to provide a middle class-income and status.[3]

---

3   The argument against nursing as a profession centers on the premise that some women label nursing as a "calling." These researchers argue that labeling it a "calling" evokes emotion and caring, which negates and distances nursing from a profession. The other argument against nursing as a profession hinges on the subordinate position of nursing within the medical profession and argues that this position make it unlikely that they could be professionals. Whereas, the affirmative position of nursing as a profession argues that the training, educational credentials, job performance, and behavior amount to professional status for nurses.

Despite scholarly debate, there is no doubt that within Black communities Black nurses represented economic stability and enjoyed social respect and prestige that located them within the communities' elite (Flynn, 2003). Not only did nursing represent an opportunity for increased social class, but it also provided a profession in which women could conduct meaningful work. According to D'Antonio (1999) the "middle-class" nature of nursing descends from the achievements of Florence Nightingale. She goes on to say, "An identity as a nurse gave these women, both by association and by virtue of their special training, a place among the more educated members of their communities" (p. 274). Nursing represents real economic and professional opportunities for women as nurses seem to be relatively privileged in comparison with women of similar racial and ethnic backgrounds. Nursing also became a profession in which women could support themselves, was highly portable, and provided job security. "Nursing women sought—each class group in its own way—to create new opportunities for themselves" (D'Antonio, p. 274). Black women especially created new opportunities for themselves as they sought out nursing as a means of transforming their economic positions, providing educational opportunities, and improving the quality and health of their communities. Nursing became a female world of almost unparalleled autonomy, control, and professional status and despite the discrimination and prejudice of the nursing profession Black women gained membership into that world.

Community College Associate Degree Nursing Programs

Nursing, traditionally seen as woman's work, has historically lacked prestige and power. Always a necessity, nurses have nonetheless lacked social status. Robinson states, "In primitive times, she was a slave, and in the civilized era a domestic. Overlooked by the plans of legislators, and forgotten in the curricula of pedagogues, she was left without protection and remained without education" (1947, 25). Earlier forms of nursing duties were equated to the chores and tasks of domestics and orderlies. It was common practice that women were not allowed to enter newly erected hospitals. Nursing in its infancy stages did not require training or education as women nurses only gained permission to enter hospitals when they agreed to carry on a wide range of activities from housekeeping and cooking to nursing the sick. The late 19th century saw a transformation in the role of nursing, as well as that of hospitals. In the earlier part of the century, nursing was a menial occupation associated with lower-class, poorly educated women; in fact, many hospital nurses were actually convalescing patients (Montag, 1963). The professionalization of nursing began in 1863 with the establishment of the first training schools for White nurses, founded originally to provide respectable work for middle-class women and to improve the moral climate of hospitals by the introduction of a different class woman to the wards (Gamble, 1995). With the increased use of hospitals and increasing complexity of hospital technology and of patient care, duties not solely attributed to nurses slowly became separated and new occupational nursing groups developed. The evolution and progress of medicine subsequently and directly impacted the evolution of professional nursing and nurse training. The push for professionalization and better training for nurses resulted in the establishment of nurse training programs, first in hospitals and later in higher educational institutions.

The development of nurse training programs has taken a dramatic change since earlier forms of nursing and nurse training in the United States. Changes in nursing include the rise of hospitals and the demise of the diploma-granting schools of nursing after World War II and their replacement by community college programs and baccalaureate-granting nursing schools (Glazer, 1991). By 1965, the American Nursing Association (ANA) had worked to standardize a formula for the education of nurses. As the ANA pushed for increasing professionalization and educational standards for the nursing profession, it described what it hoped would become the three levels of education for nurses: baccalaureate education for beginning nurse practice (BSN); associate degree education for beginning technical nurse practice (RN); and vocational education for assistants in the health service occupations (CNA, LPN) (Nelson, 2002). The three levels of nursing are categorized into basic and post-basic nursing programs. Basic programs include those awarding the diploma, bachelor's, and associate degree; post-basic programs include several non-degrees—in public health nursing and nurse-midwifery and master's and doctoral degree programs (Barbee 1993; Carnegie; 1995).

Associate degree nursing programs (ADN) are the latest and last type of basic nursing education program. Today there are more than 1,000 junior colleges with associate degree nursing programs located in all 50 states, the District of Columbia, Puerto Rico, the Virgin Islands, and Guam. Associate degree nursing programs educate approximately 60% of new registered nurses, and associate degree or diploma RNs account for 42% of nurse clinicians, 29% of clinical nurse specialists, 47% of head nurses, and 62% of supervisors (American Association of Community Colleges [AACC], 2011). Mahaffey (2002) contends that just as hospital-based diploma programs are historically intertwined with the evolution of modern hospitals, associate degree nurse education has been important in the growth of community colleges. Associate degree nursing education represents a compelling option for individuals interested in the nursing profession. Mahaffey also adds that characteristics of associate degree nursing programs such as lower tuition rates, geographic locations, completion time, reputation of graduates, dynamic curricula, and effective faculties are extremely influential in the popularity of the programs.

Community college nursing programs are argued to result from the occurrence of multiple activities including interest in and growth of junior colleges, federal involvement in funding and spending, consumer concern and support, and professional responsibility and accountability (Mahaffey, 2002). There was a burgeoning climate for a different type of nurse created by a nursing shortage, as well as a growing interest in nurse training by the government and consumers of education. The earliest two-year nursing program began as an experiment by Mildred Montag in 1952 through the Cooperative Research Project in Junior and Community College Education for Nursing, of the Department of Nursing Education at Teachers College. This program took place over five years, within eight cooperating institutions, seven colleges, and one hospital, including one historically Black university, Norfolk State University (Montag, 1963).

Associate degree nursing programs were originally initiated and developed to prepare men and women for those functions commonly associated with nursing technicians and registered nurses. According to Montag, "Its placement in the community junior college was deliberate. The structure and nature (open-access, college-based, vocational education oriented, and length of the program) of the two-year college made it ideal for a technical program" (1980, p. 248). Montag (1980) also adds "a unique feature of an associate degree in nursing is that it was the first program to be developed through research, rather than as a result of an historical accident" (p. 248). The associate nursing degree programs represented an additional opportunity for nursing to break away from the apprenticeship model as was happening with the push for baccalaureate nursing education. It also represented an opportunity for nurses and nursing faculty, usually women, to exert greater control over the educational experiences of nursing students.

The first nurses of the associate degree nursing program graduated in 1954, with a combination of general and nursing education courses, including clinical experience, developed in accordance with college policy and regulations of the state licensing authority. Graduates of two-year programs were being prepared to give care to patients as beginning staff nurses and to cooperate and share responsibility for their patients' welfare with other members of nursing and health staff (Carnegie, 1995). According to researchers, the almost instant popularity of the associate degree nursing programs was unexpected, much like the boom and rise of community colleges during this period. These programs were so successful that, in the 1960s, they were expanding so rapidly that at times a new ADN program was opening somewhere in the country every week (Haase, 1990). Haase, describing the innovation and intrigue of two-year nursing programs, stated, "They attracted innovative nurse educators who were willing to challenge traditions, experiment with new teaching strategies and take risks as they worked out a new two-year curriculum as preparation for nursing practice" (p. 86).

East St. Louis and State Community College

By the time State Community College was established in 1969, East St. Louis had undergone drastic changes from the fourth largest city in Illinois to one of the poorest cities in the state with a continuously decreasing population, and an increasing minority, particularly African American population. East St. Louis presents a wide range of struggles and angles from which to evaluate and describe the city. East St. Louis has faced a variety of struggles that characterize the overall development of the city including economic struggles stemming from an overreliance on industry as a sole economic base, followed by the collapse of the industrial base; political struggles—East St. Louis is known for its political corruption and patronage, and social struggles—the "Southern" culture and customs that characterize racial interactions in East St. Louis and the treatment of minority groups including racism, discrimination, and segregation; and finally the transformation of the population in East St. Louis from a racially and socially mixed city to one with a highly low-income African American population (Ferguson, 1981). The struggles that East St. Louis faced, and continues to face, have resulted in a city that continuously juggles the need to provide social services for its residents with the reality that services that are provided are inadequate. This includes the financial difficulty the school district has continuously faced, the slow decrease in the number of hospitals that service the city, and even the ability to provide fire and police services to the residents of East St. Louis.

East St. Louis defined and characterized by its reliance on industry and manufacturing jobs to sustain its economic and social services, similar to other industrial suburbs like Gary, Indiana, and Camden, New Jersey, suffered severely when its economic base collapsed. Between 1950 and 1970, manufacturing employment in East St. Louis decreased by more than 5,000 people. A major problem for East St. Louis was its high property assessments, compounded by "employers and employees moving from the central city to the suburbs, taking with them their tax monies, their purchasing power, and all the other attributes of the urban middle class" (Altes, 1970, p. 1). The high rate of tax assessment, coupled with a rising municipal tax rate left East St. Louis drawing more heavily on deteriorating local tax resources in an effort to provide necessary services. The overburdened services deteriorated rendering the area less attractive to self-sufficient residents and existing businesses, resulting in the relocation of more residents and businesses. These acts contributed to a never-ending cycle in which the lack of disposable income, the limited variety of retail establishments, and the high rate of abandonment lead to further out-migration, commercial closing, and severed economic relations. The massive out-migration left in its wake joblessness and a dependency that contributes to educational underachievement, crime, poor housing, inadequacy of basic services, and crippling dependence on public welfare (Donahue & Glickman, 1977).

Illinois lawmakers and East St. Louis residents turned toward education as a means of rectifying and remedying the devastating changes in East St. Louis. Educational relief came in the form of East St. Louis State Community College, established in 1969, by the 76th Illinois General Assembly through Senate Bill 1255. Bipartisan legislation authorized an experimental junior college in East St. Louis financed 100% through Illinois state expenditures (*East St. Louis Metro-East Journal*, May 19,1969). The two-year institution was designed and developed to solve many of the problems plaguing East St. Louis, as well as lead the transformation of both the community and its people. SCC was charged with easing the growing unemployment and waning jobs in the area by being both an experimental college and heavily vocational-education focused, two distinctions that would allow for job and skill training and greater ease in introducing programs and partnerships that had not been tried out in other junior colleges of the time (Smith, 1980). Proponents of State Community College hoped that the local institution would rise to the challenge that community colleges had been accepting since their inception, which included providing new educational patterns by making provisions that adjusted to a wider range of people, including women who chose both family and education, workers with jobs and families, the urban poor with insufficient finances, people in need of retraining, retired persons, the handicapped, disadvantaged, and others alienated from existing programs and institutions. State Community College was an institution established explicitly for the growing, low-income African American population of East St. Louis and joined the ranks of other educational institutions established to serve historically oppressed groups (Townsend, 1999).

Nursing at State Community College

East St. Louis State Community College (SCC) was only one of many two-year institutions to join the ranks of associate degree nursing programs. State Community College was established to educate and serve primarily the majority African American population of the East St. Louis metropolitan area as they sought educational avenues in hopes of changing their current economic position. State Community College and the nursing program were envisioned as one example of the ways in which education could serve the needs of the East St. Louis community. The Illinois Community College Board approved the nursing program at SCC in 1971. State Community College began offering the associate degree in nursing in 1972, a mere three years after the initial establishment of the institution in 1969. Then president of State Community College in 1972, Clifton Woods III, in discussing the establishment of the nursing program, espoused the hope of the future program, "It is envisioned that the two-year program should lead easily to employment as there is a great demand for registered nurses" (Canty, 1970). State Community College established its nursing program within the larger philosophy of the overall institution, which subscribed to "the belief that every individual is worthy of an education and that a planned, organized sequence of experiences can provide this individual with a vehicle that will lead to a meaningful contribution to society and to himself" (Holderman & Wellman, 1972 p. v). The creators of the nursing program pushed for the development of nursing out of an earnest awareness of the benefits of a nursing career to the students and the opportunities that nursing would provide the community, not to mention the excitement and continued development of associate degree nursing programs.

State Community College came to mean a myriad of things to many different people; however, no group held the school in such high esteem as the women and few men of the nursing program at State Community College. When interviewees for the study were asked which academic program stood out most for them during their tenure with the institution, more than half of them responded with "The nursing program!"[4] One interviewee in particular (Mr. GB) expressed his enthusiasm for the nursing program by stating, "And then at that time (1982 and beyond), the nursing program was booming. SCC had the top-nursing program in the state of Illinois. I mean if you wanted to be a nurse you went to SCC, just like they talking about going to Ranken to be a mechanic, man them girls was getting, well them girls and guys before they could get out of here, they had jobs." Mr. GB could hardly contain his excitement for the nursing program and enthusiastically explained what the program meant to him as an outsider and offered an explanation of the advantages students gained from the program. He continued by saying, "It was that many women down here to get in that nursing program. It was a waiting list. But I mean if you went to SCC and you got a nursing degree it was all over the country. You was shoo. . . you came in there, you probably come in there. . . you knew what you was doing. You knew it" (GB, personal interview, 2009). The nursing program represents only one of the numerous programs that State Community College offered to its students, but it provides a lens through which to view how students were able to utilize the academic programs of the community college in their attempts to overcome racist, sexist, and classist discriminations put in place by the larger society.

Methods

This qualitative and historical study was conducted to explore the ways in which African American women in the East St. Louis area utilized the two-year Associate Degree Nursing program at State Community College of East St. Louis as a means of economic and social mobility. More specifically, the study examined: (1) why they chose nursing as a field of study, (2) why they chose State Community

---

4   This study interviewed 23 people, and 17 individuals acknowledged the nursing program as a stellar and standout program for the institution.

College to pursue their nursing degrees, and (3) how they hoped achieving the nursing degree would enhance their lives. In an effort to capture the stories of these women and allow them to share their voices, the study was conducted using a phenomenological approach. One of the assumptions underlying phenomenological inquiry is that there is an "essence" or there are "essences" to the shared experiences of study participants (Patton, 2002). In other words, the meanings ascribed to a particular phenomenon are likely to be shared and mutually understood among participants. Moreover, from a phenomenological viewpoint, what emerges as important ultimately relies on how participants experience and interpret their world.

Purposeful sampling was used to identify participants in this study. According to Patton, "purposeful sampling focuses on selecting information-rich cases whose study will illuminate the questions under study" (2002, p. 230). Participants were selected with assistance of former faculty, staff, and students of State Community College. I contacted the president of the SCC Nursing Student Alumni Association who assisted in identifying alumni who might be interested in participating in this study. Upon receiving the names of seven potential participants, I contacted each person to explain the study and to personally invite them to participate. In the end, three participants agreed to be interviewed for the study.

Two of the participants were graduates of the State Community College nursing program who had gone on to become registered nurses (RNs) and are currently working in the nursing profession, one as a lead hospital nurse, and the other as the executive director of nursing services for a for-profit institution. The third participant, also a registered nurse, was one of the original co-founders and directors of the program at SCC who worked with the program for 23 years. I conducted semi-structured interviews lasting from 30 minutes to 1.5 hours with each participant to gain an understanding of their experiences with nursing and the nursing program at State Community College. Each participant was given a pseudonym to be used during the study. Upon completion of the data collection, each interview was transcribed and analyzed.

Each interview transcript was first read to identify and isolate the uniqueness of each participant's experience. Notes were carefully taken and summarized. A second reading of the transcripts involved content analysis in order to make sense of and identify consistencies among respondents' experiences at SCC. Content analysis of the interview transcripts served as a form of open coding in which I was able to recognize patterns among participants' experiences and allowed them to freely emerge. Following this portion of analysis, the patterns were grouped into thematic categories. Interpretations of the themes consisted of identifying the meanings of participants' experiences, and the utilization of my personal perspectives to understand and attach significance to the meanings of participants' experiences.

Upon completion of analysis, study participations were contacted and asked to offer their opinions, additional insights, and feedback on the findings of the study, a necessity in ensuring accurate representation of participants' voices. In addition, I asked two senior researchers—one of whom conducts community college research and the other a historian of African American education—to review and provide feedback on the coding of the interview data and the findings section. All suggestions were taken into consideration and used to either reconceptualize or reorganize the content and presentation of the findings.

Findings

As a result of data analysis, three central themes emerged in this study:

> (1) combating racism and discrimination, (2) providing a better life, and (3) supportive and caring environments. In the first theme, participants describe how State Community College allowed them to combat racism and discrimination felt in other nursing programs and society in general. The second theme consists of participants' views on how nursing allows them to achieve a better life. The third theme highlights participants' acknowledgment of the care and support they received from attending the community college nursing program.

Combating Racism and Discrimination

State Community College's nursing program was important to the residents of the East St. Louis metropolitan area in that it was one of a few programs in the area open to Blacks desiring to become nurses. De facto segregation and discrimination left those individuals in the East St. Louis metropolitan area interested in nursing with few opportunities to fulfill their goals. The co-coordinator of the nursing program at State Community College, in response to her biggest accomplishment with the institution, talks about the scarcity of nursing programs in the area. She states:

> You will have to know that uh there are not. . . there were not that many schools of nurses who admitted African American students and I guess I was committed to the fact that there were going to be some African American young men and women who could enter the workforce. Because on both sides of the [Mississippi] river [Illinois and Missouri] there were just not schools that were willing to admit African American students. You know, maybe one or two, three or four, so State Community College had the task of producing more African American nurses in the metropolitan East St. Louis area. (Mrs. CG, 2009)

Former students of the nursing program also echoed an awareness of the reluctance of area nursing programs in admitting Black students. One participant, NB, shares her experience in applying to a hospital-based nursing program at her place of employment, Mercy Hospital, which had a diploma training program for its employed nurse aides to become qualified registered nurses. She relates her experience as such: establishing a program of nursing sought to keep the door to professional medicine open to those disadvantaged by other programs.

> When I applied to Mercy's program they would not hire, they would not put me in the program. And they [older nurses working at the school] and the [sic] cousin instructed me about the college in East St. Louis. Now Mercy took and hired girls that didn't even have their diplomas. They hadn't even finished high school. They set up a program for them, where they brought in the GED. Well I didn't need a GED, but I was vocal in unfair [racial] treatment that I saw there. And that's probably why they wouldn't let me in their program. (NB, 2009)[5]

The reluctance of programs in the area to admit Black students was not only limited to Black women as one of the male graduates of SCC also stated his experience with resistance in a local four-year program (RW, 2009). The lack of opportunity for residents in the area made the offerings at State Community College that much more important. As with anything else, SCC sought to rectify and remedy segregation in an affordable educational institution and by establishing a program of nursing sought to keep the door to professional medicine open to those disadvantaged by other programs.

Providing a Better Life

While education is important to everyone, feminist scholar Vivyan Adair (2008) is convinced education is especially essential for those who will face the continued obstacles of racism, classism, sexism, and homophobia; for those who have been distanced and disenfranchised from U.S. mainstream culture; and for those who have suffered generations of oppression and marginalization (p. 4). She argues that no group of individuals fits all these criteria better than low-income African American women. There is common agreement that education is not only the ticket to economic success but to basic survival as well. The women interviewed for this study expressed those same sentiments. The nursing program at SCC was a chance for them to ensure their survival. The program allowed them to gain the necessary skills and knowledge base to sustain themselves and their families.

Lois Weis (1985) found that the desire to provide a better life for their family was a major reason for Black females to attend community colleges. This also proved to be a major reason given by the women who attended State Community College. They envisioned SCC as a means of improving their life station and providing the ability for them to offer a better life not only for themselves but for their children as well. They were able to provide a better life by using the com-

---

5   This quote is part of a larger quote where the interviewee is talking about her experiences with the diploma-nursing program and her knowledge of the nursing program at State Community College. She had a cousin that attended SCC and so she references her cousin as "the cousin," instead of saying "my cousin."

munity college to gain their "life career." Nursing at SCC in particular afforded women the chance to not only provide for their families but also to join the ranks of professional career women. When asked why they enrolled in SCC and particularly the nursing program the common reason was to better themselves and their economic position. One former student stated, "Everybody was trying to. . . the students were trying to further themselves, 'cause I was one of 'em" (NB, 2009). While it isn't known if the nursing program was known all over the state, what is known is that the women and men who enrolled in the nursing program at State Community College were able to utilize their education to become registered nurses and effectively change their economic positions.

Supportive and Caring Environments

Institutions such as State Community College whose impetus and focus are to provide educational and economic training for minority and underrepresented students provide an educational space that is supportive, caring, and attentive to students' needs. While studies show that most African American nurses are trained in predominantly White two-year nursing programs, they also show that these institutions are failing to provide supportive academic and social environments for African American students, making it all too important for institutions similar to State Community College, predominantly Black-serving institutions, to be supported and cultivated (Coleman, 2008). African American students are more likely to report satisfaction and succeed when there are sufficient numbers of African American faculty to assist in providing academic, social, and cultural support for African American students. Also, historically Black schools—and by extension those schools specifically devoted to serving minority and underrepresented students—have supported and participated in the struggle for inclusion of African American women in healthcare, and they have done it well. According to Laura McQueen and Lynn Zimmermann (2004), educational institutions that cater to minority populations are aware of the needs of their students and invest time and resources to ensure that their students succeed. In this case, the nursing faculty at State Community College saw to it that their students were well prepared to take and pass state licensing exams. McQueen and Zimmerman also state, "The close-knit community in an HBCU nursing program creates an atmosphere of trust and care that is often the cornerstone to students gaining that extra piece needed to 'get in the testing game'" (p. 53). Institutions committed to serving underrepresented populations have shown strong evidence in successfully educating and moving students toward nursing careers.

Instructors and administrators in the nursing program at SCC took their job of educating and preparing competent nurses very seriously and heralded the position as one of great importance. The instructors and coordinators were willing to do whatever it took for their students to succeed and ultimately become nurses.

In discussing preparing students for the National Council License Exam for Registered Nurses (NCLEX-RN), Mrs. CG, former coordinator of the program, talks about the extra study sessions available to the students as a way of making sure they could pass the exam on the first try, given the extra responsibilities of the "new" nursing students—married, working full- or part-time, children, household duties—which could prove to be a burden for the students. Former students of the nursing program also feel as if the faculty went beyond the duties of their profession in seeing to it that the students were prepared to succeed.

NB (2009), describing her preparation for the NCLEX-RN, stated:

> And it was just a, everybody looked like they cared about us progressing. But our learning. . . yeah they worked with us, they didn't want embarrassments on State Boards, so they asked you, "Are you understanding this material?" And you weren't passing because we were in the city of East St. Louis, where you feel you got to help them. [sic] You had to know your material. You didn't pass because you were a minority. The instructor made sure you knew the material. And I'm not talking about. . . it went past the classroom, we were invited to their homes, where they worked with us, one on one, if it was our choice. But in general, we had to pass the same state boards anywhere [sic] else nurses had to pass. And if we left here and went to other places and practiced nursing we had to do the same thing. So we were qualified to do it when you left SCC.

Another former nursing student replied:

> Oh, I absolutely loved my instructors at State Community College because they really prepared us for the exam, I feel. That's me. . . But yeah the nursing classes, the instructors were very concerned that we learned information because we would have to be tested at the state level. Everybody would have to undergo certification exams and they wanted to make sure that we had access to the information so that we would have successful results at State Boards. (RW, 2009)

The assistance and instruction went beyond the classroom and into the homes of instructors as some instructors constructed formal study programs for the larger population of student nurses in the area. The instructors were wedded to the belief of students succeeding and provided quality instruction and services to achieve these ultimate goals.

Interviewees' narratives make a compelling argument for the need and importance of two-year institutions and two-year predominantly minority-serving institutions in educating nurses. African American nurses, while constituting a large majority of nurses with BSNs, often get their start in associate degree nursing programs. State Community College joined the ranks of two-year educational institutions committed to providing quality, low-cost nursing education. SCC also proved invaluable to educating African American nurses by filling an educational and economic void for East St. Louis' residents and through the introduction and creation of programs that were viable to their professional and personal success.

Discussion

Associate degree nursing programs have proved extremely beneficial for women of color. Four-year nursing programs and the push for the baccalaureate as the beginning professional degree often focus on high school grades and SAT and ACT test scores, both of which are argued to reflect racial bias and can be a hindrance to admission. Since community colleges often do not adhere to stringent testing scores like four-year institutions, they provide a more viable and easily accessible option for those traditionally and continuously shut out of four-year programs (McQueen & Zimmerman, 2004, p. 52). This is not to say that community college nursing programs do not have testing standards and grade requirements but that they provide an alternative route to four-year colleges and universities whose admission policies' center on test scores. Institutions like SCC provided an alternative opportunity to the subordination and exclusion students of color often feel in predominantly White institutions (Allen, 1992).

The community college became an institution, which the nursing profession was able to utilize in making the nursing degree more affordable and accessible to countless women, particularly women of color. Community colleges became spaces women were able to utilize in garnering power. Community colleges' ideology, which emphasizes opportunity, individual development, and ready access, makes them ideal places for women who have historically been limited in their educational endeavors (Frye, 1995, p. 12). The ease and accessibility of the associate degree nursing program provided an additional avenue that women of color could take in utilizing nursing as a means of changing and challenging their current positions. Associate degree nursing programs remain a highly popular choice for students entering the field of nursing.

Limitations and Implications
The methodological approach resulted in a sample size of three interviewees, making it inconceivable that the results of this study could be generalized to all African American nurses trained in associate degree nursing programs, a concept beyond the purview of this study. This study sought to examine the reasons African American women in East St. Louis chose two-year nursing programs as a means of social and economic mobility. While these three narratives do not speak for all African American nurses, they do, however, offer an explanation of why African American women in deindustrialized cities with crumbling economic bases envision nursing and the community college as an alternate to their realities. East St. Louis and State Community College, although unlike any other community

college in that it was funded 100% by the state of Illinois, provided an exciting opportunity to evaluate the role of associate degree nursing programs in achieving their stated goals. The results of this study will also help guide future research in exploring why African American women in cities similar to East St. Louis choose associate degree nursing programs as a means of economic and social mobility.

Despite the relative success of Black women in nursing, African Americans make up only 7.1% of the registered nurse population, an indication that there still remains a great need for increased numbers of minorities in nursing schools and nursing practice and in an increase in institutions conducive to these students' needs. Beacham, Askew, and Williams (2009) contend that the lack of minority nurses exists for a number of complex reasons including past discrimination, financial barriers, problems related to academic and social adjustments, low high school achievement, and a lack of academic preparedness. Associate degree nursing programs in predominantly minority-serving institutions provide a replicable prototype for easing these problems in that their programs are readily accessible, inexpensive, and provide support systems and support programs that enable the success of minority female students.

Bibliography

Adair, V.C. (20098). The missing story of ourselves: Poor women, power and the political of feminist representation. *Feminist Formations, 20*(1), 1–25.

Allen, W. R. (1992). The color of success: African American college student outcomes at predominantly White and historically Black public colleges and universities. *Harvard Educational Review, 62*(1), 26–44.

Altes, J. (1970). *East St. Louis: The end of a decade.* Edwardsville: Southern Illinois University.

American Association of Community Colleges. (2011). *Nursing education and practice.* Retrieved from http://www.aacc.nche.edu/resources/aaccprograms/health/Pages/education.aspx

Barbee, E. L. (1993). Racism in U.S. nursing. *Medical Anthropology Quarterly, 7*(4), 346–362.

Beacham, T., Askew, R. W., & Williams, P. R. (2009). Strategies to increase racial/ethnic student participation in the nursing profession. *ABNF Journal, 20*(3), 69–72.

Buchanan, T. (1999). Nightingalism: Haunting nursing history. *Collegian, 6*(2), 28–33.

Canty, T. (1970, November 19). SCC: New president believes East St. Louis institution. *East St. Louis Metro-East Journal.*

Carnegie, M. E. (1995). *The path we tread: Blacks in nursing worldwide, 1854–1994* (3rd ed.). New York: National League for Nursing Press.

Carnegie, M.E. (2005). Educational preparation of Black nurses: A historical perspective. *ABNF Journal, 16*(1), 6–7.

Chambliss, D. F. (1996). *Beyond caring: Hospitals, nurses, and the social organization of ethics.* Chicago: University of Chicago Press.

Clinton, M. M. (1993). Black psychiatric nurses: Historical perspectives, 1964 to 1984. *Journal of Black Studies, 24*(2), 213–231.

Coleman, L. D. (2008). Experiences of African American students in predominantly White, two-year nursing program. *ABNF Journal, 19*(1), 8–13.

Collins, P. H. (2000). *Black feminist thought: Knowledge, consciousness, and the politics of empowerment* (2nd ed.). New York: Routledge.

Corley, M. C., & Mauksch, H. O. (1988). Registered nurses, gender and commitment. In A. Statham, E. M. Miller, & H. O. Mauksch (Eds.), *The worth of women's work: A qualitative synthesis* (pp. 135–149). Albany: State University of New York Press.

D'Antonio, P. (1999). Revisiting and rethinking the rewriting of nursing history. *Bulletin of the History of Medicine, 73*(2), 268–290.

Davis, A. T. (1999). *Early Black leaders in nursing: Architects for integration and equality.* Sudbury, MA: Jones & Bartlett Publishers.

Donahue, R. L., & Glickman, D. S. (1977). *The East St. Louis area: An overview of state capital projects and policies.* Springfield: Illinois Capital Development Board.

East St. Louis City Council. (1967). *Federal grant application.* Mayor Alvin G. Fields Collection. Edwardsville: Southern Illinois University-Edwardsville Archives. Accessed April 18, 2010.

East St. Louis Metro-East Journal. (1969, May 19). Junior college plan sound.

East St. Louis Metro-East Journal. (1969, November 25). 'No improprieties,' Wheadon says; Sees no reason for Ware to quit.

Ferguson, S. S. (1981). *East St. Louis: A changing population.* Edwardsville: Southern Illinois University at Edwardsville.

Flynn, K. C. (2003). *Race, class, and gender: Black nurses in Ontario, 1950–1980.* Unpublished doctoral dissertation. York University, Toronto.

Freidman, E. (1990). Troubled past of "invisible" profession. *Journal of American Medical Association, 264*(22), 2851–2852, 2854–2855, 2858.

Frye, J. H. (1995). Women in the two-year college, 1900 to 1970. *New Directions for Community Colleges, 89,* 5–14.

Gamble, V. N. (1995). *Making a place for ourselves: The Black hospital movement, 1920–1945.* New York: Oxford University Press.

Gilbert, M. K. (1998). "Race," space, and power: The survival strategies of working poor women. *Annals of the Association of American Geographers, 88*(4), 595–621.

Glazer, N. Y. (1991). "Between a rock and a hard place": Women's professional organizations in nursing and class, racial, and ethnic inequalities. *Gender & Society, 5*(3), 351–372.

Haase, P. T. (1990). *The origins and rise of associate degree nursing.* Durham, NC: Duke University Press.

Hine, D. C. (1989). *Black women in White: Racial conflict and cooperation in the nursing profession, 1890–1950.* Bloomington: Indiana University Press.

Hine, D. C. (2005). Nursing. In D. C. Hine (Ed.), *Black women in America* (pp. 441–449). New York: Oxford University Press.

Holderman J. B., & Wellman, F. L. (1972). *The public community college system of the state of Illinois.* Illinois Community College Board Papers. Springfield: Illinois State Archives.

Illinois Community College Board. (1981). *Status report/recommendation for future funding and governance of State Community College of East St. Louis.* Springfield: Illinois Community College Board.

Love, K. L. (2009). *An emancipatory study with African American women at predominantly White nursing schools.* Unpublished doctoral dissertation. University of Connecticut, Storrs.

Mabokela, R. O., & Green, A. L. (Eds.). (2001). *Sisters of the academy: Emergent Black women scholars in higher education.* Sterling, VA: Stylus Publishing.

Mahaffey, E. H. (2002). The relevance of associate degree nursing education: Past, present, future. *Online Journal of Issues in Nursing, 7*(2). Retrieved May 2002 from http://www.nursingworld. org/ojin/MainMenuCategories/ANAMarketplace/ANAPeriodicals/OJIN/TableofContents/ Volume72002/No2May2002/RelevanceofAssociateDegree.aspx.

McQueen, L., & Zimmerman, L. (2004). The role of historically Black colleges and universities in the inclusion and education of Hispanic nursing students. *ABNF Journal, 15*(3), 51–54.

Montag, M. L. (1963). Technical education in nursing? *American Journal of Nursing, 63*(5), 100–103.

Montag, M. L. (1980). Associate degree education in perspective. *Nursing Outlook, 28,* 248–250.

Mosley, M. O. P. (1992). *A history of Black leaders in nursing: The influence of four Black community health nurses on the establishment, growth, and practice of public health nursing in New York City, 1900–1930.* Unpublished doctoral dissertation. Columbia University Teachers College, New York City.

Nelson, M. A. (2002). Education for professional nursing practice: Looking backward into the future. *Online Journal of Issues in Nursing, 7*(3). Retrieved from http://www.nursingworld. org/MainMenuCategories/ANAMarketplace/ANAPeriodicals/OJIN/TableofContents/Volume72002/No2May2002/EducationforProfessionalNursingPractice.aspx

O'Connor, C. (2002). Black women beating the odds from one generation to the next: How the changing dynamics of constraint and opportunity affect the process of educational resilience. *American Educational Research Journal, 39*(4), 855–903.

Patton, M. Q. (2002). *Qualitative research & evaluation methods* (3rd ed.). Thousand Oaks, CA: Sage Publishers.

Reardon, K. M. (1997). State and local revitalization efforts in the East St. Louis, Illinois. *Annals of the American Academy of Political and Social Science, 551,* 235–247.

Robinson, V. (1947). *White caps: The story of nursing.* Philadelphia: J.B. Lippincott.

Smith, G. (1980). *Illinois junior-community college development, 1946–1980.* Springfield: Illinois Community College Board.

Theising, A. J. (2003). *Made in USA: East St. Louis, the rise and fall of an industrial river town.* St. Louis, MO: Virginia Publishing.

Townsend, B. K. (1999). Collective and distinctive patterns of two-year special-focus colleges. In. B. K. Townsend (Ed.), *Two-year colleges for women and minorities: Enabling access to the baccalaureate* (pp. 3–42). New York: Falmer Press.

United States Census Bureau. (2010). *State & County Quick Facts.* http://quickfacts.census.gov/qfd/states/17/1722255.html

Weis, L. (1985). *Between two worlds: Black students in an urban community college.* Boston: Routledge & Kegan Paul.

Chapter Eleven

Higher Education Leadership

One Black Woman's Journey

Menah Pratt-Clarke

Higher education leadership is still a field largely dominated by White males. According to the United States Census Bureau, women (including African Americans) increasingly obtain degrees in greater proportion than men and constitute a majority of the young adults in college (Mather & Adams, 2007). In spite of this increase, the number of African American women in leadership positions within higher education remains relatively low (DiGeorgio-Lutz, 2002). Howard-Vital and Morgan (1993) hold that the intersectionality of race and gender present unique challenges for women of color pursuing academic and administrative careers in postsecondary education. Jenifer (2005) echoes this sentiment as the retired president of the University of Texas at Dallas, stating "From the founding of American higher education in 1636, it has remained an institution that both overtly and inadvertently discriminates against African-Americans and women" (p. 1). Thus, as a Black female senior administrator in higher education, I represent a small but growing minority who exemplifies the motto of the National Association of Colored Women (2011): "lifting as we climb" (p. 1).

Using the personal narrative approach of critical race feminism, this chapter traces my path into higher education leadership and explores the development of my leadership philosophy. My leadership philosophy derives from a firm and unwavering commitment to actualizing my own potential and encouraging others to actualize theirs. I also believe in the fundamental importance of setting goals and creating a vision in order to transform intangible ideas into tangible achievements. This work shares the lessons I learned about leadership from my journey: the importance of having a foundation and circles; a willingness to take risks; the critical role of "other-mothers"; and the power of voice.

Early Family Experiences

My early family experiences played a critical role in the development of my leadership philosophy. My story begins as a daughter of two PhD parents. My father was born in Freetown, Sierra Leone, West Africa and received a PhD in nuclear physics from Carnegie Mellon University. He was the first citizen of his country to reach that level of achievement. My mother was born to sharecroppers in Texas and was one of eight children. She was the only child to obtain a doctorate. Her PhD was in social work from the University of Pittsburgh. She also received her MA in religion and was an ordained minister. My parents earned these degrees in the 1960s, and thus, their perspectives regarding education were closely intertwined with their passion for civil rights and their sense of justice, equality, equal opportunity, and affirmative action. Educational achievement was an important value of my parents as African Americans and was the foundation of my leadership journey.

Being aware of our foundation is an important leadership lesson. Our parents—their philosophies about life, their values, and their beliefs—often have profound impacts on our lives and career paths. Although their influence may be subtle and difficult to perceive, its effects are real and direct. As I reflect upon my career, I realize that I was not conscious of the level of influence my parents would have on my life. In fact, when I entered college, I felt a strong desire to distance myself from my parents in order to define myself—my identity, my values, my beliefs, and ultimately, my destiny. Little did I know that my search would be circular, bringing me back to the foundation that was established by my parents.

When I graduated from high school in Normal, Illinois, I was 16 years old. My graduating class had 300 students. I was the only Black. Through my early years, I was often told that I talked "White," acted "White," and did "White" things, including playing piano, violin, and tennis. The "Whiteness" of my life continued after high school on the professional tennis circuit. After two years on the circuit—an almost exclusively White environment—I enrolled at the University of Iowa, another predominantly White environment. It was at the University of Iowa that my interest in education, critical race, and feminism developed. Iowa was the foundation for my career in higher education and administration. It was also the place that I began to find myself, my voice, and my passion.

The Iowa Years

My higher education journey started with literature. I majored in English and was introduced to the beauty of words and writing. A chance encounter with William

Faulkner led to a short love affair. His novels enticed me. His stories about the South appealed to me and his use of language fascinated me. There was a connection that I felt to Faulkner as I read *Intruder in the Dust* (1948); *As I Lay Dying* (1930); *The Sound and the Fury* (1929); *Light in August* (1932); and *Absalom, Absalom!* (1936). The themes about race relations and family relations resonated with my own life. I soon realized, however, that I was seeing the world solely through the eyes and words of British, American, and Russian male and female writers. I recognized that a concrete connection to my own identity as a Black woman was missing. My search led to minors in two other disciplines: African American Studies and Philosophy.

Although I enjoyed the writings of the American pragmatists and German philosophers, I often wondered what a Black female philosopher would have written. Searching for the Black female philosopher led me to the Department of African American Studies. I began to learn about the experiences, history, and leadership of Black people, often through the eyes of Black men. I read *Invisible Man* (1952), *The Fire Next Time* (1963), *The Autobiography of Malcolm X* (1965), and other African and African American classics. I could not seem, however, to find the Black women I so urgently sought. My spirit was growing restless with undefined and increasingly racing thoughts, about race, literature, philosophy, gender, and ultimately, about leadership.

One day, as if an answer to the quiet unspoken prayer for direction, a light was shown to me. Through books, I met Nikki Giovanni, Maya Angelou, and Gwendolyn Brooks and other Black women in novels and plays such as Gloria Naylor, Toni Morrison, and Alice Walker. I was challenged by their difficult works: *The Women of Brewster Place* (1982), *The Bluest Eye* (1970), and *The Color Purple* (1982). I saw these women as leaders. Yet I had difficultly separating the authors from the characters and the characters were often women who experienced great psychological pain and emotional sorrow. These women could not serve as the role model or image for leadership that I was seeking. I knew that fictional novels—while powerful and illustrative—could not help me actualize my potential. I needed to create another vision.

The importance of creating a vision, setting new goals, and moving on to new challenges has been a powerful leadership lesson for me. I learned that personal and professional growth and advancement require a willingness to undertake new challenges. The new challenge for me at Iowa was pursuing a master's degree in Literary Studies. I thought that I might learn more about Black women and I was still fascinated by Faulkner. Several classes and a master's thesis on *Absalom, Absalom!*, did not satisfy my restless spirit. Literary Studies was too passive. I needed to move from literature to action.

My leadership path began to turn to issues of educational opportunities, justice, and equality as I worked as a tutor with Upward Bound; as an office assistant in a minority student support office; and as a program coordinator for an afterschool program for Black sixth-grade girls. I was on a path to becoming a critical race feminist. I had a clear vision and in order to actualize that vision, I needed to leave Iowa. Moving is often necessary to grow and it forces us to learn how to adapt to change. Hence, I moved to Nashville, Tennessee, to attend Vanderbilt University.

Life at Vanderbilt

Enrolling at Vanderbilt University in Nashville, Tennessee, to pursue a doctorate in Sociology and a law degree became the next step on my leadership journey. In the Sociology Department at Vanderbilt, I was exposed to the dominant White male thinkers of the discipline, as well as their theoretical and methodological approaches. My experience in law school mirrored this experience. In law school, I was introduced to the Socratic Method and the English legal tradition of stare decisis. A master's degree in Sociology and a law degree later, I still had not found the leadership approach, image, or philosophy that I sought as a Black woman. In particular, I had not found a way to talk about myself and other Black women in a manner that was not merely literary. I wanted to talk about Black women in a way that was sociological, legal, historical, political, scientific, and methodological. The absence of my voice was almost paralyzing—spiritually, socially, emotionally, and intellectually. Knowing oneself and having voice are critical leadership attributes. Leaders must be intentional in their search for voice and self-knowledge.

I began to find my voice while preparing for the comprehensive sociology qualifying exams. I developed a reading list that focused on issues related to race, class, gender, and the law. This process created a small window into the world I was trying to find. I discovered bell hooks, Patricia Hill Collins, Adrien Wing, Black female sociologists, Black feminists, and critical race feminist scholars. Through their work, I started to find the voice I so earnestly sought. The voice I wanted to find was the voice that could speak through the lens of multiple disciplines; a voice that could combine and synthesize the strengths of different fields into a cohesive system of thought; and a voice that could be used to lead and be transformational in the world. I needed a voice that was integrated and trans-disciplinary. My graduate training revealed that sociologists think one way; they ask certain questions and they arrive at different answers than legal scholars who think another way; ask different types of questions and reach different conclusions. I wanted to move from "either/or" to "both/and" thinking.

My dissertation topic, *Where are the Black Girls?: The Marginalization of Black Females in the Single-Sex School Debate in Detroit* (Pratt, 1997), was my first attempt at trying to find and use my voice. I looked at the Black male crisis from a critical race feminist perspective. From that lens, I realized that the level of compassion for Black boys in society was matched by a subtle, yet deep-seated and deeply entrenched, level of resentment, anger, and frustration toward Black females, feminism, and matriarchy. An analysis of the discourse in Detroit documented that Black boys were in crisis—a social problem that was not in dispute (Pratt-Clarke, 2010). What the work challenged, however, was the dominant discourse in the media that essentially placed the blame on Black female classmates, Black female teachers, and Black mothers for the crisis rather than on the Detroit education system, which had failed all students. As a result of how the debate was framed, the proposed solution to the crisis was single-sex schools for Black males grounded in a Black male patriarchal, nationalistic ideology and supported by an African-centered curriculum. The schools were to be led by Black male principals and Black male teachers. As such, the Male Academy proposal minimized the role and presence of females as teachers, students, and mothers. It was as if its unwritten objective was to replace matriarchy and feminism with patriarchy and masculinity. In the Detroit Male Academy debate, the dominant voices were those of Black male community leaders and Board members. The Black female plaintiff, Shawn Garrett, was silenced and marginalized, as were the Black girls she represented in the legal case (Pratt-Clarke, 2010).

The primary objective of my dissertation was to understand what happened to the Black girls. In the process, I discovered an absence of advocacy and voice on behalf of issues that affected them. The dominant voices of the Black male crisis drowned out the voices and experiences of Black girls and women. The "required" and "expected" race loyalty, as opposed to gender loyalty, resulted in Black mothers advocating and supporting the Male Academy. There was a clear leadership void in the Black community in terms of advocacy for issues impacting Black women and girls. I knew I had a role to fill, but I did not know how to fill it. In my desire to understand the role of the law, lawyers, and justice in leadership, I decided to take a risk. Taking risks is an important attribute of leaders. A willingness to take risks requires a unique combination of confidence and conviction, and often requires moving to a new place to face new challenges.

Life in North Carolina

I moved to Morganton, North Carolina, after I received my law degree to accept a judicial clerkship. I had recently gotten married and made the difficult decision to leave my husband in Nashville for a year to work as a law clerk on the Fourth Circuit Federal Court of Appeals for Judge Sam Ervin III. Judge Ervin was a leader. He did not lead in the traditional stereotypical "top-down" manner. He led with a gentle spirit of compassion, sensitivity, and wisdom. I learned many lessons about leadership in Morganton by watching the Judge, listening to the Judge, and noticing the Judge's demeanor and attitude. Judge Ervin revealed the important qualities of a leader by example: he trusted others; he empowered others; he listened to others; he looked for justice; and he was collegial and respectful. I learned that great attorneys were leaders and that writing and speaking well are not only essential skills for a great lawyer, they are essential skills for a great leader. No leader can be great if she cannot articulate her thoughts clearly and concisely in writing and in speech. A leader must write and speak with clarity and communicate confidently to large and small audiences. Just as lawyers are advocates for their clients and represent their voice, so too are leaders the voice and face of their causes. Great leaders, like great lawyers, must have a strong presence and command attention and respect. They must also be humble as they should not speak for themselves, but for the greater cause that they represent.

As a law clerk, I learned about the federal court system and the decision-making processes that affected the law. I learned how judges decide cases, how opinions are written, how lawyers advocate for their clients, and how case law is created. It was a rare and fascinating peak at what my academic-sociological lens saw as the operation of White power (all the judges on the Fourth Circuit were White and mainly male). Through the clerkship experience, I learned the power of connections, relationships, and recommendations. For example, some clerks were handed clerkship opportunities through prior familial connections. Other clerks were at the mercy of faculty relationships with the judge, alumni connections, and letters of recommendations.

As our judge relied upon current clerks to assist with the selection of future clerks, I was able to review applications and their accompanying letters of recommendation. It was an eye-opening lesson for me to see the power of letters of reference to shape individual destinies and to create and deny leadership opportunities. Upon reading *Invisible Man*, I often wondered about what others said about me in the letters they wrote. Given the secrecy surrounding them, it is often difficult to assess their impact by race and gender, though research shows that underrepresented groups are often more negatively impacted by letters (Rothenberg, 2007; Trix & Psenka, 2003). Complementing the letters, I have seen the power of networking and relationships that often allow unqualified male and White candidates to obtain unmerited advantages over women and minorities. Unfortunately, since African Americans often do not have the breadth or depth of contacts and connections that create opportunities, relationships, and positive references, we must be more aggressive in securing this vital key to opening doors for leadership. I left Morganton—grateful for the risk I took and for the opportunity to learn about the law, lawyers, leaders, and letters.

Life as a Lawyer

After the one-year clerkship, I returned to Nashville and entered the private practice of law as the first African American female lawyer at one of the largest and most prestigious law firms. I practiced real estate law, public finance law, and commercial lending law. At the firm, I learned how to be a lawyer and appreciated the attorneys who took active responsibility for training and mentoring me. Although this experience was intellectually rewarding, being in a predominantly White male environment made this an emotionally difficult, isolating, and confusing experience for me as a Black woman. For example, I remember hearing conflicting reports from my colleagues regarding how they perceived me. Several lawyers in the firm said they didn't see me as Black and that I didn't "act Black." I certainly felt "Black" when I ate lunch at exclusively White lunch clubs and was served by Black waiters wearing gloves. I remember feeling "Black" when I attended parties at the homes of my White partners' houses and saw a Black butler, a Black nanny, or a Black cook that I wanted to hang out with and talk to because they were Black like me. I felt "Black" when I went to the mailroom where most of the Black employees spent time as the runners and mailmen. Yet, as a lawyer, I was not supposed to be "caught" talking to them. It was as if being a lawyer somehow made me "White."

In addition to a conflicted racial identity, I also had a conflicted gender identity. There were very few female lawyers, and they were not visible. As mothers and wives, I learned their time was precious and devoted to billable hours, not social hours. My examination of the culture revealed that most female attorneys who were also mothers had live-in nannies and most male attorneys had stay-at-home wives. Such "cultural examination" is a critical responsibility of a leader.

I learned that leaders must learn the culture of an organization, its values, its expectations, and its norms. In this respect, it is important to understand how an organization operates and why it operates the way it does. Once an organization is understood, a choice must be made to accept the organization and conform to its culture; challenge the organization and accept the potentially negative personal and professional consequences of challenging the status quo; or attempt to navigate the middle by both challenging and conforming. The choice often depends upon the relationship between the organization's values and one's personal values. Sometimes, there is a fundamental incompatibility of values. An organization's values might not be reconciled with personal core foundations and beliefs. At the same time, leaders must accept the duality that accompanies attempts at organizational transformation, for often most leaders will not and cannot "fit" in. A leader must decide how uncomfortable she can be and yet still be effective.

As I began to understand the culture of the law firm, I tried to both conform and challenge. Once my first child was born, the burden of balancing the personal and professional worlds became insurmountable. Being a private practice lawyer, wife, and mother created daycare dilemmas at home; billable hour challenges at work; and an identity crisis within me. My child was in daycare five days a week, sometimes for up to 12 hours, and I lost my clients who had been assigned to another lawyer during my maternity leave. After four years in private practice, I felt as if I was failing both professionally and personally. Reflection led to the conclusion that I needed to move on and continue the journey.

Before I started the journey, I reviewed my life. I had earned five degrees and I had teaching experience. The master's degree in literary studies from Iowa had created the opportunity for me to teach in Nashville. I taught African American Studies, grammar, and literature to freshmen at Fisk University. It was a wonderful opportunity to serve and help others learn about the richness and depth of African American experience. I was also blessed to teach at American Baptist College, which had outreach programs for inmates at the men's and women's maximum and minimum state prisons. Teaching the college courses literature, grammar, and speech to inmates was a tremendous opportunity. Despite the conditions, the students were eager to learn and I learned about the invisible world in which masses of Blacks are living, yet hidden. While the dehumanization and demoralization was difficult to accept, it was gratifying to see inmates taking advantage of the opportunity to get an education and to change their lives. I recognized that like my parents, I valued education. In returning to my foundational value, I accepted a position at Vanderbilt University, my alma mater. Vanderbilt became my first opportunity for leadership in higher education administration.

The Return to Vanderbilt

Returning to Vanderbilt reaffirmed my belief in the power of understanding the image of a circle as a symbol of the leadership journey. Many career paths include returns to familiar places and foundations. At Vanderbilt, I was hired as the University Compliance Officer, Assistant Secretary, and University Counsel. In these capacities, I was responsible for designing and implementing a compliance program (which included creating an ethical code of conduct and a conflict of interest policy); managing the higher education governance work with the Board of Trustees; and serving as the real estate and construction lawyer for the university, and negotiating over $500 million worth of construction contracts.

At Vanderbilt, I was able to transfer many of the skills that I learned as a lawyer and law clerk. There are certain skills that are necessary to be successful. Once we learn them, we must be able to transfer them to different circumstances. These skills include strong written and verbal communication; the ability to engage in analysis; and a recognition of the importance of teamwork. At the firm and as a law clerk, I learned how to be prepared and present information in both a verbal and written manner. I learned how to answer questions. But more importantly, I learned how to look and how to listen. At the law firm, I learned how to walk into a room, be in control, and be confident—often as the only woman and the only person of color. I used this same ability at Vanderbilt where I was often the only person of color and many times the only woman.

At Vanderbilt, I had access to spaces and places involving decision making as the Assistant Secretary and Compliance Officer. I was in the room with other leaders and though I was seated at the table, I was often not really "at the table" in a decision-making role. Yet, being in the room was important, as it gave me access to knowledge and information not typically available to Black women. Although the boardroom and meetings were spaces filled with White men, as the Assistant Secretary, I was responsible for taking the minutes. In my role, I became invisible and silently learned about investments and asset allocation in the Investment Committee meeting; I learned about executive compensation in the Human Resources Committee meeting; and I learned about budgets and finances in the Budget Committee meeting. As a private university, these were private meetings, not open to the general public as they are at public universities. Thus, I was given access to a world that was often hidden. I spent a great deal of time trying to understand this "secret" world that I had been given access to as a "secretary." I began to think about how I could move from being a "secretary" to being a leader.

I began to look deeply at the operation of the university and began to deliberately assess the organization. Through this process, certain dynamics began to catch my attention. One dynamic, in particular, was the power of White women (Murrell, Crosby, & Ely, 1999). Many White women were gatekeepers—secretaries, administrative assistants, and chiefs of staff. Many of these women only had a high school diploma. In spite of their limited levels of education, these women often controlled access to power and people; records and files; knowledge and institutional history. Other White women—not gatekeepers, but in powerful positions—were rarely accessible, available, or willing to mentor me. I was often left to fight daily battles by myself against these seemingly friendly, sometimes hostile, and often powerful barriers and obstacles.

While I was watching myself fight an unseen battle with White women, I watched White men fight another battle on behalf of other White men. I saw how mentorship worked. In particular, I saw a White "father" "adopt" a White "son" at work and take care of him. A White man would hire a younger White man, introduce him at meetings, and signal that the young man would be the older man's successor. Through their "father," these sons and future "fathers" were taught the leadership ropes. They were introduced to powerful people; were mentored about critical issues; were trained in management styles; and were informed about key policies, procedures, and rules. They were taught about the structure of the institution, as well as schooled and socialized in the fine art of career development, planning, succession, and success. Since I was not blessed with this type of career "father," I realized that I needed to create a different paradigm for myself. The solution for me was finding what Collins (2000) refers to as "mothers," "sisters," and "othermothers."

Over time, I found a valuable core of othermothers—amazing Black women within and outside of the university. Some were secretaries; some were in entry-level positions; some were managers; some were at Vanderbilt; some were in churches; and some were part of civic organizations. Some were older and some were younger. These women became my family and my community. We loved each other. We helped each other. We comforted each other; we prayed for each other; we took trips together; we shared meals together; and we went to movies together. We watched and cared for each other's children. Most important, we gave each other a sacred space for our voices. We listened to each other; we laughed together; and we talked. We talked about Black people and White people; we talked about God; we talked about the Bible; and we talked about work. We talked about our children; we talked about our marriages; we talked about our families; and we talked about ourselves and our lives. We talked about how to survive racism, sexism, and oppression with grace, dignity, and wisdom.

That was a big lesson. To be a successful leader as a Black woman, mothers and sisters are critical. While it is important to make and maintain relationships with White men and women, as well as Black men, (especially those with power) it is vital to find mothers and sisters. Mothers and sisters create a space for wisdom. One of my "mothers" was in human resources and gave me some of the best advice I have ever received related to my career. She told me that Black women are too loyal and that we stay too long. Although it took me a while to understand what she meant, years later I realized that Black women often get too comfortable and are afraid to take risks. It is only in taking risks that we can advance. Heeding her advice and realizing that I had spent eight years at Vanderbilt, I began to think about moving on, taking a risk, and returning back to the circle. I learned that leaders often have to leave to have greater access to leadership opportunities.

After much contemplation, assessment, and reflection about foundations and values, our family decided to return to central Illinois to be closer to my mother who was now alone after the death of my father. As the only surviving grandparent, my husband and I felt a responsibility to nurture the grandmother relationship for our children. So, for me, it was a return to my foundation and back again to the circle. I believe, though, that my spirit knew I would return to Illinois one day because I took two bar exams when I finished law school. I took the Tennessee and Illinois exams and became licensed in both states. Being licensed in Illinois was a key asset in securing my next leadership opportunity at the University of Illinois at Champaign-Urbana—forty-five minutes from my mother in Bloomington.

The Return to Illinois

I was hired as an Assistant Provost and Associate Director of the Office of Equal Opportunity and Access. I took a risk in accepting the position that came with a substantial pay cut and a lower reporting relationship. Yet, I learned another valuable lesson. The ladder of leadership success is not always vertical and can zigzag before it ascends. By grace, I was surrounded by three Black senior administrators. With a dual reporting line, my two immediate supervisors were Black women. One was an assistant chancellor who reported to an associate chancellor, an African American man. The other was an associate provost. These were African Americans who had been at the University for at least 20 years and became adept at navigating the place, the people, and the politics.

Illinois gave me the opportunity to have two Black "mothers" who played the role of the "fathers" that I had seen at Vanderbilt. These "mothers" took time to mentor me and help me develop skills to be successful. Although Vanderbilt was an elite private institution, Illinois was an elite public institution. I needed to learn the culture, values, structure, and operations of my new setting. I was provided with a screen of protection as an associate director to learn the people, the processes, and the power dynamics of the institution. I learned about systems and technology, as well as budgets and finances. Within four years, the Director retired and I was promoted to Assistant Chancellor and Director. I had the opportunity to work with the African American male Associate Chancellor—a position that had always been held by Black men. Upon his retirement, I was promoted to Associate Chancellor. My advancement to a senior administrative leadership role at a Big Ten institution would not have happened if it were not for the Black professional "family" that guided me.

The return to Illinois was not easy. It was extremely stressful on my marriage, as my husband was initially not employed, my children had lost their community of friends, and I missed my professional mothers, sisters, and othermothers tremendously. There was not enough time for long-distance calls and the loneliness was profound. I missed Nashville tremendously. It had been a home and haven for almost 15 years. I entered a very sad space and place of silence. As painful as the silence was, I realize now that the silence was a blessing. Sometimes we need to create spaces of silence as part of our leadership journey, for there is often an unrecognized and unanticipated power in silence.

In the quiet, almost mind-numbing silence of Illinois, I began to assess my life and the circle. When I arrived in Champaign, I began the tedious task of unpacking boxes. I realized that I had carried my dissertation and degrees around in boxes that had moved to five different homes for over 15 years. There was something in those boxes that merited attention. The quietness of the cornfields one day allowed me to reflect and look through those boxes in the basement. As

I looked through newspaper articles, magazines, journal articles, and legal briefs from Detroit, I felt energy in the boxes and papers. It was as if the Black girls in Detroit were saying "tell my story." At the same time, I recognized that it was not only the Black women in Detroit saying "tell my story," it was me telling myself to tell my story. What was my story?

My story was my journey to find and define myself as a Black woman and as a leader. It was my journey to minimize the invisibility I had felt all my life—first as a Black girl and then as a Black woman. I had been searching (often in vain) for myself in classrooms, in offices, in conference rooms, and in boardrooms. I needed to create a space, a place, and a voice for myself, for Black girls, and for Black women in scholarship, in society, in academia, and in leadership. I needed to find a conceptual way of legitimizing myself and other Black women.

And so I did. I began a four-year journey to revise the dissertation into a book. I knew I needed to publish to be considered a legitimate leader in higher education. But the question for me was whether I could do it by myself—outside of the classroom, outside of a college, outside of a department, outside of the academy, without any mentors, without a community. I wondered whether I could I create a new way of thinking about law; about justice; about equality; about Black people. The challenge of the publishing journey was not just conceptual. Not only did I have to create the work, I needed to get others to see its value in order to get published. Yet, how would I get published? Once again, I was alone. Where was the network? Where were the mentors? Where were the mothers? Where were the leaders who could help me? I was scared and insecure. The ability to fight against insecurity and to conquer fear is important for leaders. I believe the strongest asset for a leader is the ability to act, to get started, and to have the persistence and discipline to see a project through to the end.

I made a decision to act and to start on the publishing journey. It was a slow journey—often a word, a sentence, and a paragraph at a time. As I began working on the book, I started writing, reading, and researching. I read about interdisciplinary work; multidisciplinary work; and transdisciplinary work. I read about Black feminism; critical race theory; and critical race feminism. As I read, I started to write about my ideas, and in the process, I saw connections: connections between theories and methodologies, connections between theories and action, and connections between disciplines. I saw issues of power and power domains (Collins, 2000); I saw interlocking social systems and structures of law and education. In the process of seeing, I was able to begin creating and conceptualized the Transdisciplinary Applied Social Justice (TASJ©) Model.

TASJ is a "theoretical and methodological tool for engaging in transdisciplinary applied social justice research and practice" (Pratt-Clarke, 2010, p. 39). It is a tool that facilitates activism. My vision was to develop a social justice tool that reflected the power of transdisciplinarity—"the use of multiple theories, methods, approaches, frameworks, and disciplines to understand, strategize, and implement transformative initiatives in society" (Pratt-Clarke, 2010, p. 19). TASJ is "the application of concepts, theories, and methodologies from multiple academic disciplines to social problems with the goal of addressing injustice in society and improving the experiences of marginalized individuals and groups" (p. 27). TASJ's goal centers upon understanding the manner in which the life experiences of individuals and groups are entangled and influenced by the operation of systems of power, with the objective of designing effective intervention strategies. TASJ asks the following questions: "What is the social problem? What form should social justice activism take? What is the best strategy to ensure success? With what theory and with what argument can transformative change be achieved? On which institutions, individuals, and/or domains should the strategy focus?" (p. 39).

A tool for leaders, TASJ enables them to recognize the roles and influences of power domains (Collins, 2000) on marginalized, oppressed, and subordinate groups based on their socially constructed and intersecting race, class, and gender statuses. TASJ serves as an important tool as it emphasizes: people in the interpersonal domain; policies, practices, and procedures in the disciplinary domain (many of which are subtle and unspoken); the structure of departments, programs, and colleges in the structural domain; and ideas, attitudes, and beliefs in the hegemonic domain. Through the operation of policies, practices, and procedures within large-scale social structures, such as the media, the legal system, and educational institutions, the hegemonic ideologies of racism, sexism, patriarchy, classism, and nationalism can be institutionalized and perpetuated. Using TASJ can empower leaders to engage in transformative strategic initiatives that address oppression, injustice, and inequality.

Social justice activism and leadership seeks to directly or indirectly improve individual lives through strategic initiatives that impact the domains of power. The TASJ model reveals that "understanding how our lives are governed, not primarily by individuals, but more powerfully by institutions, conceptual schemes, and their 'texts'. . . is crucial for designing effective projects of social transformation" (Harding & Norberg, 2005, p. 2011; Pratt-Clarke, 2010, p. 41). The model involves the fundamental components of society: power, people, systems, and the relationship among these entities. This understanding is critical for successful leadership in higher education administration.

Being in Champaign created a space and place that enabled me to find my voice: a voice to talk and write about issues of race, class, and gender; a voice to talk and write about the education system and the legal system; and a voice to talk about racism, sexism, feminism, and classism. The voice enabled me to write about Black women and Black girls using literature; using sociology; using political science; using critical race scholarship; using critical race feminism; using discourse analysis; using social movement theory; and using Black feminism.

The voice includes narrative. It is a voice that is literary and scholarly, a voice that informs social justice activism, and a voice that can create equal opportunity for women and girls, particularly those of color. The publication of *Critical Race, Feminism, and Education: A Social Justice Model* (Pratt-Clarke, 2010) was a significant milestone for me in becoming a leader and scholar-activist in higher education.

Being a Scholar-Activist and Leader

Effective leaders with a passion for social change must be scholars and activists. Scholar-activists have a responsibility to "engage in discourse analysis; deconstruct the discourse; and to strategically determine the most effective method of intervention to have a transformative impact on the lives of individuals" (Pratt-Clarke, 2010, p. 41). Since social justice involves "disrupting and subverting arrangements that promote marginalization and exclusionary processes" (Theoharis, 2007, pp. 222–23), activism must first analyze and deconstruct arrangements to understand how to address marginalization and exclusionary processes. After analysis of the problem concludes, the second step centers upon developing a strategy for "disrupting and subverting." The final step focuses upon implementation.

Transformative change in higher education requires scholars to be activists and activists to be scholars. It requires the efforts of informed scholars who translate scholarship into action within higher education leadership positions. Social justice scholar-activists have a responsibility to engage in discourse analysis; to deconstruct the discourse; and to strategically determine the most effective method of intervention to have a transformative impact on the lives of individuals (Pratt-Clarke, 2010, p. 26). In the context of higher education, these skills are particularly critical since the institution, by nature, is designed to be impervious and adverse to change; is steeped in tradition; comfortable with the status quo; and loath to make difficult decisions. An effective senior administrator, especially a minority female at a predominantly White male institution, must serve as an instrument and voice for institutional change.

Institutional transformative change (particularly in the areas of social justice initiatives in higher education administration, such as equal employment opportunity, affirmative action, and diversity) requires the voice of an advocate. Periods of silence offer time for assessment, but they must ultimately produce sound. Similarly, theories and methodologies prove valuable for academic journals, but are ineffective without praxis. Leaders must conceive and conceptualize transformative ideas and move ideas into action. Being a leader is ultimately about being a follower of a call and a conviction. It requires the ability to encourage and persuade others to follow the call and not the leader, for the call is eternal and the leader is mortal. Following a leader alone does not lead to sustained transformation unless the leader and those who follow pursue a collective call.

For scholar-activists, the call is the call for equality; the call for justice; the call for validation; the call for legitimacy; and the call for righteousness. Scholar-activists must hear and respond to this call, which is often a hushed yet persistent whisper; a stirring yet subtle breeze. It may be so subtle that it is easily and often ignored or overlooked. Effectively responding to the call requires that the leader be prepared. The preparation includes assessing her own character and being willing to be pruned, refined, sifted, and sieved during the journey so that the call shines through her character as brightly as a light. It is this light that guides others. It is the light that shines eternally, leading and guiding others in their journeys and responses to a call.

Scholar-activists must have passion, intertwined with persistence and patience. They must be disciplined, yet not rigid and inflexible. They must engage in self-reflection. They must be visionary, yet able to balance idealism with realism. They must respond in ways that are strategic, analytic, and with controlled emotion. Scholar-activists must also be resilient and able to accept criticism. Most important, they must be unafraid to speak and to give voice to justice and equality in all settings and circumstances. They must be willing to be the consciousness that eradicates the silent, and often unconscious, operation of indifference that enables and facilitates the persistence of oppression.

In my role at the University of Illinois as an Associate Chancellor, I advise and counsel the Chancellor in critical decisions. Now, rather than just being in the room as a "secretary," I am often "at the table" or at the head of the table. I still teach in the classroom; I still write; and I still publish. As I reflected back on my journey as a Black woman, mother, wife, daughter, feminist, and scholar-activist, I recognized the many lessons I learned—the role of foundations; the importance of circles; the willingness to take risks; the necessity of othermothers; the value of silence; and the power of voice. These lessons have made a difference on my journey. By lifting as we climb, these lessons can make a difference for other scholar-activists seeking to be instruments for social justice and who seek to help create a more just and fair community for all.

Bibliography

Baldwin, J. (1963). *The fire next time*. New York: Dial Press.

Barnett-Johnson, K. R. (2010, August). Moving heaven and earth: Black women in admin searches. *Women in Higher Education, 19*(8), 13–14.

Collins, P. (1991 [2000]). *Black feminist thought: Knowledge, consciousness and the politics of empowerment*. New York: Routledge.

DiGeorgio-Lutz, J. (Ed.). (2002). *Women in higher education: Empowering change*. Westport, CT: Praeger Publishers.

Ellison, R. (1952). *Invisible man.* New York: Random House.

Faulkner, W. (1929). *The sound and the fury.* New York: J. Cape & H. Smith.

Faulkner, W. (1930). *As I lay dying.* New York: J. Cape & H. Smith.

Faulkner, W. (1932). *Light in August.* New York: H. Smith and R. Haas.

Faulkner, W. (1936). *Absalom, Absalom!* New York: Random House.

Faulkner, W. (1948). *Intruder in the dust.* New York: Random House.

Gonzalez, C. (2010). Leadership, diversity, and succession planning in academia. Research & Occasional Paper Series. *Center for Studies in Higher Education, 8,* 10.

Harding, S., & Norberg, K. (2005). New feminist approaches to social science methodologies: An introduction. *Signs Journal of Women in Culture and Society, 30*(4), 2009–2015. Retrieved from http://www.journals.uchicago.edu/doi/abs/10.1086/428420

Howard-Vital, M. R., & Morgan, R. (1993). African-American women and mentoring. ERIC Document Reproduction Service No. ED360425.

Jenifer, F. (2005). Minorities and women in higher education and the role of mentoring in their advancement. Retrieved April 23, 2011, from http://www.utsystem.edu/aca/files/Mentorship.pdf.

Mather, M., & Adams, D. (2007). *The crossover in female-male college enrollment rates.* Washington, DC: Population Reference Bureau. Retrieved April 23, 2011, from http://www.prb.org/Articles/2007/CrossoverinFemaleMaleCollegeEnrollmentRates.aspx

Morrison, T. (1970). *The bluest eye.* New York: Holt Rinehart & Winston.

Murrell, A., Crosby, F., & Ely, R. (Eds.). (1999). *Mentoring dilemmas: Developmental relationships within multicultural organizations.* Mahwah, NJ: Lawrence Erlbaum Associates.

National Association of Colored Women. (2011). In *Encyclopædia Britannica.* Retrieved April 23, 2011, from http://www.britannica.com/EBchecked/topic/404462/National-Association-of-Colored-Women.

Naylor, G. (1982). *Women of Brewster Place.* New York: Viking Press.

Pratt, M. A. E. (1997). Where are the Black girls?: The marginalization of Black females in the single-sex school debate in Detroit. Doctoral dissertation. Vanderbilt University, Nashville, TN. *Dissertation Abstracts International:* Section A. 58(03), 1122.

Pratt-Clarke, M. (2010). *Critical race, feminism, and education: A social justice model.* New York: Palgrave Macmillan.

Rothenberg, P. (2007). *Race, class and gender in the United Sates: An integrated study.* (7th ed). New York: Worth Publishers.

Smith, P. (2000). Failing to mentor Sapphire: The actionability of blocking Black women from initiating mentoring relationships. *UCLA Women's Law Journal, 10*(2), 701.

Theoharis, G. (2007). Social justice educational leaders and resistance: Toward a theory of social justice leadership. *Educational Administration Quarterly, 43*(2), 221–258.

Trix, F., & Psenka, C. (2003). Exploring the color of glass: Letters of recommendation for female and male medical faculty. *Discourse Society, 14,*191–220.

Walker, A. (1982). *The color purple.* New York: Harcourt, Brace Jovanovich.

X, M. (1965). *The autobiography of Malcolm X.* New York: Grove Press.

Part Three

Leadership and Self-care among Black Women

Chapter Twelve

The "Double Outsider's" Challenges to Professional Success

Implications for Black Women's Leadership

Keisha Edwards Tassie and Sonja M. Brown Givens

According to an article in *Black Enterprise* magazine, "African American women are not advancing as far in corporate America as their White, Asian, and Latina counterparts" (Brown, 2004). In 2004, African American women represented only 1.1% of corporate officers in Fortune 500 companies (Catalyst survey, 2004). Unfortunately, recent statistics show little change in the professional upward mobility of African American women in corporate America—especially in the context of a global economic recession where minorities tend to feel the impact of hard economic times more severely than Whites.

According to the 2004 Catalyst survey, Advancing African American Women in the Workplace: What Managers Need to Know, the biggest barriers professional African American women face are negative, race-based stereotypes; more frequent questioning of their credibility and authority; and a lack of institutional support. Results indicated that 43% of Black women surveyed cited lack of an influential sponsor/mentor, 36% cited lack of informal networks, 31% cited lack of company role models of the same racial/ethnic group, and 29% cited lack of high-visibility projects as barriers to a "great extent/very great extent." Further, according to Catalyst (a nonprofit, women's research and advisory firm) the intersection of race and gender for Black women creates a "double outsider" experience not shared by White women or Black men in corporate America. African American women reported "exclusion from informal networks and conflicted relationships with White women" as additional challenges they faced on a regular basis (p.

46). Additionally, 32% of African American women surveyed believed they were perceived by their White colleagues as "underqualified" and/or that their White colleagues questioned their credibility, compared to that belief held by Latinas and Asian women, at 22% and 14%, respectively.

The report concludes by stating "while approximately 75% of Fortune 500 companies have formal diversity programs, only 33% of the women surveyed believe these programs effectively create supportive environments and only 36% say these programs foster respect for their cultural background" (p. 46). The Catalyst survey's findings were based on a quantitative study of African American women at Fortune 1000 companies and a qualitative study of focus groups of entry- and mid-level African American women, more than 50% of whom hold a graduate degree.

In a 2005 article in *Black Enterprise* magazine titled "Devalued by Diversity," Alleyne states that "the meaning of diversity over the last few decades has morphed from an altruistic opportunity to right the ills against Black Americans in this country to a business imperative that is all-embracing of other cultures, walks of life, and sexual preferences. In many cases, the broad definition has left African Americans in corporate America feeling marginalized" (p. 53). We argue that those feelings of alienation are felt to a stronger degree by Black women because their unique, ascriptive positioning in corporate America does not automatically grant them the power advantage experienced by those who have access to the 'men's club' nor the power advantage held by Whites in corporate America.

Alleyne notes that while roughly 75% of the largest Fortune 500 companies have developed some sort of diversity initiative, many continue to struggle with implementation and success. According to the Catalyst survey (2004), Black women "judge diversity policies as having limited benefits and are pessimistic about their own opportunities to advance to senior management" (p. 53). Marlon D. Cousin, managing partner of the Marquin Group, an executive search firm specializing in diverse talent, believes that "companies do a poor job of managing diversity because they don't hold employees accountable" (p. 53). Rather, Cousin believes that companies should be managing diversity by making it a part of performance appraisals, or tying it to compensation, or how employees are rated. Until companies and their employees are held accountable for inequalities in the workplace, Black women will continue to be challenged by an imbalanced work environment.

Standpoint Theory

According to Patricia Hill Collins (1990, 2000), scholar of Black feminist thought, standpoint theory refers to "historically shared, group-based experiences" (p. 375). She goes on to explain that "groups have a degree of permanence over time such that group realities transcend individual experiences" (p. 375). As noted earlier, the 'reality' of the "double outsider" existence of Black women in the workplace illustrates this group's standpoint. And while there are certainly accounts of Black women who have risen to professional success in corporate America or through entrepreneurial business without significant race-based or gender-based challenge, the overall experience of this group is more in line with the results of the previously mentioned Catalyst survey.

In analyzing the experiences of Black women, standpoint theory is not adequately discussed without attention to Black feminist thought. "Black feminist thought consists of ideas produced by Black women that clarify a standpoint of and for Black women" (Collins, 1986, p. 16). Assumptions underlying Collins' definition of Black feminist thought include: (1) although recorded by others, Black feminist thought is produced by Black women; (2) Black women possess a unique standpoint on, or perspective of, their experiences and there will be commonalities shared by Black women as a group; (3) universal themes included in the Black women's standpoint may be experienced and expressed differently by distinct groups of Black women based on age, region, sexuality, and class; and (4) while a Black women's standpoint exists, its contours may not be clear to Black women themselves (Collins, 1990, 2000). Black feminist thought serves as a guide for both the commonalities and distinctions of Black women's experiences in the workplace.

There are three key themes of Black feminist thought that offer light to the sometimes dark, lonely experiences of professional Black women. The first theme is "self-definition and self-valuation"—described by Collins (1986) as an affirmation of self and a challenge to the "political knowledge-validation process that has resulted in externally-defined, stereotypical images of Afro-American womanhood" (p. 16). Collins offers two reasons why defining one's self and valuing one's self are significant; first, a Black woman who defines and values herself in the face of established, widely known stereotypes allows her to resist the dehumanization of systems of domination. A Black female professional with the ability to define and position herself according to her prerogative and work ethic rather than through the decisions of others based on ascriptive characteristics gains not only professionally, but emotionally as well. In fact, Collins notes that self-definition and self-valuation are necessary for Black female survival.

The second theme discusses the interlocking nature of race, gender, and class oppression. Because Black women are at the intersection of multiple sources of domination, Black feminist thought focuses on this interlocking nature of Black womanhood in the contexts of class (and sexuality, region, etc.) rather than attempting to understand these elements individually. As mentioned previously, Black female professionals are positioned in the workplace without the resources naturally available to both their male and White counterparts.

The third theme involves redefining and explaining the importance of Black women's culture. In exploring this culture, ways in which Black women develop and pass on mechanisms and motivations for coping with their unique cultural position are discovered. Further, a greater understanding of self-definition and self-valuation result from this cultural exploration as well. Collins (1986) states, "there is no monolithic Black women's culture—rather, there are socially-constructed Black women's cultures that collectively form Black women's culture" (p. 22). Professional Black women understanding the nuances of Black women's culture is a necessary element for building stronger connections within the group in order to endure the setbacks, stagnation, and alienation experienced in the workplace, as well as for advancing professionally.

Coping Strategies

Networking. While some of the professional and emotional challenges experienced by Black women in the workplace are clear, suggestions for coping with these challenges can be found in the literature. For example, Elliott & Smith (2004) found that Black women, compared to Latino and White women, were less affected by perceived workplace discrimination due to their effective use of networking strategies to 'offset' the disadvantageous position of being both Black and female in a workplace environment. In fact, the results of their study were contrary to the prediction that networking strategies would be least effective for Black women due to the intersection of both race and gender discrimination for them, stating that networking strategies were "increasingly effective among Black women, relative to White men, for moving into positions of higher power" (p. 379). Results from this study showed that Black women's opportunity to rise from worker to supervisor increased by 39% when they effectively utilized network assistance, and their opportunity to advance from supervisor to manager increased by 500% when effectively negotiating network assistance. Indeed, for Black women, networking seems to be an effective strategy for coping with and responding to workplace discrimination.

Outside the office. In an article from *Essence Magazine*, "Feeling Good Being the 'Only' Sister" (1998), family psychologist Dr. Brenda Wade notes that being the only Black woman in a professional setting can be stressful and exhausting; leading to overwork, alienation, and depression. Dr. Wade suggests taking the following steps to cope:

(1) Join a Black professional group for encouragement. (2) Get involved in a Black civic organization such as the local NAACP or National Coalition of 100 Black Women. (3) Stay grounded by filling your office with cultural paintings,

symbols or books. (4) Maintain a connection with a nearby community church or mosque. (5) Preserve a balance between your inner and outer life through daily meditation, prayer and books. (p. 40)

Connection to one's culture. In a 1996 interview for *Essence Magazine*, Dr. Ella L.J. Edmondson Bell, a professor of organizational management at University of North Carolina Charlotte, and Dr. Patricia Reid-Merritt, a professor of social work and African American studies at Richard Stockton College in Pomona, New Jersey, were asked about the results of their study of Black women senior managers in the corporate sector. Both researchers stated that their motivation for conducting the study came from the 'invisibility' of Black professional women in the corporate arena. Dr. Bell notes that "when you read about corporate women, it's usually referring to White women." Various interesting findings from their study were discussed; Drs. Bell and Reid-Merritt mention the following:

> The most successful Black women are the ones who have kept their connections to their Black community strong/'Rooted in their history;' really successful Black women were true to themselves as Black people; found their bicultural mode; [engaged in] networking; could switch between their corporate roles and their roles as Black women as the situation demanded, and reach out to other people that way; inherited inner strength; [emphasized] collectivity and sense of spirituality; and they were strategic—capitalizing on [their] difference. (p. 62)

METHOD

Participants
One hundred African American women from various backgrounds were solicited for participation in this study. A convenience sample was used to contact potential volunteers through email correspondence, where they were instructed about how to access the online survey. These volunteers were then asked to share the survey link with other Black women in their social network. The women were quite diverse in age. Fifteen percent were 20–29 years of age, thirty-five percent between 30–39, twenty-eight percent between 40–49, sixteen percent between 50–59, and seven percent of the sample was over 59 years of age. Most participants (96%) had some college education and seventy-eight percent held college degrees.

Independent Variables
Standpoint Identity. Participants were instructed to complete an Identity Measure adapted from Egan and Perry's (2001) Gender Identity multidimensional measure of identity and psychosocial adjustment. The modified measure included 23 Likert-type items used to assess participant perceptions of their own Typicality, Contentedness, Felt Conformity Pressure, and Intergroup Bias as African Ameri-

can women. Sample items include "I believe that I am an average woman of color at my workplace (typicality)," "I feel annoyed that I'm supposed to do certain things just because I'm a woman of color (contentedness)," "The women of color I know would be upset if I developed close friendships with White women (felt conformity pressure)," "I think that people of color are more truthful than Whites (intergroup bias)." Reported Alpha reliabilities for the original Gender Identity scales are .78 (Typicality), .79 (Contentedness), .92 (Felt Conformity Pressure), and .73 (Intergroup Bias).

Perceived experiences with Racial Discrimination. The online survey also included items from the Schedule of Racist Events [Lifetime] (Landrine & Klonoff, 1996), which was designed to assess "the frequency with which African Americans have experienced specific racist events (types of racial discrimination) (p. 148)." Items used in this study asked participants to report their perceived experiences with specific acts of racial discrimination over their lifetime. The measure consisted of 17 Likert-type items ranging from 1 (The event happened once in a while [less than 10% of the time]) to 7 (The event happened almost all of the time [more than 70% of the time]). Sample items include "Have you been treated unfairly by your co-workers or colleagues because you are a woman of color?" "Have people failed to show you the respect that you deserve because you are a woman of color?" "Have you been called a racist name like nigger, chink, spick, or other names?" The reported Alpha reliability for the Lifetime SRE is .95.

Anti-White attitudes. The final scale included in the survey consisted of items from the Johnson-Lecci Scale (2003), a 38-item "multicomponent self-report measure of anti-White attitudes held among Blacks" that was shown to reliably "predict the interpretations of ambiguously racist scenarios (i.e., perceived racism)" (p. 299). Eighteen Likert-type items from the scale were adapted and used to assess mean ratings for participants' ingroup directed stigmatization, outgroup directed negative beliefs, negative views toward ingroup-outgroup relations, and their own negative verbal expressions toward Whites. Sample items include "I believe that most Whites really believe that Blacks are generally inferior," "I consider myself to be racist toward Whites," "I have referred to mixed couples as sell-outs," and "I have referred to a White person as a honkey." The reported Alpha reliability for the complete Johnson-Lecci measure is .79.

Items from each of these scales were adapted to create a fifty-seven-item measure of standpoint dimensions (e.g., Race typicality) associated with participants' choice(s) of coping strategies to manage a presented act of workplace discrimination.

Dependent Variables

Coping responses. After completing three demographic measures for age, race, and education participants were instructed to read the following scenario and consider how they would respond if it were a real situation for them:

> You are becoming increasingly frustrated with the behavior of your supervisor, Todd. Since your first day with the company he seems to suggest that you were hired as part of the company's efforts to diversify its staff, in accordance with its recently adopted strategic diversity plan. He even introduced you as his "affirmative action ticket" during your first official staff meeting with colleagues from your work team. Your department has just completed employee performance evaluations for the year, and you've discovered that Todd has written a negative appraisal of your job performance. In his review he specifically mentioned your absence from an important staff meeting as the motivation for his negative review. However, you know that three other members of your work team were also absent from the meeting and that none of them received negative performance appraisals for the year. Furthermore, their absence from the staff meeting was not mentioned as criteria in their evaluations.

The scenario was adapted from a cross-section of real experiences with workplace discrimination reported in a narrative analysis of six African American women who abruptly ended their employment as university professors, business managers, and office assistants without any prospects for future employment in place (Pennington, 1999). Afterward, participants completed a twenty-eight-item measure designed to assess the various strategies participants might employ to manage the tensions and emotions of the situation presented in the scenario. These items were adapted from the brief COPE inventory which identifies 14 scales used to measure how individuals deal with emotionally tense experiences (Carver, 1997). Each item was measured using a 7–point Likert scale ranging from 1 (strongly disagree) to 7 (strongly agree) to assess participant projections of response to the scenario with each of the coping types (e.g., acceptance, humor, religion). Sample items included the following, "I would pray or meditate," "I would do something to think about it less, such as going to the movies or watching TV," "I would use alcohol or drugs to help me get through it," "I would get help from other people." Reported alpha reliabilities for these scales range from poor (.50) to strong (.90) (Carver, 1997). Twenty-eight COPE items were adapted and administered as part of the online survey. These items were used to assess participant projections about how they would respond to the workplace discrimination scenario.

RESULTS

Data Reduction: Standpoint Factors. The final factors and loadings for participant standpoint items (e.g., anti-White bias, group typicality) were determined by conducting exploratory factor analyses with a varimax rotation. All of the final factors have eigenvalues greater than one and factor loadings of .60 or higher on one item and .40 or lower on all other factors. Thirteen items were excluded from the analyses because they were complex across multiple factors. Six factors emerged, accounting for 65.8% of the variance in the data. The first factor was comprised of fourteen items associated with participant's reported experiences with direct acts of racial discrimination at some point in their lives (e.g., been called a racist name, treated unfairly by co-workers/strangers/people in service jobs; α = .94). A second factor included eight items associated with participants' self-reported in-group stigmatization/discriminatory expectations (e.g., most Whites would love to return to a time in which people of color had no civil rights, really believe that people of color are genetically inferior, would harm people of color if they could get away with it; α = .95). The third factor was made up of seven items associated with out-group directed negative beliefs (e.g., I think people of color are more honest/truthful/creative/friendly than Whites; α = .91). Factor four consisted of four items associated with participant perceptions of their own group typicality as women of color (e.g., I believe that I am a typical woman of color, the things I do in my spare time are similar to what most women of color like to do, the kinds of things I'm good at are similar to the kinds of things most women of color are good at; α = 84). Factor five also consisted of four items which are associated with race contentedness (e.g., I feel annoyed that I'm supposed to do certain things just because I'm a woman of color, cheated that there are some things I'm not supposed to do just because I'm a woman of color; α = .82). The sixth, and final standpoint factor consisted of five items associated with participants' self-reported negative verbal expressions toward Whites (e.g., I have referred to Whites as "crackers," have spoken negatively to Whites without concern for their feelings, have called a White person a "redneck"; α = .86) Final factors were created by summing the items and dividing by the total number of items.

Data Reduction: Coping Factors. Items adapted from the brief COPE were entered into an exploratory factor analysis with varimax rotation. All final factors have eigenvalues greater than one and factor loadings of .60 or higher on one item and .40 or lower on all other factors. Seventeen of the original items were excluded from the analyses because they were either complex across multiple factors, or had poor sub-scale reliability. Five factors emerged, accounting for 64.3% of the variance in the data. The first factor consisted of four items associated with passive responses to the workplace discrimination scenario (e.g., I would try to see the situation in a different light/learn to live with the situation; α = .74). The second was another four-item measure associated with avoidant responses (e.g., I would use alcohol or drugs to help me get through/give up trying to deal with the situation; α = .79). The third factor consisted of two items associated with support-seeking behaviors (I would get help from other people/ get advice or help from other people about what to do; α = .83). The forth factor was comprised of two items associated with religiosity/spirituality (I would pray or meditate/find comfort in my religion or spiritual beliefs; α = .82). The final factor also consisted of two items, and was associated with diversion (I would turn to work or other activities to take my mind off of the situation/do something to think about it less, such as going to the movies or watching TV; α = .70). Final factors were created by summing the items and dividing by the total number of items.

The guiding research question for this exploratory investigation asks to what extent are the women's projected responses to perceived workplace discrimination related to the standpoint factors? The first step of the analysis was to explore the relationship of reported demographics to the available coping responses. We observed two significant relationships.

Age: We observed a positive relationship between the age of the women responding to the online survey and five of the thirteen response options. Age was positively associated with the choice to respond to the workplace scenario by *seeking comfort and understanding from a romantic partner* $F(6, 94)$ = 2.84, p < .05; *doing something to think about it less, such as going to the movies or watching TV* $F(6, 94)$ = 3.75, p < .01; *saying things to let my negative feelings escape* $F(6, 94)$ = 3.12, p < .01; *expressing negative feelings* $F(6, 94)$ = 2.45, p < .05; and *going out for a drink to make myself feel better* $F(6, 94)$ = 2.74, p < .05. In sum, the results for age suggest that older women who find themselves challenged with the situation detailed in the presented scenario are more likely to cope externally and vocally than younger women.

Level of education: Each participant was asked to disclose her highest level of education in the demographic portion of the survey. We analyzed the data on education to determine if participant responses to the scenario would be related to level of education. We found education level to be significantly related to response choices to *seek comfort and understanding from a romantic partner* $F(6, 94)$ = 2.26, p < .05; *do something to think about it less, such as going to the movies or watching TV* $F(6, 94)$ = 2.69, p < .05; *express negative feelings* $F(6, 94)$ = 2.39, p < .05; and *go out for a drink to make myself feel better* $F(6, 94)$ = 2.29, p < .05. These results support the findings for participant age.

In addition, ANOVA tests were conducted in order to assess the relationship between each standpoint factor (e.g., Grouptypicality) and each of the thirteen Likert scales used to assess participant responses to the scenario. Results of the analyses yield the following:

Grouptypicality: The degree to which participants perceived themselves to be a "typical" woman of color was significantly related to their choice to respond to the scenario by stating that they would *take action to make the situation better* for themselves $F(6, 94) = 3.88$, p < .01. In other words, the more similar participants believed themselves to be to other women of color, the more likely they would respond to the scenario with direct action. Grouptypicality was also found to be significantly related to the choice to *seek emotional support from friends and family* in order to process the event $F(6, 94) = 2.72$, p < .05. These findings indicate that social networks and comparisons could play a key role for women of color who must decide how to deal with difficult workplace situations that they perceive to be discriminatory.

Anti-White Bias: Participants self-reported bias toward Whites was found to be significantly related to their choice to cope with the presented scenario attempting to *develop a strategy about what to do* $F(2, 98) = 4.11$, p < .05. Bias against Whites was also found to be significantly related to participants' choice to *express their negative feelings* about the events $F(6, 94) = 2.23$, p < .05. These findings suggest that strong racial bias toward Whites might motivate women of color to be strategic and unabashedly vocal in this type of workplace context.

SRE mean: The number of recalled experiences with perceived racism over the course of participants' lives was found to be significantly related to the decision among participants to either *look for something good in the situation* $F(6, 94) = 2.44$, p < .05; *learn to live with the situation* $F(6, 94) = 2.23$, p < .05; or *express their negative feelings* $F(6, 94) = 2.84$, p < .05. That is to say that the women in the sample who reported few experiences with perceived racism during their lifetime also reported that they would adopt a more passive approach to coping with the scenario than women who recalled many experiences with perceived racism during their lifetime.

Negative group expectations: The degree to which participants expected to be victims of discrimination from Whites was related to their choice of response to the presented scenario. Expectations of discrimination were found to be related to some women's choice to *find comfort in religion or spiritual beliefs* in response to perceived workplace discrimination $F(6, 94) = 2.99$, p = .01. Negative expectations of Whites was also found to be related to the choice of some to *get advice or help from other people about what to do* $F(6, 94) = 2.41$, p < .05. These findings suggest that negative expectations of Whites' behavior may prompt women of color in the workplace to seek external validation of their self-worth and personal agency.

Use of Anti-White Speech: Participant self-reports of using negative verbal expressions against Whites was the final standpoint factor found to be significantly related to response choices to the workplace discrimination scenario. Higher mean scores for anti-White speech were revealed to be related to dismissive response to the scenario. Namely, to *give up attempts to cope with the person* $F(6, 94) = 2.27$, $p < .05$.

Conclusion

As an exploratory study, the results of this research propel, more so than answer, questions about the experiences of Black women in their pursuit of leadership. We found that *difference* was the common factor here, not similarity or groupings as it relates to the choice of coping strategy. We intended this research to simplify and categorize the experiences and coping strategies of Black women in the workplace; however we learned that there is no 'predictive model.' The experiences (both professional and personal) of Black women are unique to the individual.

The question most significant to understanding the results of our study is "Where is this Black woman in her life course?" We refer back to our discussion of Collins' Standpoint Theory. While Standpoint Theory describes "historically shared, group-based" experiences which we know to be true for Black women, Collins acknowledges the inherent differences of experience even within the larger social group. That is, while it is clear that there are common experiences among Black women precisely because they are both Black and female, race and sex cannot adequately explain, nor predict, the behaviors of Black women—to approach this phenomenon from a categorical perspective only serves to essentialize the Black female experience. The individual experience is, itself, a 'standpoint.'

The assumptions of Collins' (1986) Black Feminist Thought further explain the complexity of our results:

Although recorded by others, Black feminist thought is produced by Black women. The significant variation in the responses of our participants illustrates the importance of this assumption. Diversity training models and presumptions about 'effective' mentoring in the professional environment are impotent if based on the experiences of White and/or male counterparts. The shared experiences of Black women that do exist require a new, more inclusive way of thinking about the most effective ways to encourage and support Black women in their pursuit of leadership.

Black women possess a unique standpoint on, or perspective of, their experiences and there will be commonalities shared by Black women as a group. Beyond the historical and contemporary shared experiences of Black women as a result of their race and gender, this study does show that while the coping strategies of Black women are varied based on the individual's standpoint, having had experiences with, and first-hand knowledge of, the challenges in pursuing leadership are common among Black women, although the responses to those challenges vary from Black woman to Black woman.

Universal themes included in the Black women's standpoint may be experienced and expressed differently by distinct groups of Black women based on age, region, sexuality, and class. This assumption speaks to the heart of the results of our study. The responses from our participants clearly indicate that what is most influential in exploring and understanding the coping strategies used by Black women is the individual difference among Black women. In our study, race and gender were not predictive factors; rather, the individual's standpoint directed the participants' strategies for coping with workplace discrimination and challenges to the pursuit of professional leadership.

While a Black women's standpoint exists, its contours may not be clear to Black women themselves. The final assumption speaks more to us, the researchers of this study (who are ourselves professional Black women), than it does to the responses of the participants in the study. As mentioned, we set out to explore the commonalities in the experiences of Black women pursuing professional leadership so that we could create, or work toward creating, a model that would 'simply' explain and predict the types of coping strategies used by categories of Black women. By initially categorizing and collapsing factors in our analyses, we (naively) expected to find rather clean, obvious categories of Black women who would appear to follow a particular path in strategizing and negotiating their pursuit of professional leadership. As we have clearly explained, what we expected to find at the start of this research is not, in fact, what we found. Whether our presumptions were due to socialization or our own individual standpoints, we have learned that a predictive model for the coping strategies employed by Black women when pursuing professional leadership is anything but 'simple' and, in fact, is unrealistic.

The results of this study support the notion that there is more difference *within* races and genders than *between* races and genders. Our results indicate that the circumstances Black women encounter and how they choose to deal with those circumstances are more so communication issues than race and/or gender issues. The responses of our participants indicated that identity, prior experience, and standpoint are far more influential than simply their race or gender. Decisions regarding coping strategies communicate (intentionally or not) the individual's sense of identity, prior experience, and standpoint.

Our intent for this research was to highlight the challenges faced by Black women pursuing leadership in the workplace. Therefore, we feel strongly that future research must investigate the most effective ways in which Black women can be supported professionally. While it is clear that a model predicting the coping strategies of Black women seems to be unrealistic, what we can do is work from the ideals of Black Feminist Thought and Standpoint Theory to explore and share the realities experienced by Black women pursuing leadership. In order to both understand and improve the situation, we must acknowledge that there is not *one* voice to speak to their experiences, but rather many voices of 'truth' that require equal consideration. It is clear that questions in future research must go beyond those that deal with race and gender alone.

Bibliography

Alleyne, S. (2005). Devalued by diversity. *Black Enterprise*, 35(6), 53–58.

Brown, C. M. (2004). Advancing African American women in the workplace. *Black Enterprise*, 34(11), p. 46.

Carver, C. S. (1997). You want to measure coping but your protocol's too long: Consider the brief cope. *International Journal of Behavioral Medicine*, 4(1), 92–100.

Catalyst (2004). Advancing African-American women in the workplace: What managers need to know. Retrieved from http://www.catalyst.org/publication/20/advancing-african-american-women-in-the-workplace-what-managers-need-to-know

Collins, P. H. (1986). Learning from the outsider within: The sociological significance of Black feminist thought. *Social Problems* 33(6), 14–32.

Collins, P. H. (1990, 2000). *Black feminist thought: Knowledge, consciousness, and the politics of empowerment*. New York: Routledge.

Egan, S. K., & Perry, D. G. (2001). Gender identity: A multidimensional analysis with implications for psychosocial adjustment. *Developmental Psychology*, 37, 451–463.

Elliott, J. R., & Smith, R. A. (2004). Race, gender, and workplace power. *American Sociological Review*, 69(3), 365–386.

Johnson, J. D., & Lecci, L. (2003). Assessing anti-White attitudes and predicting perceived racism: The Johnson-Lecci Scale. *Personality and Social Psychology Bulletin*, 29, 299–312.

Landrine, H., & Klonoff, E. A. (1996). The schedule of racist events: A measure of racial discrimination and a study of its negative physical and mental health consequences. *Journal of Black Psychology*, 22(2), 144–168.

Little, B. (1996). Do we have to lose ourselves to succeed in the workplace? *Essence*, 27(6), 62–64.

Pennington, D. L. (1999). *African American women quitting the workplace*. Lewiston, NY: Edwin Mellen Press.

Sanchez-Hucles, J. V., & Davis, D. D. (2010). Women and women of color in leadership: Complexity, identity, and intersectionality. *American Psychologist*, 65(3), 171–181.

Wade, B. (1998). Feeling good being the `only' sister. *Essence*, 28, 11(40), 1–3.

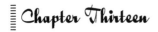

Chapter Thirteen

Working Towards Self-care

The Role of Vicarious Traumatization in Black Female Mental Health Professionals

Nakisha A. Scott

A wealth of evidence suggests that vicarious trauma is not limited to the victim alone (Lerias & Byrne, 2003). Bearing witness to an event, having to listen to explicit accounts of a traumatic event, or even having explicit knowledge of an event have been shown to cause serious, prolonged anxiety in varying degrees (American Psychiatric Association, 2000; Erikkson et al., 2001; Johnsen, Eid, Lovstad, & Michelson, 1997). As a group, Black[1] women hold a long tradition of labor force participation (Feagin, 1970).

According to the Bureau of Labor Statistics of 2010, employed persons in nonagricultural industries by age, sex, race, and Hispanic or Latino ethnicity, African American women make up 3,243,000 in the education and health services field compared to their counterparts who make up 17,212,000. Due to their personal ambitions as well as the many demands made on their time, African American professional women may find it difficult to successfully balance their careers and personal lives.

As a student therapist and an African American woman, I know firsthand the importance of self-care, particularly when dealing with clients that have experienced trauma. Given the importance of self-care, however, I have seen many experienced mental health professionals struggle with adequately providing self-care. Essentially, I believe the reason for this is because Black women in the mental health profession become so involved in their clients' lives that they sometimes

---

1 The terms *Black* and *African American* will be used interchangeably in this chapter.

feel guilty when they do something positive for themselves. As an African American woman in the mental health profession, I sincerely believe that it is important that Black women set proper boundaries and protect themselves from mental erosion. The objective of this chapter is to understand the effects of vicarious traumatization on female African American mental health professionals.

In this chapter, I discuss why this topic is important. Then, I define and provide examples of vicarious victimization. I then highlight the distinction between vicarious victimization and burnout.[2] Following this, I offer key studies regarding Black women in the helping profession and vicarious victimization. I end this chapter with coping strategies from previous scholars regarding how to avoid vicarious victimization, as well as provide personal strategies that have helped me, as a Black female helper, attain career–life balance.

Significance of the Current Topic

First, Black women have become increasingly more visible in the mental health profession. Although many of these women work in the helping "professions"[3] as social workers, therapists, and psychiatrists, more Black women have successfully secured leadership roles as heads or directors of mental health agencies. Although they occupy statuses where the occupants are normally males or White women, their success highlights many contradictions and choices within the human services profession and confronts what our society assumes is normal. Second, the reputation African American women have established as helpers has extended beyond clinics and has reached into their communities. These women have become known for fostering change and willingly implement much of what they have learned in their professional degrees to help the community.

In this respect, many Black women in the helping professions spend time in churches and other community outlets in order to educate and eradicate misconceptions regarding mental health and to promote its many benefits. In addition, these women have created successful careers in the mental health field while effectively responding to the needs of clients. Yet although they are considered successful by their professional peers and other prominent members of the African American community, their route to success usually comes with a great degree of difficulty.

Also, it is critical that Black women in the helping profession proactively protect their personal health and well-being. A large body of research supports that racism and sexism particularly undermine the mental and emotional stability of Black women in the helping professions (Feagin, 1970; Hubert, 2010; St.

---

2 *Burnout* is described more as a result of the general psychological stress of working with difficult clients.

3 The terms *helper, helping professional,* and *mental health professional* will be used interchangeably throughout this chapter.

Jean & Feagin, 1999). Thus, since they are African American *and* female, many of these women, for example, are opposed by clients who do not perceive them as adequately qualified to meet their needs. Additionally, for Black women that have earned their doctorate degrees and have a keen interest in researching mental health–related issues, their research (although sound) is frequently devalued and met with harsh criticism (Gilkes, 1985). Last, but most certainly not least, it is important for Black women in the health professions to become proactive, or leaders, in regard to protecting their mental health. Many mental health professionals work with clients who have experienced traumatic events such as being abused or witnessing abuse, victims of violent and heinous crimes, domestic violence, community or school violence, neglect or traumatic grief.

African American women in the mental health field work long hours and share a commitment to the solution of helping the needs of their clients who have faced traumatic events or other life-altering experiences. As a result, many workers in the helping profession experience many of the negative effects of a session with a client long after the client leaves. This condition not only causes the usual burnout but also vicarious trauma, which is a serious challenge that has been faced by many in the mental health profession and, if left untreated and unresolved, can have severe consequences.

What Is Vicarious Traumatization?

Vicarious traumatization, or VT, occurs when one receives indirect exposure to trauma through a firsthand account or narrative of a traumatic event. This impact comes directly from the traumatized individual's experiences and affects others who are exposed to the event through the victim's explicit accounts of the experience (Lugris, 2000). It affects the cognitive schemas or core beliefs of the professional and the way in which they may change as a result of empathic engagement with the clients and exposure to the traumatic imagery presented by clients. For example, a clinical psychologist who is working with a victim of sexual abuse may have nightmares about the horrific things that they have heard from the client's story. And in turn the helper's sex life begins to diminish, and she begins to emotionally withdraw from her partner. She begins not to trust anyone. Given this form of engagement, albeit through empathic engagement and/or exposure, this may actually cause a disruption in the helping professional's view of self, others, and the world in general.

It is important to note that vicarious traumatization unfolds over time. Rather than being based on the helper's responses to one person, one story, or one situation, it is the cumulative effect of contact with survivors of violence or disaster or people who are struggling. Vicarious trauma happens as a result of empathy. According to Pearlman and Mac Ian (2008), empathy is the ability to identify with another person, to understand and feel another person's pain and joy. It is commonly understood that one cannot work in the mental health field unless he or she is empathetic.

In this regard, it is said that "if your compassion does not include yourself, it is incomplete" and, if not clearly executed it can cause the professional to become too deeply involved. Everyone has his or her own personal history, personality, and life circumstances; however, the mental health professional must always remember to demonstrate a great deal of care in the therapeutic setting. Thus, when the helper cares, she can more easily relate to the experiences, reactions, and feelings of others. In addition, when the helper becomes skilled at caring about the pain of people who have endured traumatic life experiences, she becomes more aware of their own grief, fear, anger, and despair.

Vicarious trauma happens not only because the helper cares about people who have been hurt but also because she oftentimes feels committed or responsible to help. Vicarious trauma occurs when the mental health professional opens her heart and mind to the worst in human experience, namely natural and human-made disasters as well as human cruelty. When the helper witnesses the suffering of people that she cares about and feels responsible to help, over time, this can change how she sees herself, the world, as well as what matters to her. "Thus, VT extends beyond the latter, inasmuch as it is cumulative across clients, manifests outside the therapy hour, and permeates the clinician's life and worldview" (Harrison & Westwood, 2009, p. 205). Although they are used interchangeably, vicarious traumatization and burnout are not the same.

Distinctions between Vicarious Traumatization and Burnout

Burnout can occur to anyone working long term in an emotionally demanding job where there is inadequate support, where the workload is unmanageable, or where the person lacks the training required to do the job effectively (Baird & Jenkins, 2003). The likelihood of burnout is associated more closely with the work environment than with the presence of a trauma history on the part of either the client or the therapist (Jackson, 1999). The effects of burnout can include emotional exhaustion, de-personalization, and reduced feelings of accomplishment (Jackson). Burnout may be preventable on the organizational level, as lower levels are associated with factors such as adequate supervision, communication, and positive feedback, as well as with manageable workload and adequate training.

Vicarious traumatization, on the other hand, is the result of the cumulative effect of traumatic material and is now viewed as an inevitable effect of working with trauma survivors (Jackson, 1999). In the words of Judith Herman: "Trauma is contagious" (1992, p. 140). Unlike burnout, vicarious traumatization is seen as resulting from "the interaction of the clinician's personal characteristics. . . along with the material presented by the client" (Pearlman & Saakvitne, 1995; Cunningham, 2003, p. 452). Greater risk is associated with higher levels of exposure to traumatic material (Cunningham) and to a personal history of trauma on the part of the therapist (Jackson). Interestingly, a number of studies have found that the effects of vicarious traumatization are lower in therapists with more experience in working with trauma than in people new to this work (Cunningham; Jackson; Way, Van-Deusen, Martin, Applegate, & Jandle, 2004).

A higher level of education on the part of clinicians also is associated with fewer symptoms of vicarious trauma (Baird & Jenkins, 2003). Secondary traumatic stress (STS) or what Figley (1995) refers to as *compassion fatigue*, is related to the adverse reactions of helpers who seek to aid trauma survivors. STS is often used interchangeably with VT, although VT implies more permanent rather than temporary stress responses (Stamm, 1999). VT implies that the responses of the mental health professional are influenced by their own unresolved issues (e.g., the lingering impact of the helper's victimization experiences). Essentially, these unresolved issues may lead to avoidance and overidentification with the client and may thus cause the helper to protect the client, become the "champion" of the client, and adopt the role of "rescuer."

Vicarious traumatization occurs only among those who work specifically with trauma survivors, whereas burnout may occur among persons in any profession (McCann & Pearlman, 1990). VT and burnout also differ in that burnout is related to a feeling of being overloaded secondary to client problems of chronicity and complexity, whereas VT reactions are related to specific client traumatic experiences. Thus, it is not the difficult population with which the mental health professionals work but rather the traumatic history of a traumatized population that contributes to VT.

Last, while burnout progresses gradually as a result of emotional exhaustion, VT often has a sudden and abrupt onset of symptoms that may not be detectable in its early stage. Finally, burnout does not lead to the changes in trust, feelings of control, issues of intimacy, esteem needs, safety concerns, and intrusive imagery that are foundational to VT (Rosenbloom, Pratt, & Pearlman, 1995). It is important to note that many mental health professionals working with traumatized populations experience general burnout as well as VT.

Similarities between VT and Burnout

Despite these contrasts, VT and burnout share several characteristics. Both VT and burnout may result in physical symptoms, emotional symptoms, behavioral symptoms, work-related issues, and interpersonal problems. In addition, both VT and burnout are responsible for a decrease in concern and esteem for clients, which often leads to a decline in the quality of client care (Raquepaw & Miller, 1989). Like the construct of burnout, countertransference is also distinct from VT.

Vicarious Traumatization among Black Women Helpers

Causes for VT. Countertransference has been one of the most commonly offered explanations of how VT might occur (e.g., Blair & Ramones, 1996; Pearlman & Saakvitne, 1995a). *Countertransference* refers to a counselor's emotional reaction to a client as a result of the counselor's personal life experiences (Figley, 1995). VT, however, is a direct reaction to traumatic client material and is not a reaction to past personal life experiences. The concept of countertransference in itself is subject to debate about its meaning and components. However, most meanings of countertransference involve the helper experiencing strong responses within the psychotherapeutic relationship in relation to the client. This can include emotional and behavioral responses (both conscious and unconscious) to the patient, the material they bring to therapy, reenactments, and transference (Gabbard, 2001; Norcross, 2001; Pearlman & Saakvitne, 1995a). Herman (1992) reports that traumatic countertransference can include a range of emotional reactions to trauma survivors, such as identifying with their helplessness, grief, personal vulnerability, and rage. Unless these are understood and contained, they could lead to longer-term personal, therapeutic, and professional effects. Blair and Ramones (1996), Pearlman and Saakvitne (1995a), and Wilson and Lindy (1994) offer detailed discussions of countertransference and its relationship to VT.

It is suggested that the two processes are different but interact with each other. Countertransference describes experiences that take place within a therapeutic relationship whereas VT relates to changes taking place in the whole of the therapist's life, including her belief system. Pearlman and Saakvitne (1995a) give detailed discussion to the interaction between the two processes. They posit that unacknowledged countertransference can leave the therapist vulnerable to VT. Likewise, they suggest that VT can leave the therapist vulnerable to stronger countertransference reactions. Processes suggested to be involved in the interaction between VT and countertransference are decreased self-awareness, increased defenses, challenge and change to the therapist's own identity, decreased self-protectiveness, challenges to beliefs, and worldview.

Dynamics that are perhaps more common in therapy with survivors of abuse, such as victim perpetrator abuser–rescuer dynamics (Courtois, 1988), may also render the helper more vulnerable to VT. Helpers whose clients see them in the abuser role may find the associated feelings contradictory to their self-identity and therefore difficult to cope with (Catherall & Lane, 1992). This may be a particular risk for new or unsupervised mental health professionals (Neumann & Gamble, 1995). In summary, while countertransference processes may play a part in leaving the helper vulnerable to VT and vice versa (Pearlman & Saakvitne, 1995a), the two processes are different, with VT not being limited to the therapeutic relationship and being more generalized to affect the helper's life. The differences between countertransference and VT are not always distinct.

Although VT may involve countertransference issues (e.g., the counselor being a trauma survivor), VT is not inherent in, nor does it equate to, countertransference (Figley, 1995). An additional difference between countertransference and VT is that countertransference is specific to the mental health professional's experience during or around counseling sessions, whereas VT effects transcend the session, thus affecting all aspects of counselors' lives. Countertransference and VT, although distinct in conceptualization, are related to one another. There are several negative consequences for the Black female helpers that do not minimize VT in their lives. As the helper experiences increasing levels of VT, the related disruptions in cognitive schemas become part of the counselor's unconscious personal material that may then result in countertransference reactions toward the client (Saakvitne & Pearlman, 1995). These differences among VT, countertransference, and burnout indicate that VT is a unique construct that is worthy of consideration apart from the concepts of burnout and countertransference. The management and prevention of burnout reactions and countertransference have been addressed in the literature (James & Gilliland, 2001), yet these issues are rarely addressed with regard to VT. Thus, in addition to feelings of isolation, the Black female helper can become exhausted, emotionally drained, overwhelmed, overloaded, alienated, distant, detached, and eventually rejected by colleagues. Other feelings that have been associated with VT are feelings of anger and sadness about the client's victimization. VT is often times unreported due to the fear of breaking professional ethical codes of practicing while impaired, which could threaten job security. Cognitively, there is a preoccupation of thoughts of clients outside of their work and/or an overidentification with the client, which crosses ethical boundaries.

As a result, these women begin to question their competence, self-worth, and job satisfaction. If left unchecked, Black women may begin to challenge basic beliefs of safety, trust, esteem, intimacy, and control. In other words there is a feeling of insecurity and dubiousness surrounding safety, trust, esteem, intimacy, and control. It is not always what the client brings into the room that may cause VT, but sometimes it is the mental health worker who has unresolved issues that attribute to VT. Some of these issues include, but are not limited to, a personal victimization history that is unresolved; feelings of shame, guilt, anxiety, or anger; lack of experience—novice workers are at great risk and lack of coping skills impose excessive demands from self, others or work situation; current personal stress experience; and unrealistic expectations around recovery of patients.

Coping Strategies to Avoid Vicarious Traumatization

It is important to be mindful and aware of symptoms before they become out of control. To help Black women helpers take leadership over their mental health,

I provide the following coping strategies. According to Richards and colleagues, learning to create healthy boundaries, which will allow you to maintain respect for your client's ability to heal and to deal with their own issues, is very helpful to avoiding VT. This also means understanding your role as a helper, not a savior. You could also leave time during sessions to process with your clients so that you are not carrying their issues home with you (Richards, Campenni, & Muse-Burke, 2010). Mental health professionals should always access their own feelings, reactivity, and triggers and allow for time to address them.

Provide daily self-care, self-nurturing, balance in life activities and within self, and connection to self, to others, and to something larger (e.g., a purpose) (Richards, Campenni, & Muse-Burke, 2010). Maintain your own personal journal to write your feelings down. Additionally, learn to hold the frame—the frame is the environment of therapy, consisting of the physical, professional, and ethical boundaries of our work. Get therapy—personal therapy for mental health professionals relieves stress, assists coping with a stressful career, and distinguishes the therapist's issues from their clients. This objective view is invaluable, and it's also a tax write-off. Avoid wishful thinking and self-blame. Try to not blame yourself for your clients' progress in therapy, especially if you have done all that you can to help them. Don't take work home. Mental health professionals new to the field tend to carry a 24–hour pager, return phone calls and e-mails all weekend, and are generally on the clock all the time. Find coverage for your emergencies, finish your paperwork at your office, and let home be your sanctuary (Richards, Campenni, & Muse-Burke). Join groups, from Rotary Clubs to Toastmasters to your local association or a consultation group, opportunities for professional connection do exist. When the only people you speak with all day are clients, you become socially isolated (Richards, Campenni, & Muse-Burke). Diversify and engage in multiple activities (e.g., psychotherapy, assessment, research, teaching, supervision, consultation), work with multiple types of patients and problems (e.g., age, ethnicity, disorders), and balance professional responsibilities with personal needs. Appreciate and focus on rewards associated with clinical work that bring you life and vitality (Richards, Campenni, & Muse-Burke).

Look for ways to create a greater sense of freedom and independence in your work. Interpersonal support that could be maintaining a healthy relationship with your partner, family, and friends can serve you well in difficult times. Participating in health, physical, and recreational activities are also fun ways to relieve stress and protect against VT. Have fun with activities that are not work related. You might enjoy an exercise program, vacations and travel, hobbies or other activities, taking time off for no specific purpose, reading, and so on (Richards, Campenni, & Muse-Burke, 2010).

Benefits of Avoidance

As Black women in the mental health profession the benefits of protecting ourselves from VT and other harmful disorders extend well beyond ourselves to our
families and those closest to us. The benefit is an increased vitality in our quality
of life. Quality of life encompasses everything from our health, effectiveness in
our careers, family, and intimate relationships, minds, bodies, and souls. Additionally, and more important, stress is a leading cause of death (Whiting, 2004).
As Black women we have ascended into very great positions of influence in the
mental health profession and we need not let anything cause us to detour from
our paths or stifle us in anyway.

Conclusion

In order for Black female helpers to ameliorate many of the hazards of the mental
health profession, it is imperative that they create and implement an effective self-
care plan. Therefore, self-care is not synonymous with selfishness but is rather a
tool that Black women helpers need to be effective healers. Self-care is an ongoing
process that, to a large degree, depends on the personal history, gender, personality, developmental stage, and life changes of the helper. Thus, the self-place of the
mental health professional should start with a personal reflection of the values
that keep them committed to helping in this way. Ultimately, these values guide
the helper's life and work and make her a more effective helper and leader in the
mental health field.

Bibliography

American Psychiatric Association (2000). *Diagnostic and statistical manual of psychiatric disorders*
    (4th ed.). Washington, DC: APA.

Baird, S., & Jenkins, S. R. (2003). Vicarious traumatization, secondary traumatic stress, and burn-
    out in sexual assault and domestic violence agency staff. *Violence and Victims, 18*(1), 71–86.

Blair, D.T., & Ramones, V.A. (1996). The undertreatment of anxiety: Overcoming the confusion
    and stigma. *Journal of Psychosocial Nursing, 34*(6), 9–18.

Catherall, D., & Lane, C. (1992). Warrior vets. *Journal of Traumatic Stress, 5*(1), 19–36.

Courtois, C. (1988). *Healing the incest wound: Adult survivors in therapy.* New York: Norton.

Courtois, C. (1993). Vicarious traumatization of therapist. *National Centre for PTSD.* http://www.
    ncptsd.org/ treatment/cq/v3/n2/ruzek.html.

Cunningham, M. (2003). Impact of trauma work on social work clinicians: Empirical findings.
    Social Work 48(4), 451–459.

Eriksson, C., Vande Kemp, H., Gorsuch, R., Hoke, S., & Foy, D. (2001). Trauma exposure and
    PTSD symptoms in international relief and development personnel. *Journal of Traumatic
    Stress, 13,* 205–211

Feagin, J. (1970). Black women in the American work force. In Charles V. Willie (Ed.), *The family
    life of Black people* (pp. 23–35). Columbus, Ohio: Merrill.

Figley, C. R. (1995). Compassion fatigue as secondary traumatic stress disorder: An overview. In C. R. Figley (Ed.), *Compassion fatigue: Coping with secondary traumatic stress disorder in those who treat the traumatized* (pp. 1–20). New York: Brunner-Routledge.

Gabbard, G.O. (2001). A contemporary psychoanalytic model of countertransference. *Journal of Clinical Psychology, 57,* 983–991.

Gilkes, C. T. (1982, March 1). Successful rebellious professionals: The Black woman's professional identity and community commitment. *Psychology of Women Quarterly, 6*(3), 289–311.

Harrison, R. L., & Westwood, M. J. (June 01, 2009). Preventing vicarious traumatization of mental health therapists: Identifying protective practices. *Psychotherapy, 46*(2), 203–219.

Hatfield, E., Rapson, R. L., & Le, Y. L. (in press). Primitive emotional contagion: Recent research. In J. Decety & W. Ickes (Eds.), *The social neuroscience of empathy.* Boston: MIT Press.

Herman, J.L. (1992). *Trauma and recovery.* New York: Basic Books.

Hubert, S. J. (2002). *Questions of power: The politics of women's madness narratives.* Newark: University of Delaware Press

Jackson, P. (1999). *Gender differences in impact and cognitions among clinicians providing therapy.* Unpublished master's thesis. University of Manitoba, Winnipeg, Canada.

James, R. K., & Gilliland, B. E. (2001). *Crisis intervention strategies* (4th ed.). Belmont, CA: Brooks/Cole.

Lerias, D., & Byrne, M. K. (2003). Vicarious traumatization: Symptoms and predictors. *Stress and Health, 19,* 129–138. doi: 10.1002/smi.969

Lugris, V. (2000). Vicarious traumatization in therapists: Contributing factors, PTSD symptomatology, and cognitive distortions. *Dissertation Abstracts International: Section B: The Sciences & Engineering, 61,* 5572.

McCann, I.L., & Pearlman, L.A. (1990). Vicarious traumatization: A framework for understanding the psychological Eeffects of working with victims. *Journal of Traumatic Stress, (3),* 1, 131–150.

Neumann, D.A., & Gamble, S.J. (1995). Issues in the professional development of psychotherapists: Counter-transference and vicarious traumatization in the new trauma therapist. *Psychotherapy, 32,* 341–347.

Norcross, J.C. (2001). Introduction: In search of the meaning and utility of countertransference. *Journal of Clinical Psychology, 57,* 981–982.

Pearlman, L. A. (1995). Self-care for trauma therapists: Ameliorating vicarious traumatization. In B. H. Stamm (Ed.), *Secondary traumatic stress: Self-care issues for clinicians, researchers, and educators* (pp. 51–64). Lutherville, MD: Sidran.

Pearlman, L. A., & Mac Ian, P. S. (1993). Vicarious traumatization among trauma therapists: Empirical findings on self-care. *Traumatic Stress Points: News for the International Society for Traumatic Stress Studies, 7*(3), 5.

Pearlman, L. A., & Mac Ian, P. S. (1995). Vicarious traumatization: An empirical study of the effects of trauma work on trauma therapists. *Professional Psychology: Research and Practice, 26,* 558–565.

Pearlman, L. A., & Saakvitne, K. W. (1995a). *Trauma and the therapist: Countertransference and vicarious traumatization in psychotherapy with incest survivors.* New York: Norton.

Pearlman, L. A., & Saakvitne, K. W. (1995b). Treating therapists with vicarious traumatization and secondary traumatic stress disorders. In C. R. Figley (Ed.), *Compassion fatigue: Coping with secondary traumatic stress disorder in those who treat the traumatized* (pp. 150–177). Bristol, PA: Brunner/Mazel.

Raquepaw, J. M., & Miller, R. S. (1989). Psychotherapist burnout: A componential analysis. *Professional Psychology: Research and Practice, 20,* 32–36.

Richards, K. C., Campenni, C. E., & Muse-Burke, J. L. (2010). Self-care and well-being in mental health professionals: The mediating effects of self-awareness and mindfulness. *Journal of Mental Health Counseling, 32*(3), 247–264.

Rosenbloom, D. J., Pratt, A. C., & Pearlman, L. A. (1995). Helpers' responses to trauma work: Understanding and intervening in an organization.

Son, L., Singer, T., & Anglin, T. M. (1998). Violence exposure and emotional trauma as contributors to adolescents' violent behaviours. *Archives of Paediatrics and Adolescent Medicine, 152,* 531–539.

Stamm, H. (1997). Work-related secondary stress. *National Centre for PTSD.* http://www.ncptsd.org/treatment/cq/v3/n2/ruzek.html.

St. Jean, Y., & Feagin, J.R. (1999). *Double burden: Black women and everyday racism.* New York: M.E. Sharpe, Inc.

Way, I., VanDeusan, K.M., Matin, G., Applegate, B., Jandle, D. (2004). Vicarious trauma: A comparison of clinicians who treat survivors of sexual abuse and sexual offenders, *Journal of Interpersonal Violence, 19*(1), 49–71.

Weiss, D., Marmar, C., Metzler, T., & Ronfeldt, H. (1995). Predicting symptomatic distress in emergency services personnel. *Journal of Consulting and Clinical Psychology, 63,* 361–368.

Whiting, S. (2004). Stress can kill you. *The Institute of Nutritional Science.* http://www.healthyinformation.com/Stress.pdf

Wilson, J. P., & Lindy, J.D. (1994). *Countertransference in the treatment of PTSD.* New York: Guilford.

Chapter Fourteen

Honoring the Lateness of the Day

Opportunistic Shifts in the Personal Leadership Sojourns of African American Professional Women at Second Adulthood

S. Alease Ferguson and Toni C. King

I was raised in Harlem and from an early age I learned that anybody can reach their individual goals. My trips to the poles are symbols for everyone's personal goals. My quest transcends, race, age, gender and [is] for all of humanity.
— Barbara Hillary, Nurse, Activist, Publisher, Cancer Survivor, Adventurer and First African American Woman to Reach both Poles at Age 79 (Barbara Hillary Press Release, 2011)

A New Demographic on the Rise

As veteran African American womanist psychologists and organizational consultants we have dedicated our lives to the study of the evolving nature of African American professional women's leadership across the lifespan. Overall this work has created a montage of discovery concerning Black women's lives that includes the cultural nuances surrounding matrilineal transmission of leadership; achievement, self-directed striving and leadership; social and institutional change leadership; organizational socialization and mentoring, self-sacrifice, caregiver leadership; elder financial advocacy; housing piracy prevention; and the toll exacted by family, communal and organizational leadership responsibilities. Fundamentally, our body of work has detailed the African American professional woman's strategies for self-care and mental health self-help as critical modes of reflection and resistance to oppression (King & Ferguson, 1996, 2001, 2006, 2011). Presently, our own maturity, and the maturation of our clientele and their potentialities has given way to investigating the phenomenology of African American womanist leadership at the stage of second adulthood. Developmentally, the second adulthood is that period of human development and radical transformation spanning from age 45 years to the end of life. This developmental stage is divided into two distinct phases of achievement and contribution: (1) the Age of Mastery (45–65) and (2) the Age of Integrity (65–85 and beyond).

The second adulthood is the only phase of human development in contemporary industrialized contexts absent of any time tables of accomplishment or institutionally prescribed skill attainments. Thus, when one reaches this epoch, the sky is the limit! Our intrigue with this phase of life cycle development stems from the realities that it is a highly introspective, active, and uncharted stage. We glimpsed its excitement and wonder somewhere around the age of 50 when we and our colleagues and clientele began to muse about such things as: "What do I do with the rest of my life? I have been interested in so many things and accomplished so many things that I do not know what to do next" or, "Only God knows how much time is left and I want to make the most of it. So how do I set about discovering what to do next? And what are the steps that will get me there?" Another common contemplation is "I have spent so much time looking outward, after others and at my career. When does my turn begin and how do I seize the future?" As clinicians we do know that this period offers those fortunate enough to have achieved maturity a blank canvas with which to chart a pathway to soul satisfaction and joy, if only they are willing to take inventory and script a new path. This period also affords African American professional women leaders additional opportunities for self-exploration in ways that strengthen their individual and collective identities. It can also be a phase where the vestiges of old injuries from race, class, gender oppression, and internalized self-expectations and constraints are released. Experientially, this is a highly individualized passage that involves taking the whole of one's life in hand to reflect, reevaluate, plan, and script a pathway for individuation and self-actualization. If consciously embraced and nurtured, second adulthood is one of the most creative and fulfilling periods of a woman's life.

Baby Boomers and the Second Adulthood

> . . . the bold spirit/
> pays little heed to time. If it grows weary/
> it is through sorrow, not through age.
> —Elizabeth Coatsworth, "Body & Spirit," *Down Half the World* (1968)

In the United States baby boomers comprise the lion's share of individuals now entering second adulthood. Between the years of 2015–2030, it is expected that 65% of all Americans will be over the age of 60. According to Boyd and Bee (2010), boomers represent the first generation of elders likely to enjoy a measure of affluence far exceeding that of their parents and grandparents. Members of this cohort are also likely to be the healthiest, best-educated, and longest-living retirees and largest consumer demographic in history. In the coming decade, African American women between the ages of 45–85+ years are estimated to comprise 17.9% of the total individuals in second adulthood (U.S. Census Bureau, 2006). As members of the baby boomer generation, African American women professionals have likely attained either baccalaureate degrees or professional degrees, traveled widely, prospered financially, and lived what has traditionally been considered a middle-class existence. At the macro-levels their lives have also benefited from the American post–WWII economic boom; the rise and fall of the American middle class; the Civil Rights, women's, gay, and disabilities movements; nutritional, medical, and global technological innovations; and the inauguration of the first African American president of the United States.

In African American communities it is also important to recognize the elasticity and contextual meaning of the term *professional*. While professional in the mainstream sense connotes credentialing and admission to the ranks of a particular profession, in Black communities the term *professional* also refers to those who meet the criteria of living out a "professional ethic" in work, life, and community service *even* when their life circumstances have delimited opportunities for formal educational attainment and credentialing. Thus, in addition to the college-educated, graduate school diploma doctors, lawyers, educators, scientists, MBAs, MSWs, and the like, there have always been those women (and men) who have held their lives and spheres of work to such high standards that they too are considered "professionals." This group we refer to as "life standard professionals" and among them are skilled workers such as welders, nurse's aides, and unskilled laborers such as domestic workers, retail employees, waitresses, childcare workers, cooks, and school bus drivers. There are also a substantive number of small-business owners or entrepreneurial women: shop owners, milliners, daycare owners, seamstresses, beauty shop owners, caterers, sales representatives for pyramid marketing concerns (e.g., the Avon or Tupperware Lady, Mary Kay consultant, etc.) and those engaged in a host of other businesses, trades, and vocations. Other professional Black women might never have worked outside of the home yet may have been the mainstay of churches, PTAs, NAACPs, community fundraisers, city council and civic governments, 4–H clubs and extension centers, or other community development venues. The status of professional accrues to such a group because of their community leadership, standards of excellence in daily life, and strategic pursuit of and deployment of the resources within their reach to achieve personal, familial, and communal uplift. In short, viewing one's identity in a professional light, creating a process in all that one does to project excellence, and attaining the goals and outcomes of professional status have always signified "professional" within Black communities.

Returning to the subject of second adulthood, chronologically it is considered as the third and culminating or "crowning phase" of life. Due to increased longevity, those in second adulthood have the opportunity to enjoy a period of life that is emergent, unscripted, and likely to last for up to 40 years. It is no longer considered as a developmental phase of hastened decline, immobility, or the near terminal phase of life. In this millennium the identities of elders as the depressed and disengaged "rocking chair" generation has been outmoded. It has been replaced by the imagery of the savvy and wizened silver-haired working professional or volunteer, home-owning, sports-car driving, globetrotting, creative, civically engaged, vibrant, attractive, and physically fit human. Today, elder models of vitality and creativity are surfacing in our own families, churches, neighborhoods, AmeriCorps VISTA programs, youth afterschool tutorial programs, neighborhood centers, community recreation centers, marathons, Senior Olympics, and in the media. From the vantage point of race and gender, gone are the traditional patriarchal conceptions of women at the later years as persons of diminished capacity and collapsed or displaced identities due to the loss of spouses, childcare obligations, or career-focused functions.

This acknowledgment of the advantages of second adulthood is not to dismiss the downsides of aging or to romanticize aging and its accompanying life issues. Rather we seek to articulate the marginalized view of Black generativity at mid- and latter-life among Black populations as a basis for heightened contribution and leadership. The distinctive position of Black women professionals in second adulthood stems from prior stages of economic foundation building, personal growth, competency attainment, efficacy of life management, and communal leadership. Black communities have long been aware of models of second adulthood and have celebrated men and women of the community who have "paid their dues," "earned their props," "been the bridge others have come over on," or served as the "giants on whose shoulders we stand." For Black women such celebrations of second adulthood generativity occur through venues of church women's day events honoring church mothers, Living Legacy Awards banquets, vibrant family gatherings for mile-marker decade birthdays beginning at the 50th, and then occurring every five years at the 70th, and the daily gifting of mothers and othermothers at second adulthood as well as the conferring of special titles and terms of endearment common to a particular context or created especially for the honoree: Queen, Ma' Dear, First Lady, Church Mother, Elder, Doc, sister president, and others.

The Latter Adulthood Literature

The nearer I come to the end of my days, the more I am enabled to see that strange thing, a life, and to see it whole.
—Simone de Beauvoir, *All Said and Done* (1974)

Gains in knowledge about latter adulthood can be attributed to the fields of life-span development, adult development, and gerontology. During the midcentury to this first decade of the millennium these modern and dynamic branches of psychology have taught us much about later adulthood. This knowledge points to the interaction between demography, the society's ever-changing social and technological advancements, and the cohort's real-life dilemmas. Overall a series of major paradigms have been set forth to critically influence society's thoughts concerning the life challenges and experiential elements of the aging process. One such enduring paradigm is that of Freudian ego psychologist Erik H. Erik-son's (1962, 1974, 2000) formulation of "integrity versus despair" as the prime psychosocial challenge of latter adulthood. Scholars Bernice Neugarten, Robert Havighurst, and Sheldon Tobin (1961) are credited with robust elaborations of the diversity of elder lifestyles. Their findings affected public policy and changed society's notion of aging as a continuum of varied responses inclusive of the tra-ditional aged, graded "rocking chair" disengagement behaviors to that of the new paradigm affirming an action-oriented elder lifestyle.

Following the trend of the action paradigm of aging is Rabbi Zalman Schachter-Shalomi's psychospiritual framework *From Age-ing to Sage-ing* (1991). This model, also reflected in George E. Valliant's (2002) *Aging Well: Surprising Guideposts to a Happier Life*, has also become a worldwide movement and suggests that latter adulthood is analogous to the autumn and winter seasons of life. In 1996, pop-culture journalist Gail Sheehy, author of the famed *Passages* (1970), penned the *New Passages* (1996)—a highly accessible and practical guide to script-ing a life in second adulthood. Following from Sheehy's work there have been a variety of contributions from women scholars focusing on the issues of identity, individuation, and proactive life change. Examples of such works include feminist scholar-activist Germaine Greer's (1996) *Change*, which identified menopause as a defining event in the lives of women that commonly sparks proactive change and self-revelation. Journalist Abigail Trafford's (2004) *My Time: Making the Most of the Bonus Decades after 50* articulated the notion of "my time" and "the bonus years," followed by anthropologist Mary Catherine Bateson's (2010) notion of "Adulthood II" as the second act or the sequel to the first part of our lives. In this last work Bateson portends that Adulthood II is the most intentional and impro-visational stage characterized by active wisdom and the pursuit of adventure.

With regard to the issues of latter adulthood identity, individuation and the processes of intentional scripting of life going forward and its impact, our direct practice is informed by the works of Erikson's theory of psychosocial development (1962); Cohen's latter adulthood and creativity (2000); Giddens' discussion of the fluid nature of identity in modernity (1991; 1994); and Jungian psychologist Cla-rissa Pinkola Estes' (1992), author of *Women Who Run with the Wolves*, theory of reclaiming the wild or instinctive feminine self. At the bedrock of our perspective is Erik H. Erikson's psychosocial stages of adult development known as integrity versus despair; Gene Cohen's stages of creativity in later adulthood; and Anthony Giddens' (1991, 1994) notions of adult identity as fluid across the lifespan and evidenced by progressive steps toward individuation or liberation at the personal and interpersonal levels. Attention to advancing liberation can be construed as a matter of both identity and life politics. These politics require the turning attention away from collective identity to focus on self-understanding in ways that promote freedom for individuals as they choose to map out their own routes to selfhood in globalized and socially dis-embedded contexts.

Turning away from one's collective identity does not mean literally turning one's back on one's cultural community or disavowing the extended self. John Mbiti's (1969) concept of the extended self is integral to the structure of Black identity in which people of African descent experience personal identity as interwoven with the identity of Afrocentric community. The turning we speak of connotes a dialectical turning away to turn toward. The deeper individuation of this stage releases constraining notions of collective identity and reveals the self-actualized life as a more rooted foundation for generative cultural participation. Thus, release and liberation from overextension to others in a manner counter to self-care is tantamount in this stage. In fact, the gift to self is a deeply integrated synthesis of identity polarities guided by each woman's own interiority. This stage propels the blossoming of many aspects of individuation here-to-fore suppressed, denied, sacrificed, or kept waiting in the wings.

Theorist Erik H. Erikson provided the earliest conceptual model of adult aging relative to the stage of integrity versus despair. He suggests that the key accomplishment at this phase is a sense of integrity based upon the awareness and appreciation of life achievements and accomplishments. Despair will be the lot of those with unresolved regrets. Women find themselves coming to terms with lifelong lesions, patterns of self-negation, self-denial, deferment of actualizing impulses, and what Pinkola Estes (1981) refers to as "sneaking a soul life." Making peace with regrets can spark a woman to start a business, finish college, leave a job to become an artist, say good-bye to a marriage, insist that her grown up live-in children leave the roost, take up marathon running, or an infinite number of liberatory moves that bring a deep foundation of peace with self and all that has gone before.

Developmental psychologist Gene Cohen's (2000) research on elders and the phases of creativity also lends much to our thinking about the processes of individuation and integration possible at second adulthood. Cohen suggests that around the age of 50, individuals enter a phase of reevaluation during which they reflect upon past accomplishments and formulate new goals. Reevaluation is prompted by the awareness of mortality and time limitations that lead to an intense desire to shore up life details, stabilize areas of turbulence, create, and produce. Near the age of 60 individuals experience a sense of liberation and find that they are more able to create and simultaneously become more tolerant of their own limitations, failings, and frailties. Thus they are willing to take more risks than in previous years. In the 70s comes a desire for summing up one's life accomplishments into a cohesive and meaningful story. All earlier life accomplishments are a prefiguring of later life accomplishments. Albeit at this age and beyond a deep satisfaction with "being" rather than "doing" descends into one's understanding. The African-centered cultural premise that right being leads to right doing finds its way to center and taps a wellspring of satisfaction with simply being in the fullness of one's selfhood. In their 80s, many individuals experience an encore phase that is evidenced as the desire to pick up unfinished business and move it toward completion or closure and to fulfill desires that were put aside in the past. This stage includes and may emphasize accomplishments that occur because one has or wishes to set the stage for other generations to perform and collectively exceed one's own achievements. When entering this stage from the basis of generativity, empowering others to excel can counter the pain of having had to pioneer alone. In contrast, non-resolution of generativity versus despair can result in bitterness that begrudges the success and apparent ease that current generations encounter relative to one's own struggle.

The Black Woman Leader at Second Adulthood

The things that grandmothers can see while sitting on the ground, younger people cannot see even if they climb to the top of the tree.
—Senegalese Proverb

Across the ages there have always been older women and clear delineations between Eastern and Western worldviews of women. The societal imagery of the older woman is both a reflection of the outer world perceptions and the woman's own sense of regard. Jungian psychiatrist Jean Shinoda-Bolen (2002) notes that in the Western world, the ushering in of Christian patriarchy in 3100 BCE marked the beginnings of the demise of the older woman as a valued social entity. Prior to this epoch elder women were celebrated as crones or glorious crowns of wisdom and healing and as powerful symbols of beauty, wisdom, and divinity. In contrast, with the onset of patriarchy came the defamation of the elder woman as: hag, cunning, wicked, contaminated feminine, unholy beings. Within the Eastern worldview, peoples of the tribally based societies of Sub-Saharan Africa and the African Diaspora have continued to worship the cult of the Mother and Grandmother as the sustainers of life and cultural wisdom despite the incursion of patriarchy into their cosmologies of motherline veneration.

Still, across the African Diaspora the elder woman is a symbol of reverence perceived to preserve communal wholeness and wisdom. As such, old women are "recognized authorities" on a variety of topics relative to general and reproductive health and nutrition, male-female relationships, parenting, well-child care, effective discipline, household management, nature, farming, gardening and animal husbandry, civic participation and representation, and self-advocacy. According to Aubel (2006) the World Bank funded Grandmother's Project has coined the terms *Indigenous Knowledge Keepers* (IKKs), and *Indigenous Knowledge Systems Managers* (IKSMs) to honor the role of matrilineal leadership instrumental in changing community health and life-skills knowledge standards among tribal people in Sub-Saharan Africa.

Throughout, the African American literary tradition has been steeped in the celebration of the lives of the African American grandmother and elder woman as cultural, communal, and family icons. Some of the most memorable accounts of elder women in the genre of fiction reflect this group's diversity. Examples include the stalwart Lena Younger in Lorraine Hansberry's (1959) *A Raisin in the Sun*; the resourceful unifying matriarch Big Mamma "Jo" Joseph in *Soul Food* (Tillman, 1997); the widow Avey Johnson seeking spiritual growth and rebirth in Paule Marshalls' (1983) *Praisesong for the Widow*; or Joyce Mitchell's return to love and romance in Pearl Cleage's (2009) *I Wish I Had a Red Dress*. In the genre of nonfiction Brian Lanker and Maya Angelou's *I Dream a World* and Michael Cunningham and Connie Briscoe's (2009) *Jewels, 50 Phenomenal Women Over Age 50* celebrates the life and times of the dynamic elder woman.

The mass media also pays homage to the over 50s Black woman. On any given day it is possible to see these women in the media. African American women over 50 are being celebrated in human interest stories and the news as popular culture icons. Overall, their accomplishments counter stereotypes and serve to change prevailing attitudes about women of this generational cohort. We are also seeing all sorts of opportunistic life shifts in the lives of African American women such as Tina Knowles, fashion entrepreneur and chief designer of the House of Dereon; the naming of Dr. Shirley Jackson as the first African American woman president of Rennselaer Polytechnic Institute; Joanne Harrell, hearing impaired Microsoft Service Manager; and, Oprah Winfrey's announcement at 57 of a planned retirement from the *Oprah Winfrey Show* to establish the OWN cable network. An exemplar of this pattern of opportunistic shifts among Black senior women is seen in the most recent exploits of 79–year-old New Yorker Barbara Hillary, retired nurse, publisher, community activist, and cancer survivor and the first African American woman and oldest person ever to cross both the North and South Poles in 2007 and 2011. At this stage of life, these accomplishments become universal symbols of inspiration and of a woman's capacity for change and growth.

Finding the Will to Seize the Opening for the Return to Self

Sometimes you have to put yourself first, I'm doin' me.
  —Fantasia Barrino, *Back to Me* (2010)

It asks that women not be forced to choose between public justice and private happiness.
  —Susan Faludi, Backlash, *The Undeclared War Against American Women*

The psychological concepts of identity and individuation rest at the center of personal leadership at second adulthood. Identity is defined as the understanding of one's unique characteristics and how they have been or are and will be maintained across ages, situations, and roles (Boyd & Bee, 2010; Zucker, Ostove, & Stewart, 2002). Individuation is a Jungian concept referring to the process of becoming whole, solid, and indivisible and can be likened to embarking on the archetypal night sea journey or search for the Holy Grail. The quest for individuation requires that one open up the inner psyche by addressing dreams, longings, and the natural world of the collective unconscious. In so doing, the unconscious will inform and guide one through a process with a unique subjective wisdom (Jung, 1971, 2006). Each of these states of self-awareness develops across the lifespan in age appropriate ways. However at second adulthood these capacities are mature, flexible, and ready for further refinement and shaping to support the individual for the remainder of the lifespan.

To achieve what we call personal leadership is to fund the will to momentarily detach from the concerns of others to reflect upon one's own life, unfulfilled aims, and desires as a precursor to moving forward on a self-directed course that ultimately retains a deeper and more profound leadership thrust because of its life-stage appropriateness. Taking the sojourn of personal leadership requires detachment from such oppressive forces as the perceived constraints of what other individuals think the woman should or should not be doing with her time, talent, and energies. This sojourn also requires detachment from the controls levied by others' beliefs about what they themselves will lose should a woman fully define her boundaries and chosen modes of life expression. At the start of this personal leadership sojourn women must be willing to ask themselves: (1) What does it mean to authorize and exercise my own abilities for personal leadership because I now view myself at the center of my life? (2) Am I willing to use those new discoveries about myself in ways that are personally authentic and agentic? And (3) Will I make committed plans and implement those plans for the betterment of all phases of my life going forward?

If one remains alive past the age of 50 second adulthood will come. However, the question is whether and how women at this stage will take an inventory of their personal lives in order to consciously script the chapters ahead. Honoring the gift of this upcoming period requires intentionality. Reaching the age of mastery provides the time, motive, and opportunity for African American women leaders to explore their own sense of divinity, selfhood, and interiority. Despite the highly varied lives of African American female professional leaders and the similarly varied qualities of their arrival at second adulthood, they generally all need to mark a clearing for self-exploration and discovery after a lifelong outflow of care to others. At this point, African American womanist leaders awaken to the need for retreat, life examination, and preparation for future levels of generativity.

The second adulthood womanist leader's opportunity for some form of retreat permits the exploration of: (1) one's own mortality, (2) the totality of the life experience and the self-in-relation; (3) unmet personal needs and the practical use of time remaining to fulfill one's innermost aims; (4) the resolution of salient inner and interpersonal conflicts; and (5) the formulation of plans for intergenerational leadership legacy sharing to assure continuity of one's lifetime contributions and the transfer of social, intellectual, and monetary prosperity. When considering that more of the life has been lived than is left to live, one must engage in a process of evaluation to assess and work through these five developmental areas. This internal assessment process constitutes a woman's recognition of the "lateness of the day." The leadership development task is one of using this recognition as impetus for mounting a path to progression in the second adulthood and allowing one's individuation process to drive her leadership contributions. This leading from the center of one's self-hood outward is what we refer to as "honoring the lateness of the day."

Such leadership that honors individuation at this stage cannot commence without a deep and vital seizing of the opening for the return to self. When a woman seeks alignment with this stage-appropriate return to her own process of individuation, she is electing to face into a morass of such life clean-up dilemmas as unsuccessful marriages and partnerships, financial irresponsibility, addictions and workaholism, neglected health, fitness and self-care, the void of spirituality, or conversely uncritical participation in or reliance on religiosity.[4] She may also be electing to transition in consciousness by scripting new ways to see old issues. New scripts might include reframing what it means to take time for self as well as to create personally gratifying physical, emotional, and spiritual space, reevaluating what it means to be needed, altering intrusions and boundary incursions from others including adult children, and assessing personal desires that others might see as self-serving, frivolous, or foolhardy.

There is a clear distinction between ignoring and embracing the needs of second adulthood. Those who ignore the gift this stage of life can offer tend to

---

4   *Religiosity* in this context refers to institutionalized dogma that prohibits or suppresses critical engagement, questioning, or intellectual freedom of dissent, or that emphasizes privileged hierarchical position holders within the religious establishment to the detriment of an ethic of care to all members of the community within and outside of the religious institution's embrace.

live life void of reflection, cognizance, or awareness of the need for a change from the external to the internal source points for guiding one's life. Those taking the stance of embrace are active in leading their own paths to growth and positive change. In the clinical setting we have observed those African American professional women who do not embrace second adulthood go into a tailspin as they encounter fears about getting older. Many balk at facing into the less than ideal aspects of their marriages or relationships with aged parents or adult children and the lack of financial preparedness for the retirement years. Those who resist the opportunity of the moment can enter a state of emotional paralysis and burrow down into a state of denial. Denial allows them to downplay the need to pause, reflect, and strategize. The research of Unson, Mahoney-Trella, and Chowdhury (2004) suggests that financially limited and physically unhealthy African American elder women typically lack the wherewithal to obtain beneficial access to supportive physical and mental health resources. This group also fears any suggested interventions by agencies that specialize in areas of financial, physical, or mental self-help and corrective strategies. While the group that is more independent due to financial circumstances and/or physical well-being is likely to benefit from preventive and corrective psychological or physical health activities. The complexity of each woman's life structure and ability to seize the opening for a return to self lays the groundwork for resolution versus demise. What follows are descriptions of re-scripting with respect to four areas of productive life movement: (1) career and work, (2) marriage or life partnering, (3) fitness and health, and (4) forgiveness and peace making. The following examples all derive from our clinical work and the personal growth and leadership development workshops we have conducted with African American professional women.[5]

Living in Full Larder[6]:
Broadening a Career to Change the Economic Tide

> I am really not prepared financially for my retirement years. So if you look up and see me as the Wal-Mart Greeter, don't be surprised!
> —P.L.B.[7]

At second adulthood women will lament that they have not adequately prepared for the financial rigors of the retirement years. There are a host of reasons account-

---

5   All names used are pseudonyms. We have changed identifying details to the extent needed to protect identities and applied modest paraphrasing and editing for the purpose of brevity.

6   *Full larder* is a folk term used in the family of co-author S. Alease Ferguson. While we do not know the origins of this term, in her family's use it referred concretely to having a full pantry and, symbolically, to the process of being well stocked with provisions for times of crises or need. In S. Alease's family this term became discursive shorthand to refer to self-sufficiency and the capacity to contribute to an interdependent web of community.

7   P.L.B. is a friend of the family for S. Alease Ferguson, co-author of this work.

ing for this lack. Some women married early and got late starts with education and workforce entry. Many have earned modest salaries across the lifespan. Others, though working diligently over the years, have accrued financial burdens over the years from student loans, educational expenses incurred for self or offspring, help-giving to disadvantaged family members, medical expenses, limited life-long saving patterns, economic downturns affecting stock markets, 401ks, SEPIRAs, and sometimes living beyond one's means.

Second adulthood can bring on a strong realization about the need to secure financial destinies long term. Many women begin this process by evaluating: What marketable skills of a professional, paraprofessional, or vocational nature do I possess, and what new skills would I like to obtain? At the same time they explore the entirety of their lattice of social and network supports and potential new contacts to develop in making the final determination to embark upon a path. Today's Black professional women at second adulthood are testing their own creativity and ingenuity in order to keep a full larder in the golden years. In the following example, Ann Kimbrough, a 59–year-old African American licensed social worker discusses how she began creating a hedge against the financial strains of the retirement years. She notes:

> I have spent the majority of my career working at small and mid-sized social services agencies. Having earned a modest salary most of my life I have only managed to save half of what experts say is reasonable for adding to a pension and living comfortably. When I was fifty-seven years old it hit me that I had to do something fast. At that age it's not easy to find a new full time job with comparable wages and benefits. I knew I had to improve my post retirement economic outlook. Two years ago, I initiated a plan to fulfill a life-long dream to teach as an adjunct faculty in sociology and psychology at a local university. For years I had worked with student interns and I had an excellent record of mentoring women who have gone on to become highly regarded social workers here in the city. So I started shooting out applications to become an adjunct faculty member. To my surprise I got two bites on the line; and I took both of them. . . rapidly boosting my income. Instead of dragging in each night exhausted and worried, I got into the thick of preparing for classes and got a new resolve and energy. Besides helping me to jump start my savings account, I found a new career niche, formulated a research agenda and began writing journal articles and presenting collaboratively at national conferences with other faculty. . . .I found out I had a lot to say that was meaningful. Overall the experience has been a win-win. I am rewarded by working with students and my new collegial network in ways that have enlarged my personal and professional identities. I feel more confident now in my ability to provide for myself long term and to be better prepared for retirement.

Another interesting story concerning making the opportunistic shifts for financial growth and momentum can be found in Cyndi Bowles experience.

Bowles is a 68–year-old public health administrator who unexpectedly became an entrepreneur nearing the close of her formal working life. She recalls:

> It's been my plan all along to retire at age 70. I went to college while my children were growing up and started working as a professional late in the game. I started in the non-profit arena and then entered the public sector in my late forties. So I needed to compensate by working a few years longer. When I was 66 my only living Uncle became critically ill and came to live with us. Two months prior he bought a new twelve passenger econoline van to haul his fishing buddies around in. With the awareness that the van was no longer of use to him he signed the title over to me and said make good use of it, Cyn. The vehicle was humongous and nothing that I ever wanted to drive. Yet there was no way to get comparable value by selling it. So for about a month I explored a variety of business options involving transportation. I looked into things like medical transport, and school pick-ups for kids. But there were so many licensing regulations, insurance costs, rising gasoline prices, and time constraints that I had to put the idea aside. One day a woman at church, Miss Marva, got up to testify. After thanking God and the good people of the church she called out for assistance, she shared that she was now living in a senior high rise and had two sons in two different penitentiaries that she had been unable to see for over a year due to lack of transportation. After Church I went up to her in the fellowship hall and offered my services to her. At that Moment Wings of Hope Transportation Services was founded. Ms. Marva became my booking clerk and within two months Wings of Hope was operating as a weekend venture taking families to see their loved ones in prison. Today, we have three additional vans and three drivers who work weekdays doing prison runs and elder shopping excursions. My uncle is ecstatic that the van is being put to good use and comforted by the fact that I will be able to live a more comfortable life.

These examples show the creativity of the second adulthood, the internal orientation of impulses to forge gratifying expansions to career, and the underlying impetus of solidifying and deepening financial solvency.

Releasing the Ties that Bind:
Moving Beyond Dead Ends and Toward Relational Synergy

Another large looming concern at the dawning of second adulthood is the issue of one's marriage-life partnership and intimate relational lives. At second adulthood the realization of discomfort or overarching relational misfit can become intensified. Many of these women married young before realizing their own potential and may not have ever been fully compatible with their spouses. Other couples have grown apart over time due to workaholism, changing interests and associations, or chronic relational dynamics. When the status of the marriage comes into question, women at this stage are sometimes able to engage their partners in jointly working to revive their relationships into a mutually satisfying whole.

Yet others have spouses or partners who refuse to communicate openly or to seek relational counseling to maximize the odds of improvement. When women feel improvement is not possible, some will take the necessary measures to change the tone and tenor of their intimate relational lives. The choice to divorce at this juncture often meets with a variety of admonitions from friends concerning the risks of social isolation and ostracism, the slim pickings available for new intimate relationships, the perils and risks of such things as financial predators, HIV/ AIDS, and exploiters of the woman's emotional and material advantages. Yet the overwhelming need for and possibility of being loved and appreciated prompts some women to navigate toward either a single life of companionship with a committed partner or the love of family and friends, or to seek the option of becoming choicefully well mated. Leslie Stotomyer is a 62–year-old auditor. She recalls the painful decision to end her marriage of 40 years:

> Prior to my divorce I had been married for forty years. I would term the union as ill fated from its beginnings, because we did what so many young people who were sexually attracted to one another did back then—we married. Over the years we grew apart. My ex-husband did not have a college degree so my going to college, earning a bachelor's degree and getting an MBA stuck a sour note with him. Somehow we managed through the tough years of raising kids, getting every one of the kids off to college and completion; and caring for all of our parents until their deaths. Just as I thought all the care giving was done and we could live a little and perhaps get more in touch with one another. . . we ended up having to care for a young grandchild. After our grandchild came to live with us, Frank would come home from work have dinner with Sonny and I and then say that he had to take go back to the office. Often he wouldn't return until three or four in the morning. When I confronted him he had nothing to say for himself—not a word—nor did his behavior change. Even though he wouldn't reply I continued to question, and suggest counseling. After a month, I took his non responsiveness as a sign of guilt, disinterest and disengagement. I filed for dissolution of marriage without issue of minor children. The thought of staying in a relationship where there was no mutual commitment, communication or love did not match me or my self regard. I could imagine something better for myself—even if it meant being alone.

"Pushed Back to Strength"[8]: Dialoguing with Life-threatening Illness & Deciding on Fitness for Life

What dwells behind and what dwells before us are small matters compared to what dwells inside of us.
  —Ralph Waldo Emerson

---

8 *Pushed Back to Strength* (1993) is the title of a book by Gloria Wade-Gales (see bibliography).

During mid-life many women find themselves encountering issues of health due to the aging process, unhealthy habits, the stress and strain of family, career, and leadership involvements, and physical disposition factors such as those inherited genetically. In addition, women find that the decades of launching careers and contributing to family and community make it difficult to be consistently intentional regarding the lifestyle habits that enhance health. Given the ways that stress contributes to disease, biopsychosocial research has shown (Clark et al. 1999) that race can be a complicating factor in maintaining health or succumbing to illness. Herein, Black women have the multiplicative effects of both race and gender to contend with and the ways this influences life events and psychosocial overload in their lives and the lives of loved ones. It is not uncommon for such crises to arise at midlife and become increasingly more likely throughout the aging process.

Brenda is a successful attorney who has never been married and talked in our workshop about a recent diagnosis of Lupus. She recounts a series of critical events that have marked her life:

> I dated the love of my life off and on for several years until he broke it off one evening by saying that he was getting married in two weeks. I was devastated, but I continued to work as I had gotten a full time job right out of high school. . . . I worked and attended college until I got my degree. From then on I continued my education, earned a law degree, and began a full-fledged career in law working for the state government. I dated several men and had some long term relationships, but things just never worked out. I never fell for any of them the way that I had for Marcus. Life went on, my career continued to soar until I left to go into private practice for myself in my mid forties. Then. . . just after I rounded my 50th birthday, Marcus came back into my life. He just got back in touch after years of being apart and we began seeing each other. We went to museums, strolling in the park, out for coffee and dessert, and other cultural events. We talked like best friends, understood each other's moods, and shared confidences, problems and dreams. After several months, realizing my feelings had grown beyond friendship, I finally asked Marcus where all of this was headed. Of course he could say nothing because yes, he was still married. I broke things off. But it seemed that soon after my health began to decline. I gained weight, my skin lost it healthy texture, and I seemed to lose vital stamina and strength. I was diagnosed with Lupus and had chronic flare ups so severe that I felt as if my hold on life was being tested. I began to meditate, pray, cry. . . sometimes sitting for hours and reflecting on my life. I got in touch with my feelings of being abandoned, of "never being chosen", and with the rage that was eating at me from the inside out. I cannot tell you how much emotional purifying I have done. Now I can truly say I've found emotional peace. I just hope that God will restore me physically.

Brenda's story exemplifies the ways in which a life crisis, often one accompanied by physical manifestations of strain, can be the impetus for reclamation of physical and psycho-emotional health. Typically, in our practice we have found that the women themselves who face such challenges construct meaning that connects their physical health to the life crisis they are facing and that such interpretations guide the forms of therapeutic and medical treatments they select. Many become active partners with practitioners, but most important, once physical and psycho-emotional health are restored, they institute life practices that will support fitness for life across a broad range of areas. The range of fitness practices may include nutrition, spiritual practices, therapeutic support (e.g., support groups or other wellness activities), recreational activities, and other escapes from pressure and stress (e.g., social outings, personal retreats) regular exercise regimes, and health care.

Making Peace with Past and Future: Choosing Forgiveness that Includes the Self

> When have you been through enough? When does who you are, what you have learned, and how you have grown, become enough to sustain you?
> —Iyanla Vanzant, *Peace from Broken Pieces*, p. 295

The issue of forgiveness is central to forward movement in life. The inability to forgive is tantamount to doggedly clinging to past injustices and injuries. The compulsion to remain mired in hurts can prevent healing and the reconstitution and reconnaissance of self. The story of Genevieve Parsons' forgiveness of herself and her husband Albert after a shattering betrayal illustrates how crisis response and intensive self-reevaluation can alter prior life and social expectations in ways that illuminate the need for forgiveness. Parsons is a shaker and mover in the world of the theater arts. She gives the following account of her life over the last decade:

> At the age of 54 my husband of thirty-two years developed a crack addiction. He had been laid off from his job three months prior to having enough hours to claim a full pension. Though he had given me every assurance that he was out looking for work, he was really hanging out with a group of men in the neighborhood. When it became clear to me that he had developed a drug addiction to crack cocaine I gave him the choice to leave and never come back or work it out by getting into treatment. He chose treatment; and, did pretty well for a while. He participated in Twelve Step programs and got a job with the help of his Sponsor. . . Later on though, he got back with the guys he'd been hanging out with, relapsed, refused treatment and ended up committing an armed robbery. He was convicted and sentenced to ten years. In those years, I put money on his books, sent care packages, wrote letters, communicated by phone and visited him monthly. During this period my parents were furious and even attempted to force me into divorcing Albert. Their pressure and old acquaintances' expressions of their concern for me went on non-stop. Despite my outward defiance, I too wondered if he would ever achieve sobriety or would collapse and break my heart again. . . . The struggles of this experience forced me into therapy. I was

very honest with my therapist, and she really helped me to cope with my anger, shame, disappointment, and fear. Outside of counseling I did a lot of self reflection and journaling work on my own. The ten years passed slowly but not without major growth experiences for both me and Albert. At age 64, after his release from prison, I reunited with him. In this instance it was a conscious reunion that came about because I was freed by forgiveness of both myself and Albert.

To be laden with memories of only the tragedies and bleakness of one's own past reifies a sense of defeat and anger. Forgiving the self for choices that appear to have brought about the undoing of hard won life gains and victories can release women to begin anew, forgive others, and return to the potentiality of the present, rather than become controlled by past tragedies.

Refusing to Let Anything Steal Your Joy: Reclaiming the Years Which the Locust Hath Eaten

A large issue in second adulthood is that of feeling one has lost time that can never be reclaimed. For women in general—and Black women in particular—who have led lives of leadership to family, community, and society, the existential issue of whether one has given away too much of the self and paid too high a price can loom large and overshadow the future. Emma Jean Randall is a 70–year-old widow, a retired nurse, and civic leader. Over the last 20 years she has been there to serve as a relative care giver for the twins, her granddaughter Madison and grandson Micah, in the wake of her daughter's sudden death. At the same time, she gave hands-on care for all of her ailing family elders. Here she talks candidly about the present and the future:

> Everyone who knows me and the challenges I have faced has always said, "the Lord is gonna' bless you girl or He's got something really special in store for you." I also felt that I was doing exactly what I was supposed to be doing. Sometimes I was tired or lonely or it was just plain ole rough! But I never wavered in doing the right things for my loved ones who depended on me. My family elders who gave me everything I needed to be successful in this world have passed on; and now Maddie and Mic are both graduating from college. I can't believe that the time has just flown by. Over these last four years, I have discovered what everyone meant by that notion of an avalanche of blessings. You know once the kids left, I started taking up time with myself, I took classes in yoga, Pilates, and quilt making. I also joined a book club and a travel club. The most surprising blessing is that I was introduced to Mr. Bennett, a retired teacher and the brother of my book club leader. . . . In those years after my husband died and the years of doing family work, I never dated, or had a fella'. Even when my friends goaded me about living like a nun, I always rationalized things by saying that I had a great childhood, great college years and a great marriage and that I had been given enough love to last me three lifetimes. Thus, I shut out the sexual and romantic parts of myself. Long and short of it is that Mr. Bennett—well—Harold, and I

are committed life partners now. We travel, entertain, lunch, play golf, take long walks after dinner, and lounge around reading. Our life together is as simple as it is elegant. Best of all, we dote on each other—and it that is my reward!

We share this example to show that many women resolve the issue of self-sacrifice prior to second adulthood by reveling in a newfound freedom that gives room for their self-actualized selves to emerge. Of essential import here for womanist leaders is the need to assess when one has "done enough" for others to shift gears. Assessing the life structure is a necessary task for individuation and following through with the tough choices about what to take off of one's plate, if the segue toward downshifting from responsibility levels that no longer feel appropriate does not naturally occur as it did in the case described above.

Crossing the Great Leadership Divide: Toward a Cohesive Theory of Black Women Leaders across the Life Span

My Grandmothers were strong. . . with veins rolling over quick hands/
They have many clean words to say/
—Margaret Walker, *Daughters of Africa*, p. 267

The African American professional woman's Crossing the Great Leadership Divide refers to her sojourn, evolution, and rites of passage as leader. Across the lifespan, there are clear differentials in the organization and demonstration of African American womanist leadership between the first and second adulthoods. In the first adulthood (ages 18–45 years) the African professional woman as womanist leader evolves and gains mastery as an agent of change and progress in family, communal, and organizational life. As wives, mothers, extended family, and communal leaders and careerists, they create, fuel, energize, and maintain what bell hooks (1992) calls *homeplaces*. Homeplaces are sites of love and nurture based upon the integration of age-old motherline leadership wisdom and the immediacies of protecting their spouses, children, and kin from the psychological and soul destroying effects of macrocosmic racism and sexism. During these years they become efficacious in the womanly and "reproductive arts" of household management, hospitality, and entertainment; child and grandchild nurture; fosterage of the community's children; cross-generational mentors of leadership; extended family and friendship bonding; fellowshipping and re-unioning (of family, schoolmates, friendship groups, etc.); church and communal uplift; community crisis prevention, intervention, interdiction, and advocacy; elder care; family and communal grief and bereavement supporters; and guides to supports and resources. At the same time, they have become seasoned careerists. By virtue of their very presence they have led by scaling the heights of higher education, diversifying organizational life and various fields of endeavor, mounting their own paths to progression, mentoring others, delivering direct services, enriching the corporate bottom line, seeding both field-based and technological innovations, and creating new organizational entities and enterprises. By the close of the first adulthood, African American women have amassed demonstrated skills in leadership across myriad domains that can be construed as mastery.

The second adulthood (ages 45–65 years; 65–85+ years) offers a unique view of the interplay of life-cycle human development and the women's own select approaches to redistributing the balance of leadership from other-centered social contribution to a brand of complimentary self-governance and nurture. This re-contextualizing or repositioning of the self-in relation-to-the-self rather than self-in-relation-to-others marks a shift in the locus of control, identity, and individuation. Here, African American professional women transition from the physically active roles of family, communal, and career leadership to the practice of more personally circumscribed and agentic forms of leadership. In this phase of the life cycle, the directionality of the leadership thrust shifts from meeting the all-encompassing requirements for other-centered leadership to a more personal and inward guided leadership thrust.

Though women at second adulthood evidence tremendous peak vitality and a passion for their families, careers, and communal pursuits, many are quietly engaged in the life-cycle second adulthood work of personal leadership mastery and self-governance. This work is based upon the developmental needs for self-recognition, reconnaissance and recovery, and coming full circle in life. Seizing the opportunistic window through which to glimpse one's identity as a mature woman, leader, and social contributor are the hallmarks of the African American womanist leader at second adulthood. Summarily, this facing inward at the second adulthood offers new pathways for personal leadership development and the capacity with which to fund the physical and emotional stamina needed for healthy self-awareness, personal goal attainment, continued pro-social contribution, relational potency, consolidation of one's lifetime achievements, and preparation for conscious and successful living and forward momentum followed by life closure.

Until recently, the imagery of African American women as leaders has been fairly recessed due to their history of subjugation, marginality, and struggles for liberation (Hine, 1994). At the same time Black women have often parsed their leadership efforts as mere expedience or strides for living and communal uplift rather than leadership. In *Families in Peril* (1989), child welfare activist Marian Wright Edelman highlights the "both/and"[9] dilemmas of Black womanist lead-

---

9   "Both/and" refers to a characteristic of an Afrocentric epistemology that inclines itself toward knowledge that values the simultaneity of or interrelatedness of supposed opposites. In the context of this epistemology one can value both sides of a polarity and perhaps discover the dialectical value of both. This pattern exists in contrast to the kind of either/or assumptions commonly underlying Eurocentric thought.

ers. She notes: "We must not, in trying to think about how we can make a big difference, ignore the small daily differences we can make which over time add up to big differences that we often cannot foresee" (p. 107). Further, in this technological age, the notion of African American female leadership is often obscured by the notion that one must possess some form of popular culture acclaim and celebrity. In contrast, historian Mildred Hill-Lublin's (1991) analysis of the writings of Fredrick Douglas', Langston Hughes', and Maya Angelou's exaltation of the grandmother indicates that these women can be viewed as the paragons of action, hope, involvement, and dignity. The hallmark of the grandmother's leadership legacy rests in the ability to act, fuel involvement, instill hope and dignity in an effort to promote survival, preserve family history, wisdom, and Black lore, and retain and transmit values and ideals that support and enhance her humanity, her family, and community.

In *Black Womanist Leadership: Tracing the Motherline*, King and Ferguson (2011) define African American womanist leadership as a survivalist motif that encompasses the leadership of African American mothers evidenced by their issuance of tactical nourishment critical to their offspring's survival and abilities to outwit oppressive forces. The issue of African American professional women having been bred on tactical nourishment aimed at teaching the life skills that prevent internal defeat and annihilation is even more critical at the stage of second adulthood. As the ante goes up on maintaining wellness and physical health, self-efficacy, integrity, and dignity, the prior attainments of mastery can be parlayed into an enriched quality of elder life necessary for the redirection of self and the tutelage of subsequent generations. Survival of communities assaulted by multiplicative oppressions of sexism, classism, heterosexism, and racism would benefit exponentially from an elder class of survivors who themselves have not succumbed to paradigms of leadership that remain externally defined and framed despite lifespan needs to fuel the self from an internal locus of control.

It is critical to our understanding of Black women's leadership across the lifespan to move toward theories that differentiate the woof and warp of leadership at different phases of life and that also frame an Afrocentric motif surrounding Black women's leadership—a leadership centered in Black community values becoming increasingly alien to pre- and postmillennial generations. The values and defining characteristics of such Black womanist leadership at second adulthood elevate the principles of being versus doing, right relationship to self, calibration of leadership strivings with stage of life. These values signal to family and community that leadership need not be sacrificial and consumptive but rather seeks to balance giving of self with giving to self. Differentially, efforts to understand the phenomena of self-oriented leadership among African American women at the age of mastery is of vast importance to the advancement of knowledge in the realms of African American feminist and womanist psychology, lifespan development, and leadership studies. As such it is imperative that scholars and clinicians keep pace with the elder African American female population demographic and the myriad oppressions, as well as the socioeconomic, technological advances, and especially the socio-cultural meanings impacting their lives and informing their leadership.

Bibliography

Aubel, J. (2006). *Grandmothers promote maternal and child health: The role of indigenous knowledge systems managers, IK notes.* New York: World Bank.

Barbara Hillary Press Release. Retrieved from www.BarabraHillary.com

Barrino, F. (2010). *Back to me* [sound recording]. New York: Sony Music.

Bateson, M. C. (2010). *Composing a further life: The age of active wisdom.* New York: Knopf.

Beauvoir, S. de (1974). *All said & done.* New York: Putnam.

Boyd, D., & Bee, H. (2010). *Lifespan development* (5th ed). Boston: Pearson Education.

Clark, R., Anderson, N. B., Clark, V. R., & Williams, D. R. (1999). Racism as a stressor for African Americans: A biopsychosocial model. *American Psychologist, 54*(10), 805–816.

Cleage, P. (2009). *I wish I had a red dress.* New York: Avon Press.

Coatsworth, E. (1968). *Down half the world.* New York: Macmillan.

Cohen, G. (2000). *The creative age: Awakening human potential in the second half of life.* New York: Avon Books.

Cunningham, M., & Briscoe, C. (2009). *Jewels: 50 phenomenal women over 50.* Boston: Little Brown.

Emerson, R. W. Retrieved from http://www.quotesdaddy.com/author/Ralph+Waldo+Emerson

Erikson, E. H. (1962). *Young man Luther: A study of psychoanalysis and history.* New York: Norton.

Erikson, E. H. (1974). *Dimensions of a new identity.* New York: Norton.

Erikson, E. H. (2000). *The Erik Erikson reader.* (Robert Coles, Ed.). New York: Norton.

Faludi, S. (2006). *Backlash: The undeclared war against American women.* New York: Three Rivers Press.

Ferguson, S. A., & King, T. C. (1996). Bringing organizational behavior and therapy together: Counseling the African American female on job socialization failure. *Women and Therapy, 13*(1), 45–55.

Giddens, A. (1991). *Modernity and self-identity: Self and society in the late modern age.* Cambridge, MA: Polity Press.

Giddens, A. (1994). Living in a post-traditional society. In U. Beck, A. Giddens & S. Lash (Eds.), *Reflexive modernization. Politics, tradition and aesthetics in the modern social order* (pp. 56–71). Cambridge, MA: Polity Press.

Greer, G. (1993). *Change: Women aging and menopause.* New York: Ballantine Books.

Hansberry, L. (1959). *A raisin in the sun.* New York: Random House.

Hill-Lublin, M. A. (1991). The African American grandmother in autobiographical works by Fredrick Douglas, Langston Hughes and Maya Anglou. *International Journal of Aging and Human Development, 33*(3), 172–175.

Hine, D. C. (1994). *Hine sight: Black women and the re-construction of American history.* Bloomington: Indiana University Press.

hooks, bell (1992). *Teaching to transgress: Education as the practice of freedom.* New York: Routledge.

Jung, C. G. (1971). *The portable Jung.* (R. F. C. Hull, Trans.). New York: Viking Press.

Jung, C. G. (2006). *The undiscovered self.* New York: Signet.

King, T. C., & Ferguson, S. A. (1996). "I am because we are": Clinical interpretations of communal experience among African American women." *Women and Therapy, 18*(1), 33–45.

King, T. C., & Ferguson, S. A. (2001). Charting ourselves: Leadership development with African American professional women. *National Women's Studies Association Journal, 23*(2), 123–141.

King, T. C., & Ferguson, S. A. (2006). "Carrying our burden in the heat of the day": Mid-life self-sacrifice within the family circle among Black professional women. *Women & Therapy, 18*(2), 148–169.

King, T. C., & Ferguson, S. A. (2011). *Black womanist leadership: Tracing the motherline*. Albany, NY: SUNY.

Levinson, D., & Levinson, J. (1996). *Seasons of a woman's life*. New York: Knopf-Doubleday.

Marshall, P. (1983). *Praisesong for the widow*. New York: Putnam.

Mbiti, J. (1969 [1990]). *African religions and philosophy*. African Writers Series. Portsmouth, NH: Heinemann.

Neugarten, B. (1968). *Middle age and aging. A reader in social psychology*. Chicago: University of Chicago Press.

Neugarten, B. L., Havighurst, R., & Tobin, S.J. (1961). The measurement of life satisfaction. *Journal of Gerontology, 16*(2), 134–143.

Pinkola Estes, C. (1992). *Women who run with the wolves: Myths and stories of the wild woman archetype*. New York: Ballantine.

Schachter-Shalomi, Z. (1995). *From age-ing to sag-ing: A profound new vision of growing older*. New York: Warner Books.

Sheehy, G. (1970). *Passages: Predictable crises in adult life*. New York: Bantam.

Sheehy, G. (1996). *New passages: Mapping your life across time*. New York: Ballantine.

Shinoda-Bolen, J. (2002). *The goddess in older women: Archetypes in women over 50*. San Francisco: Harper.

Shinoda Bolen, J. (2003). *Crones do not whine: Concentrated wisdom for juicy women*. Berkeley, CA: Conari.

Tessler-Lindau, S., Leitsch, S. A., Lundberg, K. L., & Jerome, J. (2004 [2006]). Older women's attitudes, behaviors and communication about sex and HIV: A community based study. *Journal of Women's Health, 15*(6), 663–665.

Tillman, G. (1997). *Soul Food* [video recording]. George Tillman, writer and director. Tracey Edmonds, Producer. Beverly Hills: 20th Century Fox.

Trafford, A. (2004). *My time: Making the most of the bonus decades after 50*. New York: Basic Books.

Unson, C. G., Mahoney-Trella, P., & Chowdhury, S. (2004, May 27). *Older African American women's strategies for living long and healthy lives*. Paper presented at the Annual Meeting of the International Communication Association, New Orleans, LA.

U.S. Census Bureau (2007). Current population survey, annual social and economic supplement, 2006. Table 1.4 Population by Age, Race, 2006. Internet Release date July 27, 2007.

Valliant, G. E. (2002). *Aging well: Surprising guideposts to a happier life from the landmark study of adult development*. Boston: Little Brown.

Vanzant, I. (2010). *Peace from broken pieces*. Los Angeles: Smiley Books.

Wade-Gayles, G. (1993). *Pushed back to strength: A Black woman's journey home*. Boston: Beacon.

Walker, M. B. (1994). *Daughters of Africa*. New York: Ballantine.

Wright-Edelman, M. (1989). *Families in peril*. Boston: Harvard University Press.

Zucker, A., Ostove, J.M., & Stewart, A.J. (2002). College educated women's personality development in adulthood perceptions and differences in age. *Psychology and Aging, 17*(2), 236–244.

Chapter Fifteen

Overcoming Gender and Race Issues in the Workplace

Jacqueline Fancher Marn

The conceptualization of leadership evokes images of ideological values, intrinsic motivation, integrity, and accountability. While there are varied theoretical approaches to define leadership, many researchers conceptualize leadership as a compilation of traits or behaviors involving complicity or negotiation. Over the past century in mainstream literature on leadership theory, researchers identified leadership as relational practices between leader and group members' exchanges (Jablin, Miller & Keller, 1999), establishing a "social influence process where influence is exerted by a person or group over other people or groups to structure the activities and relationships in an organization" (Yukl, 1994, p. 3).

Early influential research was theorized in terms of power relations that were hierarchical, authoritative, and power influenced. Surveys conceptualizing leadership predominantly studied male leaders, which emphasized male behavior as the standard against which both men and women would be judged (Daft, 2002; Harris, Smith, & Hale, 2002). The traditional roles of women in workplace activities were neither acknowledged nor evidenced in early research with much of this research conducted in larger companies, usually in the United States. During the postindustrial era of sociocultural changes, emerging multicultural perspectives, and globalization, the leadership paradigm shifted. Different classification systems were developed from power relationships, to transformational process, to a skills perspective (Rost, 1991). As women's presence increased in the workforce and as they began occupying positions of leadership, their effectiveness and style of leadership were the focus of increasing studies (Powell & Graves, 2006).

A factor analysis of 176 male managers' responses to a survey of their attitudes toward women in the world of work completed by Bass, Krusell, and Alexander (1971) depicted women as poor prospects for managerial positions. Additional surveys reported large differences in the attitudes and traits of women. While some studies found women as a group described themselves different from men on traits required for management (O'Leary, 1974), Fletcher (2002) noted that women have certain skills that result in distinct expectations within organizational structures. Thus Fletcher observed that women are often expected to be nurturing, selfless, less bureaucratic, and hierarchal in their interactions. The perception of women when characterized as emotional, sympathetic, affectionate, slow to anger (Thio, 2000) fueled the gender stereotypes and created the impression that women are less effective in leadership positions. In reality, conclusive evidence shows that women in leadership positions have to maintain a desired balance in which they do not appear expressly masculine or feminine. Males, however, do not have this difficulty, for there is an inherent set of characteristics considered desirable for men managers (Powell & Butterfield, 1986). Loden (1985) contended that the masculine style of management is characterized by qualities such as hierarchical authority competitiveness and analytic problem-solving positions (e.g., Taylor & Ilgen, 1981). "Other studies have shown that male and female managers both have characteristics required for effective performance as managers, such as potential capability, cooperativeness and understanding, and competitive drive and leadership ability" (Dubno, 1985, p. 235).

According to Fondas (1997) empirical research supports small differences in leadership style and effectiveness between men and women. Some evidence indicates that men and women may differ in personality characteristics that could, in fact, affect leadership style and effectiveness (Templeton & Morrow, 1972; O'Leary & Depner, 1975). Fondas posited women experience slight effectiveness disadvantages in masculine leader roles whereas more feminine roles offer them some advantage. Research further showed that women experience both advantages and disadvantages as leaders, with the disadvantages resulting primarily in the masculine-defined roles (Eagly & Carli, 2003). Such incongruity according to Eagly and Carli requires women leaders to seek leadership styles that do not unnecessarily provoke resistance to their authority and instead complement managerial competence. The resulting male-female perceptions plague expectations and aspirations and increase the challenge of women, particularly African American women within the workforce.

Yet the developmental antecedents of leadership for African American women indicate a dearth of empirical literature that is less than optimal or comprehensive. Historically, by the 1960s there was a growing impetus to address the disparate effects of workplace inequality, motivated by decades of social turbulence associated with the women's liberation movement, sociocultural changes, and federal legislation on discrimination in employment (specifically Title VII of the Civil Rights Act, 1964, and Affirmative Action) (Bass, 1981). Supported by commissions on women's development and governmental legislation, the advent of impending shifts in opportunity amplified the concept of women's centrality within the workforce. The decades following the 1960s experienced an increase in African Americans entering a wide range of occupations, becoming more visible as chief executives of many cities (Biles, 1992) with the rate of representation in state and bureaucratic jobs increasing substantially as well (McGlowan-Fellows & Thomas, 2004). Some African Americans were able to benefit from affirmative action efforts that helped add to Black representation in professional and managerial positions (Allen & Farley, 1986). The evolution in leadership research inspired new concepts and substantive divisions that began the contextual frameworks for understanding women's levels of participation in the economy. The context for understanding women's roles and styles of leadership became an important consideration for corporate planning and policy decisions. Study results continued as a foundation for discussion surrounding women in the labor force.

In recent decades shifts in organizational demographics with respect to race, gender, and national origin supporting cultural diversity became the new corporate objective (Edwards, 1991) and a measure designed to influence organizational change. The number of women leaders and those competing for leadership positions likewise increased scholarly interest in response to the global trend in which women are disproportionately relegated to lower-level leadership positions (Powell & Graves, 2006). Yet, while some measured gains may exist for women and specifically Black leaders, additional studies of women's entry into management recorded limitations because of discriminatory practices in personnel decisions, retaining, promoting, and supervision (Rosen & Jerdee, 1974). Petersen and Saporta (2004) noted impediments to women's upward movement diminished in the early 1980s, however, with women promoted at increased rates to upper-level positions. Using Equal Employment Opportunity Commission (EEOC) data collected on sex by race/ethnic employment and occupational segregation from U.S. employers, recent research methodically addressed how women and minorities access management positions (Tomaskovic-Devey, Zimmer, Stainback, Robinson, Taylor, & McTague, 2006).

Assumptions from earlier studies created a paradigm to explain racial and gender inequality revealing barriers created by behavioral and cultural corporate practices associated with workplace recruitment, retention, promotion, stereotyping, and quotas resulting in wage inequality and job segregation (Huffman & Cohen, 2004). While findings from previous workplace studies continue to show that some gains have been made and have generated meaningful information, there remains a critical need to examine factors that explain disproportionate gains for Black women in leadership positions and how those who join the leadership ranks negotiate contextual relations in the workplace. When negotiating the workplace dynamic, Black women's resiliency depends on a number of variables: identifying gender and race issues; embracing ethnic distinction to move beyond the stereotype; understanding the organizational culture; and creating an expectancy of success.

Gender and Race Issues and Their Strained Effects on Black Women Leaders

Built on a class structure with inherent inequality, our culture has established gender and race as organizers in Western society. Individuals often rely on these categorizations to synthesize information in order to provide identifiers about people (Smith, Smith, & Markham, 2000). Investigations of how humans differ by sex dominated the literature throughout the 1970s (Goetz & Grant, 1988). The early years of the feminist movement influenced scholars committed to equality in which many sought to discover no genetic gender differences beyond those involving procreation or they hoped to establish unambiguous biological imperatives of the superiority of one sex over the other (Nihlen, 1975). Jaggar (1983) posited the basic differences between the sexes as social constructions emanated from the different roles that men and women play in a patriarchal society. However, what resulted was a perspective that focused on women's attributes of confidence, pride, and hope (Eisenstein, 1983).

Studies show that widely held gender beliefs do exist in the contemporary United States (Lueptow, Garovich, & Lueptow, 1995; Huffman & Cohen, 2004). A significant body of research documents the underrepresentation of women leaders in the workplace (Wright & Baxter, 2000) and has specifically examined how normative conceptions of men and women vary across time, ethnic group, and social situation. "In many contexts where gender is effectively salient, then hegemonic cultural beliefs about gender acts like a weight on the scale that modestly, but systematically differentiates the behavior and evaluations of otherwise similar men and women" (Ridgeway & Correll, 2004, p. 520). Lorber (1994) suggested that gender is an institution that is embedded in all the social processes of everyday life and social organizations, which creates a double standard for judging ability from performance. Its use as a modern social institution is to construct women as a group to be subordinate to men as a group (Lorber).

According to Ridgeway and Correll (2004) one of the significant achievements in gender knowledge in the past decade is the theoretical conceptualization of defining gender as a social phenomenon. Ridgeway and Correll contended gender as a social phenomenon reinforced by social contexts created a hierarchy assigning more status and power to men. The research literature primarily confirmed that gender is a foundational element of organizational structure in processes, practices, and distributions of power (Acker, 1990; Huffman & Cohen, 2004). Gendered and race-based social groups have different access to social capital because they are situated in different positions in the social hierarchy and often outside of the social mainstream (Acker). Kanter (1977) argued social network variables can explain workplace achievement beyond work-style assumptions of masculine versus feminine. Social relational contexts can be insidious, building systems of inequality (Kanter), and thus amplify the significance of gender in its creation of a cumulative effect within organizations.

Moreover, as a whole, the research results concerning leadership and gender are complex and contradictory. Much of the research relies on extensive measurement of personal attributes that reveal the degree to which gender differences are due to the measured individual attributes (Pinnick, 1994). First, "leader and gender stereotypes put aspiring female leaders at a distinct disadvantage by forcing them to deal with the perceived incongruity between the leader role and their gender role" (Powell & Graves, 2006, p. 86). Increasingly, however, women's leadership is characterized by inclusiveness, receptiveness, shared decision making, concern for relationships, cooperativeness, and a climate of openness (Daft, 2002; Harris, Smith, & Hale, 2002). Such characteristics that dominate explanations for gender disparity produce exclusionary practices, creating a myriad of challenges for women leaders.

Socially constructed, gender asserts certain expectations in male-female power relations. Many of the behaviors and traits traditionally associated with specific gender and racial/ethnic groups are inaccurate and greatly influence conditions and opportunities available to women and persons of color (Smith, Smith, & Markham, 2000). For African American women the result is added discriminatory treatment that is reflected in the tenor of their workplace relationships. It is important to note, according to Cole (1995): often, "women of color also incorrectly assume that to struggle for gender equality means that they have to set aside their struggle against racism"—a particularly powerful and burdensome perception that is exacerbated by these women's knowledge that they also face what Cole called the "sting of sexism" (p. 550). Despite moderate gains made by women and racial minorities, White male advantage has remained essentially undisturbed in the most sought-after blue-collar and white-collar occupations (Stainback, Robinson, & Tomaskovic-Devey, 2005).

Glass Ceiling

Access to information can be an obstacle for women and minorities' efforts to gain access to leadership positions. Unquestionably, their struggle is aggravated by information about jobs, which is often passed through gendered and racialized social networks (Green, Tigges, & Diaz, 1999). White males are assumed to have access to higher-quality jobs through old boy networks (Saloner, 1985). Kanter (1977) explained that women are less often successful because they are more often blocked from network advantages. Gender as a socially constructed category contains inherent power differences (Weber, 2001) while some theorize women may benefit from networking with males, and members of minority groups may benefit from associating with members of dominant groups.

Leadership development for women is often limited because of what has been termed the *glass ceiling*, "an often invisible but formidable workplace barrier" (Shaw, Champlin, Hartmann, & Spalter-Roth, 1993, p. 1). Auster (1993) observed that the glass ceiling is not one ceiling or wall in a single, defined location; instead, it is frequently a pervasive type of gender bias. Many African Americans believe that they have been kept from getting the optimal jobs, thus facing the impenetrable glass ceiling in their attempt to move into leadership positions (Sigelman & Welch, 1991; Williams & Chung, 1997).

For African American women, however, the glass ceiling impeding their career advancement may be more than mere glass with significant, potential economic implications. According to Anderson (1998), the glass ceiling has, instead, been referenced to concrete. Corporate policies and practices in career development, operations training, hidden rewards systems, and hierarchal prerequisites often serve as identified barriers preventing women from reaching upper-most management positions (Davies-Netzley, 1998). The 1989 Department of Labor instituted the "Glass Ceiling Initiative," examining the issue of the glass ceiling and succession plans in Fortune 500 companies (Powell & Butterfield, 1994). This initiative spoke to the persistent biased stereotype, lack of systemic corporate efforts that created impediments to complete women and minority participation. The study results determined minorities and women were employed well below the executive level in staff rather than line positions that were a career track to executive positions (Morrison & von Glinow, 1990). The study further noted there was a glass ceiling beyond which few minorities and women advanced (Morrison & von Glinow).

African American women have to challenge the use of gender as well as race to limit the types of positions that are available to them. Organizational behavior associated with discrimination and institutional prejudices narrow perspectives with regard to the ability of African American women to be effective in leadership positions. Motives for the disparity are caught between race, gender, and cultural beliefs. Within the prevalence of gender-role stereotyping there is the confusion over the ambitions and abilities of women as observed by Maddock and Parkin (1993). However, the increasing number of African American women in leadership has fueled scholarly interest and has challenged narrow conceptions and distinctions of gender patterning addressing the vast, divergent views of Black women and their potential for leadership.

Race History

Despite the passage of the 14th Amendment in 1868, which guaranteed Blacks equal rights under the law, equality was uncommon in most of the nation for nearly a century. Coakley (1998) noted that since the 1700s, racial categorization led to race logic, which positioned the logic that White-skinned people were intellectually superior to people of color, who were labeled as physically superior or beastlike savages. Later, in the nation's history, the Civil Rights Act of 1964 banned racial practices and made it unlawful to discriminate because of a person's race, national origin, religion, or sex in areas such as employment, housing, or public services. In spite of this legal progress, however, ideologies of racial differences and efforts to expose race and racism using race logic continued (Stepan, 1982). According to Adam and Allen (1995) the area of race inquiry in the social and behavioral sciences is principally affected by willingness to accept unconfirmed and oversimplified statements without query. Hare (2002) observed "such scientific confusion may have complex explanations, such as the difficulty of disentangling race from culture from history" (p. 571). Allen further noted the explanations may be simpler, as in the failure to recognize that race is not a perfect predictor of a person's values, or even experiences. The substantial research on issues of race and class centers, in part, on race perspective that stresses the persistent nature of both past and present institutional discrimination across all class levels limiting the life chances of all Blacks (Willie, 1978). Sociologists and critical race theorists assert that racism is permanent, whether it exists or is ideologically supposed (Winant, 1994). It is important to understand racial beliefs and practices have become far more contradictory and complex and that it is necessary to move naive assumptions and revive discussions of racism as a multidimensional social force (Winant).

Racism in the Workplace

Throughout the history of the United States, African American women have been challenged by issues of race, class, and gender (Collins, 1991; Hunter, 1998; Peterson, 1992). Within the social, cultural, and economic changes stemming from the Civil Rights movement and the women's equal rights movement, one might expect minorities' gains to be relatively greater (Menges & Exum, 1983). Motivated, in part, by threats of federal sanctions, White companies during the 1960s and 1970s incorporated a new stratum of college-educated Blacks into previously closed managerial jobs (Landry, 1987). Though not a widely recognized and uniformed improvement, it informed corporate change and accentuated the relationship between human capital and race-based systems of job allocations. Despite some progress in the socioeconomic status of working women and minorities, race and gender inequalities in workplace power continue. The reality, however, is women are not present in leadership in critical numbers.

There has not been substantial empirical data to sanction the belief that the race-based discrimination in the workplace has been eliminated (Stuart, 1992). It is not easy to assess situations since data for minority leaders is collected less carefully and less frequently than for women in the dominate group, and it is not always clear whether data pertain to all ethnic minorities or only to African Americans (Menges & Exum, 1983). Even with heightened concern, and often constrained by issues of race, itinerant research minimally documents the experiences and perceptions of African American women leaders in particular.

In the midst of changing culture and now in a more globalized market, some companies now understand the need to embrace racially diverse environments (Forsyth, 2006). Thus companies will suffer a competitive disadvantage if they fail to utilize Black workers who are fully competent to perform the job. Essentially, the utilization of African American workers is increasingly required if firms are to remain productive and competitive (Forsyth). Paradoxically, there are acknowledged gains in entry to upper-level positions for African Americans; yet, disproportionately African Americans clearly stagnate in their ascent through the managerial vertical alignment, and thus fail to achieve positions of power. The result over time for corporations is underdeveloped human capital, which marginalizes the employee and the employee's abilities (Elliott & Smith, 2004). According to Elliott and Smith such patterns suggest that workplace power constitutes a central battleground in struggles for equalizing opportunities sometimes creating an environment where Black women feel peripheralized and discredited. Specific findings indicate that, relative to White men, all groups encounter increasing inequality at higher levels of power, but only Black women seem to experience this form of inequality as a result of direct discrimination (Elliott & Smith).

Whether overt or covert, discrimination intervenes in the everyday cultural logic of race (Banton, 1997). Racism is the foundation of discrimination (Banton) and as an existential fact continues as a vehicle of oppression, challenging opportunities in the employment arena (Fosu, 1997; Spaights & Whitaker, 1995). Fundamentally, systemic racism viewed as incontrovertible disproportionately burdens African Americans while within some companies using a façade of equality attempts to supersede the canon of racism (Spaights & Whitaker). While the tolerance for overt racism has changed the outward corporate appearance, corporations at large have not created and maintained a radically new paradigm for equality.

Discrimination, even when it is not observed, must be inferred as a residual significant effect within workplace stratification hierarchies (Moss & Tilly, 2001). Covert racism proves equally as damaging as a "subtle and subversive institutional or societal practice, policy and norm utilized to mask structural racial apparatus. Consequently, covert racism often undetected, is often inherently inculcated" (Coates, 2008, p. 212). The centrality of employer preconceptions and especially the ways in which subjective biases translate into discriminatory behaviors against women of color may contribute to exclusion and stagnation in mobility, an important mechanism for the effect on the Black population's racial wage gap (Padavic & Orcutt, 1997).

Negotiating the Workplace Dynamic: Black Women Resiliency

Embracing Ethnic Distinction and Moving Beyond the Stereotype

In recent decades racial worldview continues to maintain its momentum supporting an intrinsic connection inhibiting the development of and access to the wide range of options available to African Americans in American labor markets. While results of research on ethnic attitudes during the 1970s gave rise to the conclusion that negative stereotypes about African Americans in the United States had decreased (Pettigrew, 1979, 1985), not everyone, however, shared this optimism. This is especially true because many Black women have been an abstraction unadorned with symbols of reward and unrecognized in positions of power with limited allocation of privilege and wealth.

Scholars debated during the 1840s and 1850s whether Europeans, White Americans, and Negroes were created equal (Gould, 1981). While there was disparity in determining whether non-Whites were a separate species or a subspecies, there was the general consensus that "Negro inferiority was an unchangeable fact of nature" (Fredrickson, 1971, p. 83). "In the United States the biophysical features of different populations, which had become markers of social status, were internalized as sources of individual and group identities" (Smedley, 1999, p. 695). During the 19th and 20th centuries the concept of race was linked with biological features, such as skin color and facial traits (Guthrie, 1976). Guthrie described the early work of anthropologists who tried to classify races according to skin-color measures, hair texture, and lip thickness. Studies showed biological markers were analogous to the controversial theory that intelligence and some social behaviors could be related to a particular type of race, considering it as a biological designation (Smedley, 1999). Some scientists prefer to use such race-based concepts in biological ways, asserting that race remains useful as an analytic category (Wade, 2004). While other discourses range from bio-determinism to other attributable characteristics, Weber (1978) argued race is a matter of consciousness, not biology. Attributable to the inferiority paradigm built on the belief that people of color are biologically and genetically inferior to Whites (Carter & Goodwin, 1994), however, continues a fluidity establishing a societal disposition that makes these tenets seem natural to some.

Following the Civil War the advent of racial ideology strengthened defining and subsequently stereotyping African Americans as the lowest-status group in American society. Stemming from the cultural imperative of race ideology, portrayals of their inferiority pronounced them intellectually inferior and morally dubious to some. Within the dominant view of racial disparities as a product of stereotypical characteristics for African Americans, many in the majority population now believe that since they are no longer racially prejudiced there are no barriers to opportunity for Blacks (Kluegel & Smith, 1986). Yet, despite significant progress in the socioeconomic status of working women and minorities, race and gender inequalities in workplace power perpetuate and abound. Studies of the possibility of discrimination by analyses of employer attitudes of women in organizations demonstrated that employers may hold biased views that may influence hierarchal, corporate decisions surrounding hiring, firing, and promotions (Kirschenman & Neckerman, 1991; Bass, Krusell, & Alexander, 1971). For African American women, detrimental employer biases might position them as less dependable, segregate them into lower-skilled, race-typed jobs involving menial tasks and poor working conditions, and lead to stagnation in upward mobility (Gruber, 1998; Padavic & Orcutt, 1997).

Beyond the Stereotype

African American women continue to encounter obstacles resulting from stereotypic beliefs rooted in race. Inasmuch as it is a normative expectation for women to insist that they be responsive to the needs of others sacrificing their own goals and desires, the perception of Black women as sympathetic is often compromised by stereotypical images of sharp-tongued, easily dismissed and sexualized, aggressive or indecisive leaders (Collins, 2000; hooks, 1981).

To combat the stereotype and the imposed depreciation, inequity, and disdain that Black women experience within the sphere of the workplace culture, Black women leaders must do several things. First, they must work to construct a new image of pride by moving beyond the contempt many hold regarding their African past. A central component is to embrace their own sense of dignity understanding African American women's ancestral patterns of resistance that were vital ingredients in ensuring the survival of their community from slave revolts to the present female notions of resistance (Davis, 1971). According to Davis, during slavery African American women endured a double oppression, and their survival-oriented activities made them heirs to a tradition of perseverance and heroic resistance, thus allowing them to create self-definitions. Davis (1981) asserted that slavery constructed for Black women an alternative definition of womanhood, one that included a tradition of "hard work, perseverance and self-reliance, a legacy of tenacity, resistance and an insistence on sexual equality" (p. 29).In spite of this oppression, Black women have been endowed with the capacity to be successful beyond the stereotypic view many may hold to raise their voices in leadership roles. Studies of Black women have emphasized that from adversity and oppression come the formation of womanhood and the ability of these women to turn adversity into strength and courage (Giddings, 1984).

W. E. B Du Bois (1990) noted that historic, cultural cores must be integrated into the economic and social life of the settlement within which they are embedded, which involves balancing identity. As such, for African American women he suggested that African Americans have to fight part of this battle against racial stereotypes and exclusion on the terrain of identity. Thus, developing an identity beyond stereotypical designations can become a means to empowerment prompting self-determination for Black women leaders.

Afrocentric African American intellectuals have argued for the need to establish an autonomous cultural identity "from the Negro point of view" (Cruse, 1984, p. 71) gaining historical perspective, which fuels ambition, motivates determination, and supports achievement. According to Cruse (1984), African American women leaders who gain perspective surrounding successes and failures of their predecessors are better equipped to construct new intellectual paradigms of inspiration and liberation. Inasmuch as Afrocentricism constructs a positive identity beyond the sphere of traditional Western ideals of women leaders popularized in the literature, it also repositions the philosophy of Black women as a means to negotiate and resist race-based identification when detrimental.

Cultural Identity

The importance of cultural identity to people of African descent has been emphasized repeatedly (Asante, 1983; Cruse, 1967; Karenga, 1983) as it repositions Black consciousness. For decades the African American community identity has been influenced by definitions assigned to it by the larger society from images of beauty to its definition of success (Oliver, 1989). Within the school of Du Bosian thought he warned of the impact that hundreds of years of enslavement, oppression, and institutionalized racism could have on the collective and individual psyches of African Americans (Du Bois, 1990, 1939; Akbar, 1984). African Americans, Du Bois argued, were constantly reminded of their supposed inferiority and kept in a quasi-state of slavery. Du Bois believed that to respond to their psychological oppression in Western society, African Americans would have to surround themselves in African and Black culture. Surrounding themselves with positive images of African and Black culture and history would put African Americans in parity with European Americans, allowing them to deflect prominent negative images of themselves (Du Bois). Resulting from what often appears to be an immediate assimilation and abandonment of cultural tradition and its social character, the challenge remains to advance the status of African Americans beyond the confines imposed by the larger society. According to Dr. John Clark:

"A race is like a man. Until it uses its own talents, takes pride in its own history, and loves its own memories, it can never fulfill itself completely" (n.d).

Within the scope of cultural identification for Black women who lead and are concentrated in non-representative management structures, they must move beyond corporate derailment techniques, in part, by embracing and capitalizing on their understanding of their cultural identity. Black women will need to recognize that culture can be the core of the matrix that underlies character, influences behavior, and becomes essential to making them leaders. As Hine and Thompson (1998) asserted: "Quite simply the way Black women approach life works. The cultural traditions of survival, resistance and change have enabled Black women to shape the raw materials of their lives into an extraordinary succession of victories" (p. 5).

Understand the Organizational Culture

Organizational culture has been the focus of many studies. Organizational culture typically is defined as a complex set of values, beliefs, assumptions, and symbols that define the way in which a firm conducts its business (Barney, 1986). "Based on an analysis of questionnaires obtained from more than 100,000 respondents in more than 50 countries, Hofstede (1980, 1997, 2001) identified five major dimensions in which cultures differed: power distance, uncertainty avoidance, individualism-collectivism, masculinity-feminist, and long-term-short-term orientation" (Northouse, 2004, p. 305).

Organizational cultures encompass both individual and group-level subcultures assembled by age, race, and gender that perpetuate different behaviors. These splintered employee groups have the propensity to alter and sometimes even replace the official culture (Harris, 1994). According to Harris most organizational scholars agree that sharing beliefs and values captured in schemas is a prerequisite for the existence of culture in organizations. Schemas as observed by Harris serve as mental maps that enable individuals to orient themselves within their experiential terrain.

While the organization should ideally embody core values of acceptable behavior (Block, 1991), organizational cultures typically develop specific categories relating to the organization's power structure and use of symbolic mechanisms to establish and maintain control (DiMaggio, 1997). Misuse of such categories constitutes the principal means by which culture is shaped and biases are formed and solidified (DiMaggio). Such divisional practices create a foundation where African Americans experience a disproportionate share of social liabilities. Because social knowledge is generally contextually bound (Holyoak & Gordon, 1984), women may see themselves as preparing for inconsequential ranking. Social stereotypes may strengthen the perception that women in organizations are members of a lower-status group (Ely, 1995).

African American women work to negotiate the organizational terrain by several approaches. Researchers seem to agree that culture may be an important factor in determining how well an individual assimilates into an organizational culture (Schein, 1985). Since leaders design organizational systems and shape organizational cultures, leadership implies identification of core organizational goals (Schein). African American women leaders then must create standards for excellence and identify ways to achieve these standards. Learning to effectively navigate their interactions with people from different ethnic and cultural backgrounds can help build credibility. Studies show that distrust of management is pervasive (King, 2004), thus building quality relationships will generate improved performance. Black women leaders must also garner meaning from workplace experiences from changeable structures that alienate them. Black women must use cultural challenge to become a mobilizing force in an effort to develop a voice to identify struggles and negotiate resolution and to create processes that address contradictions in perceptions toward collaboration. Black women leaders must likewise capitalize on the predictable measures. Such predictability is essential for the establishment of trust between employees and management (Granovetter, 1985).

African American women leaders serve as role models for standard behavior within the organization as they play a critical role in managing organizational diversity and establish and present a set of behaviors motivated to reduce discrepancies among impressionistic images. Professional image construction has important implications for achieving social approval, power, well-being, and career success (Ibarra, 1999; Rosenfeld, Giacalone, & Riordan, 2001; Schlenker, 2003). Some women may use impression management employing behaviors to protect their self-images and behaviors that influence the way they are perceived by significant others. According to Meyerson and Fletcher (2000) women seem to prefer to rely on extra high performance and commitment for visibility to their seniors rather than networking. Greenwald (1980) and Steele (1988) argued that people strive to affirm their self-concepts and women in the workplace create assertive self-presentation strategies to garner a desired impression (Tedeschi & Norman, 1985).

Within organizations minority workforces may demand increased access to good jobs or fair treatment from management (Smith & Elliott, 2002). Studies have emphasized the overtly discriminatory actions of employers (Neckerman & Kirschenman, 1991) and the sociocognitive stereotyping processes that predicate differential treatment (Ridgeway, 1997). A study by Steele (1999) noted that the mere presence of stereotypes can have debilitating effects on minorities' performance. Exposing African American women to stereotypic beliefs when thought to be less competent in a given domain has been shown to raise anxiety and lead to lower performance (Steele). Consequently, a sizeable percent of African Americans in the workplace expect race and race-related issues to potentially impede their corporate evolution and subsequent leadership progression. Thus, Black women must work to understand the interplay between structural factors and race-based, situational assumptions regarding their merit that extend beyond cultural stereotypes to address exclusionary decisions. They must understand what is essential as corporate discourse, what is capricious, and what is intended for the purpose of discrimination within the complex, hierarchical employment structure. To this end, Black women must discover points of convergence that challenge the status quo and subsequently Black oppression (Kitano, 1985).

Entrepreneurship can also be significant to addressing the challenges of stratification within organization culture that limits opportunity for Black women who stagnate in the traditional male-dominated, hierarchical structure. In the last decade small business has been an increasing contributor to growth in the American economy. A report by the National Women's Business Council (2004) showed 365,110 majority-owned, privately held firms were owned by African American women in the United States in 2004, amassing approximately $14 billion in revenues. As Black women become more attuned to the struggle of being perceived as nonproductive and as they are overlooked for promotions into higher-level positions within the vertical corporate structure, they can begin the process of identifying and pursuing opportunities of entrepreneurship. Their increasing entrepreneurial involvement will empower women, providing directions for others, and will have economic implications for corporations and companies that fail to promote Black women (Baumol, 1990).

Creating an Expectancy of Success

Self-efficacy. There are a number of interconnected reasons for the stagnation of Black women vying for leadership positions. The differential distribution of Black women leaders in the workplace has been attributed to many factors, among which include a convergence of economic forces and social processes and the opportunities available to them. Narrow perspectives with regard to the ability of African American women to be effective in managerial positions have likewise barred many from obtaining senior-level leadership positions (Smith, 1982).

At the national level the percentage of Black women in professional occupations doubled between 1960 and 1980 (Sokoloff, 1992), which is significant because of their exclusion from these occupational sectors in the past. While there are Black women leaders numerically disproportionate in the hierarchal structure, the practice of *tokenism* (Kanter, 1975) also represents blocked opportunity. However, when given the opportunity and when seeing people similar to oneself succeed by sustained effort, observers' beliefs are raised that they too possess the capabilities to master comparable activities required to succeed (Bandura, 1994). When African American women in particular are exposed to the success of other

African American women, a general self-efficacy builds a global confidence within the sphere of demand, isolation, and marginalization, and provides a greater sense of personal competence. Studies show when women occupy low-mobility positions, they confirm generalizations made about women's organizational behavior: limited aspiration, socialization with peers that is sometimes disruptive, and low morale, and job interest (Kanter, 1982).

While the present normative conditions persist surrounding gender and race articulation in the workplace, Black women persevere, in part, from self-efficacy. Bandura (1978) defined self-efficacy as "a judgment of one's ability to execute a particular behavior pattern" (p. 240). Bandura suggested that self-efficacy beliefs form an essential role in the governing process of one's motivation and performance attainments. African American women leaders must rely on their efficacy and its influence on their workplace behavior and performance, beliefs at the foundation for human motivation and personal accomplishment (Schwarzer, 1994). Bandura (1997) further identified self-efficacy as "one's capability to organize and execute the courses of action required to produce given attainments" (p. 3). Consequently, "the higher the sense of self-efficacy, the greater the effort, persistence, and resilience" (Pajares, 2002, p. 5). As Baumeister (1993) observed, the focus on self-esteem presents a number of positive outcomes for the individual and for society as a whole and for African American women in the workplace it lessens the effects of social disenfranchisement.

Black women leaders with strong self-efficacy beliefs exert greater efforts to master challenges and through continual personal assessment can build greater employee flexibility and facilitate communication confidently among the corporate power structure. As Bandura (1997) observed, the development of coping capabilities and skills in managing one's motivation, emotional states, and thought processes increases perceived self-regulatory efficacy. The higher the sense of self-regulatory efficacy Bandura noted, the better the occupational functioning. In short, personal values lie at the core of leadership; therefore, leadership with character is a powerful means of building company cultures that have both moral as well as economic imperatives (Goffee & Jones, 1998). Efficacy-based self-esteem helps individuals deal with various stressors within the social structures within which they exist (Baumeister, 1993), thus promoting self-knowledge, increased motivation, and intellectual efficacy.

Career Development

Education. The emergence of new knowledge-based economies has placed increasing emphasis on education. During the last few decades organizations have become increasingly more interested in career development in their response to a more global economy, economic drives, and productivity demands. Professional development in the workplace requires some of its employees to enroll in structured courses and company professional development classes. "Formal professional education courses and programs may be directed either toward people who are inexperienced and seeking to gain entry to a particular profession or toward experienced professionals who seek some form of continuing education outside their usual place of work" (Dall'Alba & Sandberg, 2006, p. 384). Increasing the access of women to educational opportunities in the workplace may improve their mobility within the company to achieve organizational success.

Gandhi saw education as a necessary means for enabling women to uphold their natural rights (Kishwar, 1985). Historically, African American women have valued the role education has played in their lives, particularly in the workplace dynamic. Education underlies a range of managerial systems—including those used for appraisal, career progression, and incentives—that encourage the development of professional skills (Dall'Alba & Sandberg, 2006).

The increasing proportion of African American women with high levels of education has allowed more of them to take advantage of expanding labor market opportunities. Educational credentials are the primary mechanism through which professions reserve employment positions for similar others (Mezirow, 1997). Mezirow further observed educational achievement sustains the organizational infrastructure, facilities, personal redefinition, and empowerment (1997) and as a means to increase potential advancement and wage compensation. In short, education increases marketability in the workforce. According to Khumoetsile-Taylor (2000), success resulting from education creates broad implications across social and economic lines.

Training. Despite the gains that women have made in the workplace, African American women remain underrepresented in positions of leadership besieged by negative attitudes and stereotypes (Klenke, 1996); thus, the goal must be to direct, support, and nurture these women in what is often a climate steeped in the ambivalence of race and gender. Gradually, companies have now begun to recognize that career development for its employees means profitability and improved efficiency (Walker, 1973) and is a necessary response to globalization of economies (Gilpin, 2002). Education and training are the most important investments in human capital.

While career development lies with both employees and employers (Orpen, 1994), for African American women in the workplace, the decision regarding corporate training and education must be driven by personal choice to generate opportunity. Aspiring professionals are expected first to acquire basic knowledge and skills relevant to their chosen profession and, later, more advanced knowledge and skills through formal and informal training (Dall'Alba & Sandberg, 2006). African American women leaders must assume a posture that repositions them in their respective hierarchal structure by garnering career-path information, locating available employment, and availing themselves to required training. The process may begin by attending career workshops to analyze interests, goals, and capabilities. African American women interested in upward mobility must identify possible policies which advance people of color as they work to illuminate and subsequently eliminate barriers to advancement.

Mentoring. Initial theory on mentoring was based on White male samples (Levinson, Darrow, Klein, Levinson, & McKee, 1978), which was limited to explaining homogeneous relationships among members of the dominant power group in most organizations (Ragins, 1997). Women in the labor market in both public and private sectors reportedly have no role models, no mentors, and little psychological support (Bruce, 1995). Sizeable weight is often placed on Black women leaders because of the lack of organizational support. There are few with whom to share experiences or with whom to identify, often creating themselves without model or precedent (Bruce). There is evidence that women who receive mentoring are more rapidly socialized into the culture. Individuals who do not have mentors or sponsors may be at a disadvantage or experience slower progress toward the attainment of career aspirations and development (Boice, 1992). African American women professional success depends, in part, not only on what they know but also on who they know for support, guidance and advocacy. Eberspacher and Sisler (1988) maintained that mentors may be the single most important factor in the career development of leaders inasmuch as mentors share values, career counseling, and information. Studies show the guidance and direction provided by role models, mentors, or sponsors determines an individual's future career path and pattern (Moore, 1982).

Race, ethnicity, and gender along with issues of access, compatibility, and organizational cultures influence the mentoring of African American women. When African American women meet with these obstacles, and in the absence of organizational support, they capitalize on their spirit of resiliency. First, they must advocate for themselves. Set high expectations for personal achievement. Use their personal dignity, intelligence, ambition, the spirit of strength and courage, the power of independent thinking, and initiative in their quest for achievement to sustain them in their negotiation of the workplace. Network with other peer leaders as well as with potential leaders. According to Miller and Vaughan (1997), formal and informal professional support networks are critical when making both personal and professional decisions within the workplace culture.

Beyond the workplace establish community and family involvement to provide the emotional support often important to career growth. Studies have shown that outside of the formal organization, support from community and familial systems are significant for Black women (see also Chaney, Lawrence, & Skogrand, 2012; Green, 1997; McAdoo, 1999).

Conclusion

In the midst of growing interest in explaining why and when historically marginalized groups experience success, accounts of resilience have, however, emphasized the characteristics of those who are beating the odds (O'Connor, 2002). Resilient individuals are said to have dispositions that make them attractive to others, who then intercede in their lives in meaningful ways (Masten, 1994). Such individuals are reported to be intelligent (e.g., Werner & Smith, 1982, 1992) and are commonly described as confident, optimistic, and goal directed (Masten, 1994). Therefore, resilience suggests that it is an individually determined phenomenon that seemingly rests on inherent traits, natural abilities, or personal character and temperaments (O'Connor, 2002). But what happens to resilient Black women leaders when they are disempowered, their sustainability compromised because of systemic, institutionalized forces, or when they are beleaguered as they work toward both personal and professional achievement? What we have discovered is that many African American women thrive despite their organization's general disregard. Gandhi realized that there was the imposition of a psychological fear and helplessness, culturally imposed upon women by society that relegated them to the lowest rung. His message to them was that bravery and courage should not the sole domain of men. It is clear that Black women accept the responsibility of creating a strategy of advocacy addressing the predatory corporate practices illuminating through rhetoric a voice for intolerance and by growth and professional and personal development.

In sum, leadership implies competence in both setting standards for excellence and identifying ways to achieve these standards. Black women must understand both the formal and the informal criteria that exist in the workplace under the guise of equal opportunity when it disadvantages them and react when there is opportunity. The expansion of women leaders requires a context that shapes a positive experience (Turner & Myers, 2000). There is a need for a continuous generation of paradigms, empirical testing of paradigms, and an examination of present paradigms to determine how they illuminate, obscure, or predict experiences of African American women (Howard-Vital, 1989).

Bibliography

Acker, J. (1990). Hierarchies, jobs, bodies: A theory of gendered organizations. *Gender and Society*, *4*(2), 139–158.

Adam, B. & Allen, S. (1995). *Theorizing culture: An interdisciplinary critique after postmodernism*. London: UCL Press.

Akbar, N. (1984). *Chains and images of psychological slavery*. Jersey City, NJ: New Mind Productions.

Allen, W. R., & Farley, R. (1986). The shifting social and economic tides of Black America, 1950–1980. *Annual Review of Sociology, 12*, 277–306.

Anderson, D. (1998). Reclaiming the power: Empowerment strategies for African American women in higher education. Paper presented at the 11th Annual Nation Conference on Race and Ethnicity (NCORE) in Higher Education. May 28–31. Denver, CO.

Ani, M. (1994). *Yurugu: An African-centered critique*. Trenton, NJ: Africa World Press.

Asante, M. (1983). African linguistics and communication continuities. Presented at the Fifteenth Annual Conference of the African Heritage Studies Association. April. New York.

Auster, E.R. (1993). Demystifying the glass ceiling: Organizational and interpersonal dynamics of gender bias. *Business and the Contemporary World, 5*, 47–68.

Bandura, A. (1978). Self-efficacy: Toward a unifying theory of behavioral change. *Psychological Review, 84*, 191–215.

Bandura, A. (1994). Self-efficacy. In V. S. Ramachaudran (Ed.), *Encyclopedia of human behavior* (Vol. 4, pp. 71–81). New York: Academic Press. (Reprinted in H. Friedman [Ed.], *Encyclopedia of mental health*. San Diego: Academic Press, 1998).

Bandura, A. (1997). *Self-efficacy: The exercise of control*. New York: Freeman

Banton, M. (1997). Power and prejudice: The politics and diplomacy of racial discrimination. *New Community, 23*(1), 133.

Barney, J. B. (1986). Organizational culture: Can it be a source of sustained competitive advantage? *Academy of Management Review, 11*(3), 656–665.

Bass, B. M. (1981). *Stogdill's handbook of leadership: A survey of theory and research*. New York: Free Press.

Bass, B. M., Krusell, J., & Alexander, R. A. (1971). Male managers' attitudes toward working women. *American Behavioral Scientist, 15*, 221–236.

Baumeister, R. F. (1993). Preface. In R. F. Baumeister (Ed.), Self-esteem: The puzzle of low self-regard. New York: Plenum.

Baumol, W. J. (1990). Entrepreneurship: Productive, unproductive, and destructive. *Journal of Political Economy, 98*(5), 893–919.

Biles, R. (1992). Black mayors: A historical assessment. *Journal of Negro History, 77*, 109–125.

Block, P. (1991). *The empowered manager: Positive political skills at work*. San Francisco: Jossey-Bass.

Boice, R. (1992). *The new faculty member: Supporting and fostering professional development*. San Francisco: Jossey-Bass.

Bruce, M. A. (1995). Mentoring women doctoral students: What counselor educators and supervisors can do. *Counselor Education & Supervision, 35*(2), 139–149.

Carter, R. T., & Goodwin, A. L. (1994). Racial identity and education. Review of *Research in Education. American Educational Research Association, 20*, 291–336.

Catalyst. (2006). 2006 Catalyst member benchmarking report. Retrieved July 31, 2006, from www.catalystwomen.org

Chaney, C., Lawrence, F., & Skogrand, L. (2012). An exploration of financial coping strategies for college educated African American working women: A Research Note. Published in Fall 2012 Issue of *Black Women, Gender, and Families (BWGF)*.

Coakley, J. (1998). *Sport in society: Issues and controversies* (6th ed.). Boston: McGraw Hill.

Coates, R. D. (2008). Covert racism in the USA and globally. *Sociology Compass, 2*(1), 208–231.

Cole, J. B. (1995). Epilogue. In B. Guy-Sheftall (Ed.), *Words of fire: An anthology of African American feminist thought* (pp. 549–551). New York: New Press.

Collins, P. H. (1990). *Black feminist thought: Knowledge consciousness, and the politics of empowerment*. New York: Routledge.

Collins, P. H. (1991). *Black feminist thought*. New York: Routledge.

Collins, P. H. (2000). *Black feminist thought: Knowledge, consciousness, and the politics of empowerment* (2nd ed.). New York: Routledge.

Cruse, H. (1984). *The crisis of the Negro intellectual*. New York: Quill.

Cruse, H. (1967). *The crisis of the Negro intellectual*. New York: William Morrow & Co.

Daft, R. L. (2002). *The leadership experience.* Fort Worth: Harcourt.

Dall'Alba, G., & Sandberg, J. (2006). Unveiling professional development: A critical review of stage models review of educational research. *American Educational Research Association, 76*(3), 383–412.

Davies-Netzley, S. (1998). Women above the glass ceiling: Perceptions on corporate mobility and strategies for success. *Gender and Society, 12,* 339–355.

Davis, A. (1971). Reflections on the Black woman's role in the community of slaves. *Black Scholar, 3,* 2–15.

Davis, A. (1981). *Women, race and class.* New York: Random House.

Department of Labor. (1991). A Report on the Glass Ceiling Initiative. Washington, DC: U.S. Government Printing Office.

DiMaggio, P. J. (1997). Culture and cognition. *Annual Review of Sociology, 23,* 263–287.

Du Bois, W. E. B. (1939). *Blackfolk then and now: An essay in the history and sociology of the Negro race.* New York: Henry Holt.

Du Bois, W. E. B. (1970). *The gift of Black folk: The Negro in the making of America.* New York: Simon & Schuster.

Du Bois, W. E. B. (1970). *The Negro.* New York: Oxford University Press.

Du Bois, W. E. B. (1990). *The souls of Black folk: Essays and sketches.* New York: Vintage Books.

Dubno, P. (1985). Attitudes toward women executives: A longitudinal approach. *Academy of Management Journal, 28*(1), 235–239.

Eagly, A., & Carli, L. (2003). The female leadership advantage: An evaluation of the evidence. *Leadership Quarterly, 14,* 807–834.

Eberspacher, J., & Sisler, G. (1988). Mentor relationships in academic administration. *Journal of the National Association of Women Deans and Counselors, 51,* 27–32.

Edwards, A. (1991). The enlightened manager: How to treat all employees fairly. *Working Woman, 16,* 45–51.

Eisenstein, H. (1983). *Contemporary feminist thought.* Boston: G. K. Hall & Co.

Elliott, J., & Smith, R. (2002). Race, gender, and workplace power. *American Sociological Review, 69*(3), 365–386.

Ely, R. (1995). The power in demography: Women's social constructions of gender identity at work. *Academy Management, 38,* 589–634.

Essed, P. (1990). *Everyday racism: Reports from women in two cultures.* Alameda, CA: Hunter House.

Fletcher, J. (2002). The greatly exaggerated demise of heroic leadership: Gender power, and the myth of female advantage. *CGO Insight.* Retrieved March 1, 2007, from http://www.simmons.edu

Fondas, N. (1997). Feminization unveiled: Management qualities in contemporary writings. *Academy of Management Review, 22*(1), 257–282.

Forsyth, D. R. (2006). *Group dynamics* (4th ed.). Pacific Grove, CA: Brooks/Cole.

Fosu, A. K. (1997). Occupational gains of Black women since the 1964 Civil Rights Act: Long-term or episodic? *American Economic Review, 87,* 311–314.

Fredrickson, G. M. (1971). *The Black image in the White mind: The debate on Afro-American character and destiny, 1817–1914.* New York: Harper & Row.

Giddings, P. (1984). *When and where I enter: The impact of Black women on race and sex in America.* New York: Bantam Books.

Gilpin, (2002). *The challenge of global capitalism: The world economy in the 21st century.* Princeton, NJ: Princeton University Press.

Goetz, J. P., & Grant, L. (1988). Conceptual approaches to studying gender in education: Women, culture, and education. *Anthropology & Education Quarterly, 19*(2), 182–196.

Goffee, R., & Jones, G. (1998). *The character of a corporation.* New York: Harper Business.

Gould, S. J. (1981). *The mis-measure of man.* New York: Norton.

Granovetter M. (1985). Economic action and social structure: The problem of embeddedness. *American Sociology, 91*(3), 481–510.

Green, G. P., Tigges, L. M., & Diaz, D. (1999). Racial and ethnic differences in job search strategies in Atlanta, Boston, and Los Angeles. *Social Science Quarterly, 80*, 263–278.

Green, P. S. (1997). Rites of passage and rights of way. In L. Benjamin (Ed.), *Black women in the academy: Promises and perils* (pp. 149–157). Gainesville: University Press of Florida.

Greenwald, A. G. (1980). The totalitarian ego: Fabrication and revision of personal history. *American Psychologist, 35*, 603–618.

Gruber, J. E. (1998). The impact of male work environments and organizational policies on women's experiences of sexual harassment. *Gender and Society, 12*, 301–320.

Guthrie, R. V. (1976). *Even the rat was White: A historical view of psychology.* New York: Bantam Books.

Hare, B.R. (2002). *Race odyssey: African Americans and sociology.* Syracuse, New York: Syracuse University Press.

Harris, C. M., Smith, P. L., & Hale, R. P. (2002). Making it work: Women's ways of leading. Advancing women in leadership. Retrieved June 24, 2007, at http://www.advancingwoman.com/awlfall 2002/Harris.html

Harris, S. G. (1994). Organizational culture and individual sensemaking: A schema-based perspective. *Organization Science, 5*(3), 309–321.

Harrison, F. V. (1992). The Du Boisian legacy in anthropology. *Critique of Anthropology, 12*(3), 239–260.

Hine, D. C., & Thompson, K. (1998). *A shining thread of hope: The history of Black women in America.* New York: Broadway Books.

Hofstede, G.H. (2001). Culture's consequences: Comparing values, behaviors, institutions, and organizations across nations. Thousand Oaks, CA: Sage Publications, Inc.

Hofstede, G. H. (1997). *Cultures and organizations: Software of the Mind.* London: McGraw Hill.

Hofstede, G.H. (1980). Culture and organizations. *International Studies of Management & Organization 10*(4), 15–41.

Holyoak, K. J., &. Gordon, P. C. (1984). Information processing and social cognition. In R. S. Wyer & T. K. Srull (Eds.), *Handbook of social cognition* (Vol. 1, pp. 39–70). Hillsdale, NJ: Lawrence Erlbaum.

hooks, b. (1981). *Ain't I a woman: Black women and feminism.* Boston: South End Press.

Howard-Vital, M. (1989). African-American women in higher education: Struggling to gain identity. *Journal of Black Studies, 20*(2), 180–191.

Huffman, M. L., & Cohen, P. N. (2004). Racial wage inequality: Job segregation and evaluation across labor markets. *American Journal of Sociology, 109*(4), 902–936.

Huffman, M.L., & Cohen, P.H. (2004). Occupational segregation and the gender gap in workplace authority: National versus local labor markets. *Sociological Forum, 19*(1), 121–147.

Hunter, M. L. (1998). Colorstruck: Skin color stratification in the lives of African American women. *Sociological Inquiry, 68*(4), 517–535.

Ibarra, H. (1999). Provisional selves: Experimenting with age and identity in professional adaptation. *Administrative Science Quarterly, 44*, 764–791.

Jablin, F. M., Miller, V. D., & Keller, T. (1999). Newcomer-leader role negotiations: Negotiation topics/issues, tactics and outcomes. Paper presented at The Annual Conference of the International Leadership Association, Atlanta, GA.

Jaggar, A. M. (1983). *Feminist politics and human nature.* Totowa, NJ: Rowman & Allanheld.

Kanter, R.M. (2004). The middle manager as innovator. *Harvard Business Review, 82*(7/8), 150–161.

Kanter, R. M. (1977). *Men and women of the corporation.* New York: Basic Books.

Karenga, M. (1983). Nationalism: The problematics of collective vocation. Presented at the Seventh Annual Conference of the National Council of Black Studies, Berkeley, April.

Khumoetsile-Taylor, P. (2000). The triumphs and challenges of historically Black colleges and universities. Retrieved April 14, 2011, from www.bhcc.mass.edu/PDFs?TFOTHigherEducAfricanAmerica

King, R. (2004). The corporate antitrust problem. *Workforce Management,* 22.

Kirschnman, J., & Neckerman, K. M. (1991). "We'd love to hire them, but. . .": The meaning of race for employers. In C. Jencks & P. E. Peterson (Eds.), *The urban underclass* (pp. 203–232). Washington, DC: Brookings Institution.

Kishwar, M. (1985). Gandhi on women. *Economic and Political Weekly, 20*(40), 1691–1702.

Kitano, H. L. (1985). *Race relations.* Upper Saddle River, NJ: Prentice Hall.

Klenke, K. (1996). *Women and leadership: A contextual perspective.* New York: Springer.

Kluegel, J., & Smith, E. (1986). *Beliefs about inequality: Americans views about what is and what ought to be.* New York: A. de Gruyter.

Landry, B. (1987). *The new Black middle class.* Berkeley: University of California Press.

Levinson, D. J., Darrow, C. N., Klein, E. B., Levinson, M. H., & McKee, B. (1978). *The seasons of a man's life.* New York: Alfred A. Knopf.

Loden, M. (1985). *Feminine leadership or how to succeed in business without being one of the boys.* New York: Times Books.

Lorber, J. (1994). *Paradoxes of gender.* New Haven, CT: Yale University Press.

Lueptow, L. B., Garovich, L., & Lueptow, M. B. (1995). The persistence of gender stereotypes in the face of changing sex roles: Evidence contrary to the sociocultural model. *Ethology and Sociobiology, 16,* 509–530.

Maddock, S., & Parkin, D. (1993). Gender cultures: Women's choices and strategies at work. *Women in Management in Review, 8*(2), 3–9.

Masten, A. (1994). Resilience in individual development: Successful adaptation despite risk and adversity. In M. Wang & E. Gordon (Eds.), *Educational resilience in inner-city America* (pp. 3–26). Mahwah, NJ: Lawrence Erlbaum.

McAdoo, H. P. (Ed.). (1999). *Family ethnicity: Strength in diversity* (2nd ed.). Thousand Oaks, CA: Sage.

McGlowan-Fellows, B., & Thomas, C. S. (2004). Changing roles: Corporate mentoring of Black women. *International Journal of Mental Health, 33*(4), 3–18.

Menges, R., & Exum, W. (1983). Barriers to the progress of women and minority faculty. *Journal of Higher Education, 54*(2), 123–144.

Meyerson, D. E., & Fletcher, J. K. (2000, January). A modest manifesto for shattering the glass ceiling. *Harvard Business Review,* 127–136.

Mezirow, J. (1997). Transformative learning: Theory to practice. *New Directions for Adult & Continuing Education, 74,* 5–12.

Miller, J. R., & Vaughan, G. G. (1997). African American women executives: Themes that bind. In V. Benjamin (Ed.), *Black women in the academy: Promises and perils.* Gainesville: University Press of Florida.

Moore, K. M. (1982). *Creating strengths out of our differences: Women and minority administrators.* New Directions for Higher Education Series, 72, 89–98. San Francisco: Josey-Bass.

Morrison, A. M., & von Glinow, M. A. (1990). Women and minorities in management. *American Psychologist, 45,* 200–208.

Moss, P., & Tilly, C. (2001). *Stories employers tell: Race, skill, and hiring in America.* New York: Russell Sage Foundation.

National Women's Business Council (NWBC). (2004). *Fact sheet: African American women and entrepreneurship.* Washington, DC: NWBC. R.

Neckerman, K. M., & Kirschenman, J. (1991). Hiring strategies, racial bias, and inner-city workers. *Social Problems, 38*(4), 801–815.

Nihlen, A. S. (1975). Assumptions about female learning styles and some implications for teaching. *Anthropology and Education Quarterly, 6*(3), 6–8.

Northouse, P. (2004). *Leadership: Theory and practice.* Thousand Oaks: Sage.

O'Connor, C. (2002). Black women beating the odds from one generation to the next: How the changing dynamics of constraint and opportunity affect the process of educational resilience. *American Educational Research Journal, 39*(4), 855–903.

O'Leary, V. E. (1974). Some attitudinal barriers to occupational aspirations in women. *Psychological Bulletin, 81*(11), 809–826.

O'Leary, V. E., & Depner, C. E. (1975) College males' ideal female: Changes in sex-role stereotypes. *Journal of Social Psychology, 95*, 139–140.

Oliver, W. (1989). Black males and social problems: Prevention through Afrocentric socialization. *Journal of Black Studies, 20*(1), 15–39.

Orpen, C. (1994). The effects of organizational and individual career management on career success. *International Journal of Manpower, 15*(1), 27–37.

Padavic, I., & Orcutt, D. (1997). Perceptions of sexual harassment in the Florida legal system: A comparison of dominance and spillover explanations. *Gender Society, 11*, 682.

Pager, D. (2003). The mark of a criminal record. *American Journal of Sociology, 108*, 937–975.

Pajares, F. (2002). Self-efficacy beliefs in academic contexts: An outline. Retrieved March 23, 2005, from http://www.emory.edu/EDUCATION/mfp.efftalk.html

Petersen, T., & Saporta, I. (2004). The opportunity structure for discrimination. *American Journal of Sociology, 109*, 852–901.

Peterson, E. A. (1992). *African American women: A study of will and success.* Jefferson, NC: Mcfarland & Co.

Pettigrew, A.M. (1985). Contextual research: A natural way to link theory and practice. In E.E. Lawler (Ed.) *Doing research that is useful in theory and practice*, San Francisco: Jossey-Bass.

Pettigrew, A. M. (1979). On studying organizational cultures. *Administrative Science Quarterly, 24*(4), 570–581.

Pinnick, C. (1994). Feminist epistemology: Implications for philosophy of science. *Philosophy of Science, 61*(4), 646–657.

Powell, G. N. & Butterfield, D. A. (1986). The good manager: Does androgyny fare better in the 1980s? Paper presented at the Academy of Management, Chicago.

Powell, G. N., & Butterfield, D. A. (1994). Investigating the "glass ceiling" phenomenon: An empirical study of actual promotions to top management. *Academy of Management Journal, 37*(1), 68–86.

Powell, G. N., & Graves, L. M. (2006). Gender and leadership: Perceptions and realities. In K. Dindia & D. J. Canary (Eds.), *Sex differences and similarities in communication* (pp. 83–97). Mahwah, NJ: Lawrence Erlbaum Associates.

Ragins, B. R. (1997). Diversified mentoring relationships in organizations: A power perspective. *Academy of Management Review, 22*(2), 482–521.

Ridgeway, C.L. (1997) Interaction and the conservation of gender inequality: Considering employment. *American Sociological Review, 62*(2), 218–235.

Ridgeway, C. L., & Correll, S. (2004). Unpacking the gender system: A theoretical perspective on gender beliefs and social relations. *Gender and Society, 18*(4), 510–531.

Ridgeway, C. L., & Correll, S. (2000). Limiting gender inequality through interaction: The end(s) of gender. *Contemporary Sociology, 29*(1), 110–120.

Rosen, B., & Jerdee, T. H. (1974). Effects of applicant's sex and difficulty of job on evaluations of candidates for managerial positions. *Journal of Applied Psychology, 59*, 511–512.

Rosenfeld, P., Giacalone, R., & Riordan, C. (2001). *Impression management: Building and enhancing reputations at work.* New York: International Thompson Business Press.

Rost, J. C. (1991). *Leadership for the twenty-first century.* Westport, CT: Praeger.

Saloner, G. (1985). Old boy networks as screening mechanisms. *Journal of Labor Economics, 3*(3), 255–267.

Schein, E. (1985). *Organizational culture and leadership.* San Francisco: Jossey-Bass.

Schlenker, B. R. (2003). *Self-presentation.* In M. Leary & J. Tangney (Eds.), *Handbook of self and identity* (pp. 492–518). New York: Guilford Press.

Schwager, S. (1987). Educating women in America. *Journal of Women in Culture and Society, 12*(2), 333–372.

Schwarzcr. R. (1994). Optimism. vulnerability. and self-beliefs as health-related cognitions: A systematic overview. *Psychology and Health: An International Journal, 9*. 161–180.

Shaw, L., Champlin, D. P., Hartmann, H. I., & Spalter-Roth, R. M. (1993). Impact of the glass ceiling and structural change on minorities and women. Retrieved from http://ww.ilr.comell. edu/ library/e archive/glassceiling/12/12front.htlm/

Sigelman, L., & Welch, S. (1991). *Black Americans' views of racial inequality*. New York: Cambridge University Press.

Smedley, A. (1999 [1993]). *Race in North America: Origin and evolution of a worldview* (2nd ed, revised and enlarged). Boulder, CO: Westview Press.

Smith, C. H. (1982). Black female achievers in academe. *Journal of Negro Education, 51*(3), 318–341.

Smith, J., Smith, W., & Markham, S. (2000). Diversity issues in mentoring academic faculty. *Journal of Career Development, 26*(4), 251–262.

Smith, R. A., & Elliott, J. R. (2002). Does ethnic concentration influence employees' access to authority? An examination of contemporary urban labor markets. *Social Forces, 81*, 255–279.

Sokoloff, N. J. (1992). *Black women and White women in the professions*. New York & London: Routledge.

Spaights, E., & Whitaker, A. (1995). Black women in the workforce: A new look at an old problem. *Journal of Black Studies, 25*, 283–296.

Stainback, K., Robinson, C. L., & Tomaskovic-Devey, D. (2005). Race and workplace integration: A politically mediated process?. *American Behavioral Scientist, 48*(9), 1200–1228.

Steele, C.M. (1999). Thin ice: Stereotype threat and Black college students. *Atlantic Monthly, 248*, 44–54.

Steele, C. M. (1988). The psychology of self-affirmation: Sustaining the integrity of the self. In L. Berkowitz (Ed.), *Advances in experimental social psychology*, Vol. 21 (pp. 261–302). San Diego: Academic Press.

Stepan, N. (1982). *The idea of race in science: Great Britain, 1800–1960*. Hamden, CT: Archon Books.

Stewart, J. B. (1984). The legacy of W. E. B. Du Bois for contemporary Black Studies. *Journal of Negro Education*, 296–311.

Stuart, P. (1992). What does the glass ceiling cost you? *Personnel Journal, 70*, 99–105.

Taylor, S., & Ilgen, D. R. (1981). Sex discrimination against women in initial placement decisions: A laboratory investigation. *Academy of Management Journal, 24*(4), 859–865.

Tedeschi, J. T., & Norman, N. (1985). Social power, self presentation, and the self. In J. T. Tedeschi (Ed) *The self and social life*. New York: McGraw Hill.

Templeton, J. F., & Morrow, N. S. (1972). Women as managers: Still a long way to go. *Personnel Journal, 49*, 30–37.

Thio, A. (2000). *Sociology: A brief introduction*. Boston: Allyn & Bacon.

Thomas, D. A. (2001). The truth about mentoring minorities: Race matters. *Harvard Business Review, 79*(4), 98–107.

Tomaskovic-Devey, D., Zimmer, C., Stainback, K., Robinson, C., Taylor, T., & McTague, T., (2006). Documenting desegregation: Segregation in American workplaces by race, ethnicity, and sex, 1966–2003. *American Sociological Review, 71*, 565–588.

Turner, C., & Meyers, S., Jr. (2000). *Faculty of color in academe: Bittersweet success*. Boston: Allyn & Bacon.

U.S. Equal Employment Opportunity Commission. (1972). Sixth Annual Report. Washington, DC: U.S. Government Printing Office.

Wade, P. (2004). Human nature and race. *Anthropological Theory, 4*(2), 157–172.

Walker, J. W. (1973). Individual career planning: Managerial help for subordinates. *Business Horizons*, 65–72.

Weber, L. 2001. *Understanding race, class, gender and sexuality: A conceptual framework*. Boston: McGraw-Hill.

Weber, M. (1978). *Economy and society. An outline of interpretive sociology*. G. Roth & C. Wittich, Eds. Berkeley: University of California Press.

Werner, E. E., & Smith, R. S. (1992). *Overcoming the odds: High-risk children from birth to adulthood*. Ithaca, NY: Cornell University Press.

Williams, D. R., & Chung, A.-M. (1997). *Racism and health. Health in Black America*. R. C. Gibson & J. S. Jackson, Eds. Thousand Oaks, CA: Sage Publications.

Willie, C. V. (1978). The inclining significance of race. *Society, 15*(10), 12–15.

Willie, C. V. (1979). *The caste and class controversy*. Bayside, NY: General Hall.

Winant, H. (1994). *Racial conditions: Politics, theory, comparisons*. Minneapolis: University of Minnesota Press.

Wright, E. O., & Baxter, J. (2000). The glass ceiling hypothesis: A comparative study of the United States, Sweden, and Australia. Gender and Society. *Journal of Sociology, 93*,141–165.

Yukl, G. (1994). *Leadership in organizations* (3rd ed.). Englewood Cliffs, NJ: Prentice-Hall.

Dannielle Joy Davis, Ph.D.

Dr. Dannielle Joy Davis, a graduate of the University of Illinois at Urbana-Champaign, has studied and conducted research in Ghana, South Africa, Egypt, Germany, the Netherlands, and Belgium. Her interdisciplinary, K-20 research examines the experiences of marginalized groups in educational settings and the role of organizational policy and practice in the promotion or inhibition of egalitarian academic and occupational outcomes. She has published over 20 refereed journal articles, book chapters, academic commentaries, volumes, and reviews. Dr. Davis serves as an Associate Editor for *Learning for Democracy: An International Journal of Thought and Practice* which is sponsored by the American Educational Research Association's Special Interest Group, Democratic Citizenship in Education. Her work has been published in various journals, including: *Journal of Educational Administration and History; Mentoring and Tutoring: Partnership in Learning; To Improve the Academy; Planning and Changing: An Educational Leadership and Policy Journal;* and *The Urban Review: Issues and Ideas in Public Education.*

Cassandra Chaney, Ph.D.

Dr. Cassandra Chaney earned her B.S. degree in Psychology from Southern University and A&M College (Baton Rouge, Louisiana), and her M.S. and Ph.D. in Human and Community Development (HCD) from the University of Illinois at Urbana-Champaign (UIUC). As an Associate Professor in the College of Human Sciences and Education, School of Social Work, Child and Family Studies at Louisiana State University (LSU), Dr. Chaney is broadly interested in the dynamics of African-American family life, yet under this umbrella her interests are focused on two main areas. Her primary research focuses on the narratives of African-Americans in dating, cohabiting, and married relationships, with a particular interest in relationship formation, maintenance, and stability. Her secondary research explores the ways that religiosity and spirituality support African-Americans. In additional to publishing several sole and first-authored manuscripts, she has also presented her research during local, state, and national conferences. In addition to utilizing quantitative and qualitative methods to explore the aforementioned areas, Dr. Chaney is also interested in the representation of African-American couples and families (e.g., structural and functional dynamics) in popular forms of mass media (i.e., television shows, music videos, songs). Given the unique challenges of Black families, her research provides recommendations regarding how policy can better meet the needs of Black families who experience heightened rates of incarceration, unemployment, weakened family structures, and racism. Most important, her scholarship is rooted in a strengths-based perspective and is devoted to emphasizing the various ways that Black families remain resilient in the face of these challenges. Her work has been published in *Family Relations, Marriage & Family Review, Journal of Family Issues, Ethnicities, The Journal of African American Studies, Forum for Family and Consumer Issues, The Journal of Religion and Spirituality in Social Work: Social Thought, Religion & Society, The Western Journal of Black Studies, International Journal of Qualitative Studies in Education,* and *Mental Health, Religion, & Culture.*

ROCHELLE BROCK &
RICHARD GREGGORY JOHNSON III,
Executive Editors

Black Studies and Critical Thinking is an interdisciplinary series which examines the intellectual traditions of and cultural contributions made by people of African descent throughout the world. Whether it is in literature, art, music, science, or academics, these contributions are vast and far-reaching. As we work to stretch the boundaries of knowledge and understanding of issues critical to the Black experience, this series offers a unique opportunity to study the social, economic, and political forces that have shaped the historic experience of Black America, and that continue to determine our future. Black Studies and Critical Thinking is positioned at the forefront of research on the Black experience, and is the source for dynamic, innovative, and creative exploration of the most vital issues facing African Americans. The series invites contributions from all disciplines but is specially suited for cultural studies, anthropology, history, sociology, literature, art, and music.

Subjects of interest include (but are not limited to):

- EDUCATION
- SOCIOLOGY
- HISTORY
- MEDIA/COMMUNICATION
- RELIGION/THEOLOGY
- WOMEN'S STUDIES

- POLICY STUDIES
- ADVERTISING
- AFRICAN AMERICAN STUDIES
- POLITICAL SCIENCE
- LGBT STUDIES

For additional information about this series or for the submission of manuscripts, please contact Dr. Brock (Indiana University Northwest) at brock2@iun.edu or Dr. Johnson (University of San Francisco) at rgjohnsoniii@usfca.edu.

To order other books in this series, please contact our Customer Service Department:

(800) 770-LANG (within the U.S.)
(212) 647-7706 (outside the U.S.)
(212) 647-7707 FAX

Or browse online by series at www.peterlang.com.